IMAGES
of America

SOMERS POINT

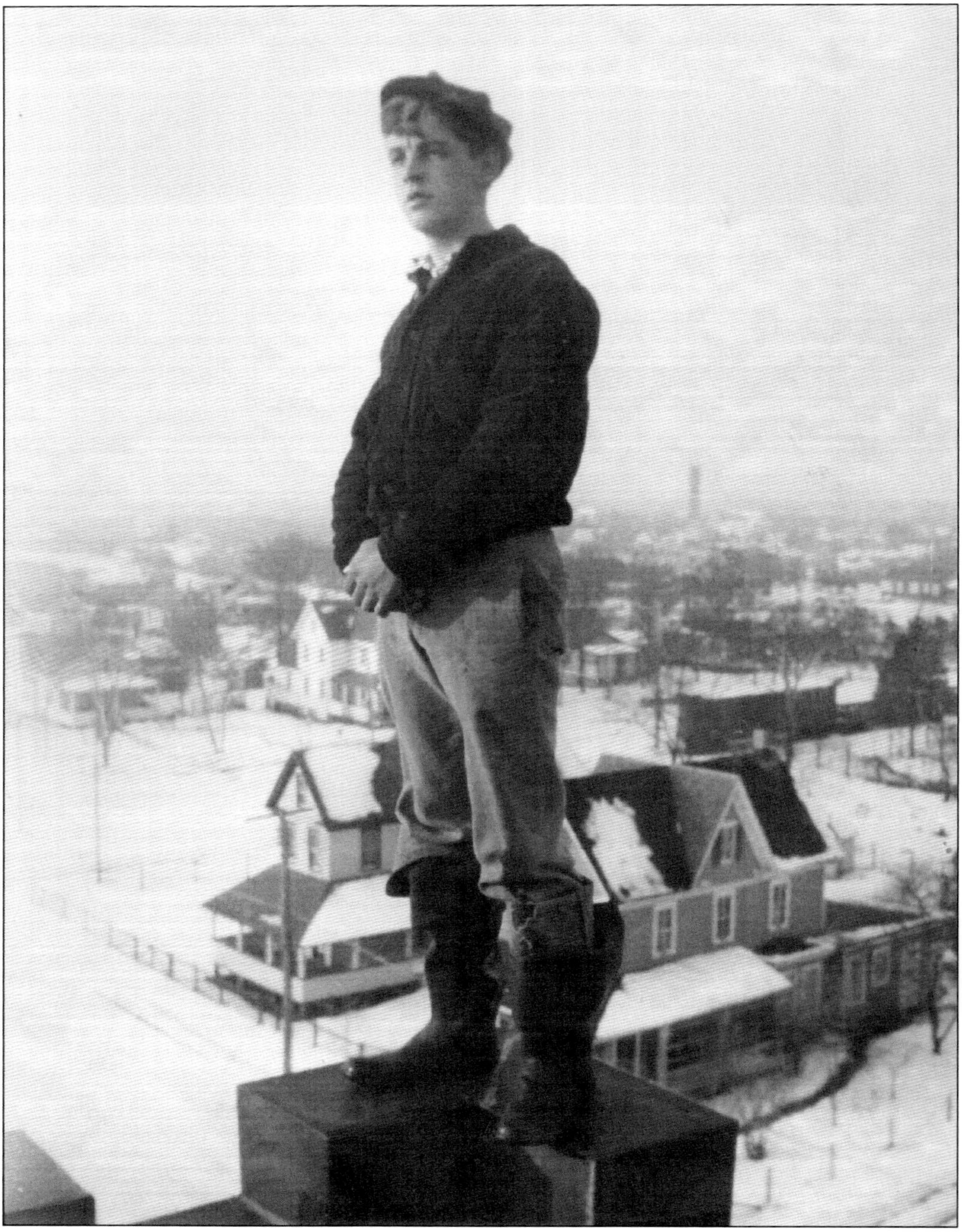

Donald Balsley looks out towards the Great Egg Harbor Bay while standing atop the hose-drying tower on the old city hall. A member of Somers Point Volunteer Fire Company No. 1 and the Republican Club, Donald would later serve the city of Somers Point as city clerk for 25 years. (Courtesy Genevieve DeVito—The Don Balsley Collection.)

On the Cover: Schoolchildren, dressed in their patriotic outfits, prepare to take part in the annual Memorial Parade. (Courtesy Ruth Mulford Newsome.)

IMAGES
of America

SOMERS POINT

Lynn Newsome MacEwan

ARCADIA
PUBLISHING

ISBN 978-1-4671-2005-0

Published by Arcadia Publishing
Charleston, South Carolina

Printed in the United States of America

Library of Congress Control Number: 2013930973

For all general information, please contact Arcadia Publishing:
Telephone 843-853-2070
Fax 843-853-0044
E-mail sales@arcadiapublishing.com
For customer service and orders:
Toll-Free 1-888-313-2665

Visit us on the Internet at www.arcadiapublishing.com

This book is dedicated to my mother, Ruth Mulford Newsome. Without her help and patience, I would not have been able to complete this project.

Contents

Acknowledgments

When undertaking a project like this, it is impossible to do it alone. I am amazed and humbled by the number of people who have helped me and the enthusiasm they have shown during the writing of this book. I would like to thank Michael and Barbara Bohs, Genevieve DeVito, John Dunn, Kirk and Margie Gerety, Bob Loper, Carmen Marotta, Jeff Miller, Ruth Mulford Newsome, Wes Swain, and Joan Bird Wilson for allowing me to use their photographs and helping me to identify people where needed. I would also like to thank Lois Mulford Broomell for all of her help researching and confirming facts. Thanks go to Richard Gray and Phil Huber for the help they gave me in identifying people in the basketball pictures. Thanks go to Ally Larned—I have tried, as you suggested, not to make it too boring even though it is history. An extra special thanks goes to my mom, Ruth Mulford Newsome, for spending endless hours with me at the computer and for all of her help in fact-finding; without her help, I would not have been able to complete this book. To my children Michael and Jennifer MacEwan—who asked me over and over again: "Aren't you done with that book yet?"—I can finally answer, "Yes, I am done." Thanks go to all of my friends and family for your support and patience and for putting up with the endless hours spent on this book and the piles of papers I had to accumulate while putting it together. I hope everyone enjoys this little piece of Somers Point history.

Unless otherwise noted, all images appear courtesy of the author from her private collection.

INTRODUCTION

Somers Point, the first settlement in Atlantic County, was settled around 1693 by Englishman John Somers on 3,000 acres of property that he purchased from Thomas Budd. Somers Point was originally known as Somerset Plantation. Somers was a Quaker who left England because of religious sentiments. He held the first Quaker meeting in Somers Point in 1695. There would later be a Quaker meetinghouse on Shore Road near New York Avenue.

On March 20, 1693, at the first meeting of the court in Cape May County, Somers was appointed supervisor of roads and a constable. He also served as justice of the peace from 1695 until 1714 and as assessor for Egg Harbor Township in 1708; in 1709, he was elected to be a member of the Province Assembly. He lived in Somers Point until the time of his death (around 1723) and was buried on his estate in the family cemetery.

Richard Somers, John's eldest living son, built the Somers Mansion, which overlooks the Great Egg Harbor Bay, around 1725. The mansion was constructed of brick in the Flemish Bond pattern. During the Victorian era, renovations on the mansion gave it a more Victorian look with the addition of two-story porches, a second-story addition in the back, and attic dormers in the front. All of these were removed when the Work Projects Administration (WPA) restored the building to its original state in the early 1940s. Somers Mansion is currently owned and maintained by the State of New Jersey Department of Environmental Protection. The mansion is open to the public for tours.

Somers Point was also home to Master Commandant Richard Somers, great-grandson of John Somers. Richard was born in Somers Point in 1775, though he attended school in Philadelphia, Pennsylvania, and Burlington, New Jersey. While away at school, he became friends with Stephen Decatur and Charles Stewart; all three would go on to become naval heroes. In 1803, Richard was commander of the *Nautilus*, part of Decatur's fleet, as they fought with the Barbary pirates in Tripoli. September 4, 1804, still found the friends involved in the battle at Tripoli. This was the day that Richard Somers would command the ketch *Intrepid*. While blockading Tripoli harbor, the frigate *Philadelphia* had run aground, and that boat's crew was taken prisoner. In an attempt to rescue them, Richard and his crew were to explode a fireboat in the middle of the pirate fleet so as to cause confusion and enable the rescue of the *Philadelphia* crew. During this rescue attempt, something went wrong, and the *Intrepid* exploded before Somers and his crew could get off of the ship. Because of his heroic act, there will always be a USS *Somers* in the US Navy fleet, and a monument honoring Richards Somers and his men stands at the US Naval Academy in Annapolis, Maryland.

Since Somers Point is located on a peninsula bordered by the Great Egg Harbor Bay, Great Egg Harbor River, and Patcong Creek, water became the source of income and livelihood for many of the families that lived there. Many men were ship captains or seamen, as well as fishermen and clammers. Shipbuilding became a major industry, with shipyards located not only on Great Egg Harbor Bay, but also along Patcong Creek. At one time, four shipyards on the Great Egg

Harbor Bay were constructing clipper ships. Although the shipbuilding industry may be long gone, the bay continues to provide for both residents and visitors alike. Many marinas are now located along Bay Avenue and provide space for docking a boat or renting a boat for the day to go fishing or crabbing. The marinas also provide a place for anglers to fulfill their fishing needs and maybe even hear a fish story or two.

The Borough of Somers Point was incorporated in 1886 and went on to become the City of Somers Point in 1902. George Anderson was the first mayor, serving from 1886 to 1887. The city now runs under a mayor-council form of government.

Many businesses have come and gone through the years, but two businesses that have become synonymous with Somers Point are Bay Shores and Tony Mart's. Located at the south end of Bay Avenue, these bars were the hot spots of the area for many years. Bay Shores was located at the bottom of Goll and Bay Avenues and was on the bay. Many locals may remember sitting on the remains of the old trolley bridge listening to the music play and watching the building—constructed on pilings over the bay—sway (or appear to sway) as the people inside danced. Tony Mart's, which was located at the corner of George Street and Bay Avenue from 1945 until 1982, hosted popular acts such as Bill Haley and His Comets, Duane Eddy, Conway Twitty, and Del Shannon. In the summer of 1965, Levon and the Hawks had been hired to play at Tony Mart's for the entire summer when bandleader Levon Helm received a call from Bob Dylan; later that year, the group backed Dylan on his first rock 'n' roll tour and became known as The Band. One of the final things to happen at Tony Mart's was the filming of the 1983 movie *Eddie and the Cruisers*. Featuring Tom Berenger and Michael Paré, as well as many locals who served as extras, the movie forever immortalized the excitement that surrounded Tony Mart's. Although it has been closed for more than 30 years, Tony Mart's is still commemorated today during memorial events held to honor this legendary bar and nightclub.

In the summertime, locals and visitors alike can enjoy free beach concerts every Friday night at the Somers Point beach, located at New Jersey Avenue and Bay Avenue. These popular concerts offer a variety of bands and different musical sounds. Each year, on the last Saturday in April, Somers Point hosts the Bayfest block party along Bay Avenue, featuring food and craft vendors, environmental exhibits, and plenty of free music. Every September, on the Saturday after Labor Day, the Good Old Days Festival is held at John F. Kennedy Park (formerly known as High Banks Park). The celebration includes a 5K run, food and craft vendors, and—again—lots of free live music. Over the years, Somers Point may have lost some of its historic buildings and charm, but it is still true to its roots and offers many events that foster a feeling of community spirit.

One

Along the Bay

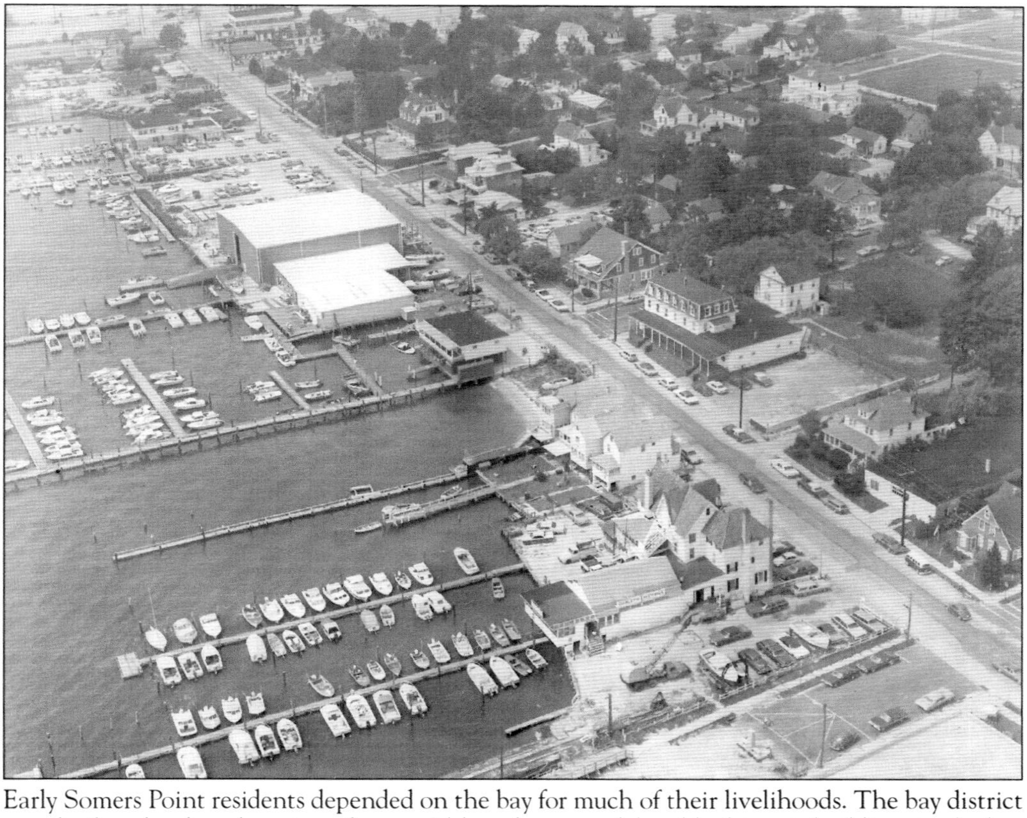

Early Somers Point residents depended on the bay for much of their livelihoods. The bay district was the first developed section of town. Although many of the older historic buildings in the bay area have been lost to newer development, some still remain, making this a quaint part of town. (Courtesy William E. Swain.)

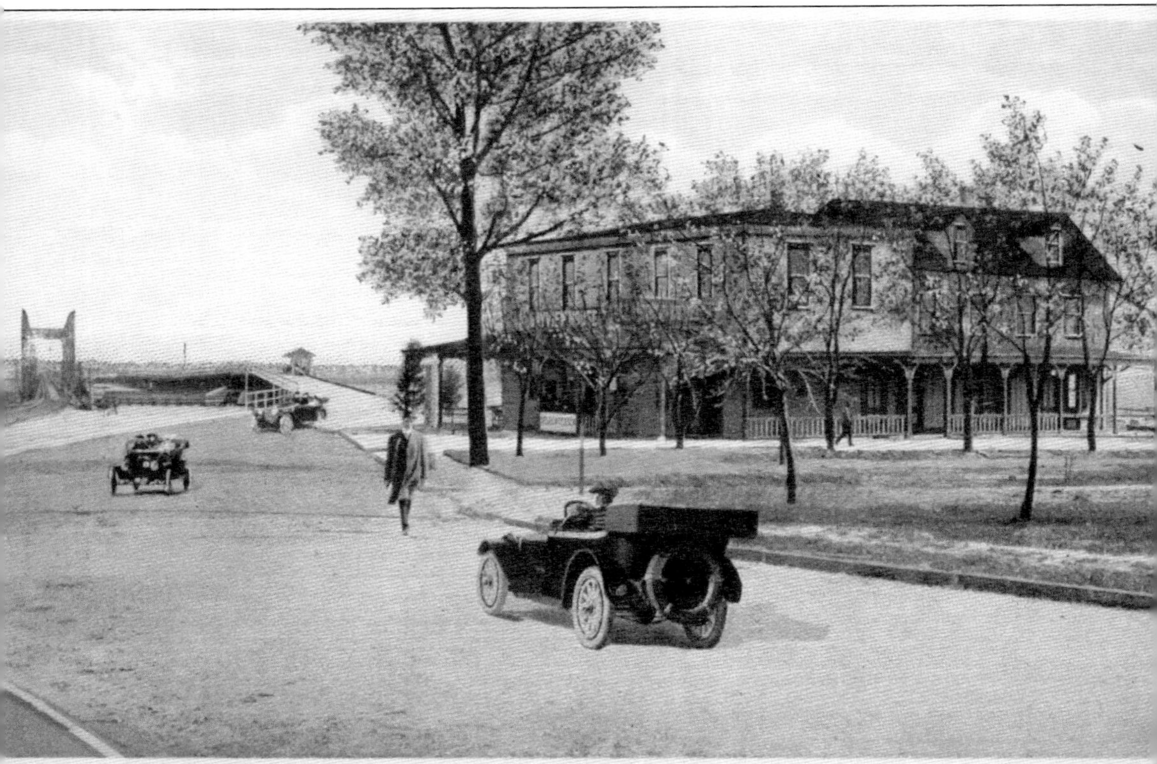

SOM⁻RS POINT, ENTRANCE TO NEW AUTO BRIDGE CONNECTING SOMERS POINT AND OCEAN CITY, NEW JERS

The Bayview House was located at the base of the first wooden bridge connecting Ocean City and Somers Point. Today, the house's location would be on the right side of Goll Avenue heading towards the bay. The Bayview House was originally built by former sea captains turned politicians John Townsend and Henry VanSant. Townsend was a councilman on the first borough council in 1886, and VanSant was a chosen freeholder at the same time. Charles J. Collins operated the Bayview House for many years. Offering "Pure Beer" and a literal bay view, it was a prime location for an overnight stay for visitors or a night out for local residents.

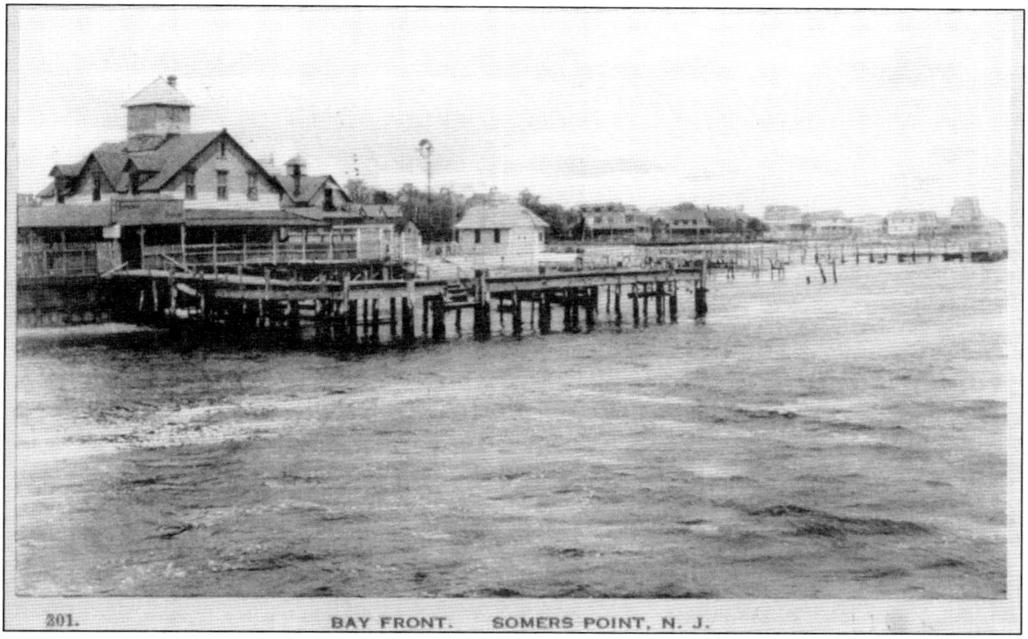

In this view looking toward Somers Point from the old wooden bridge, it becomes obvious that the landscape has changed quite a bit over the years. In the left foreground is the boathouse that would go on to become the popular Bay Shores bar. Farther down the street are more familiar buildings that still stand and remind locals of earlier times.

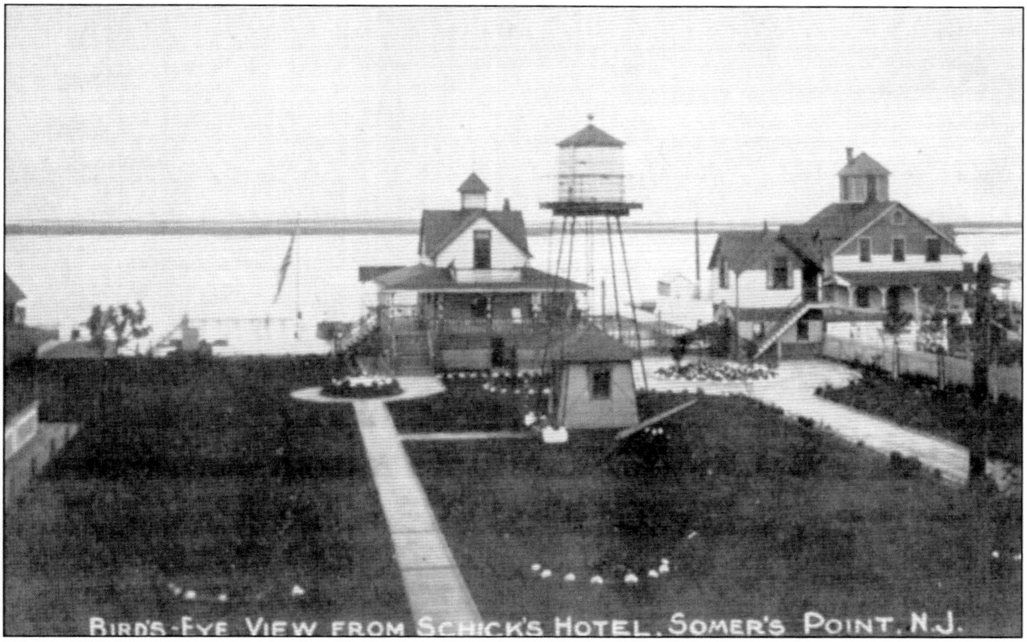

This c. 1908 image shows a bird's-eye view of the area looking across Bay Avenue from Schick's Hotel towards the bay. A postcard from that era identifies this area as fishing headquarters. The bay has long provided good fishing—for both survival and recreation—to Somers Point residents and visitors alike.

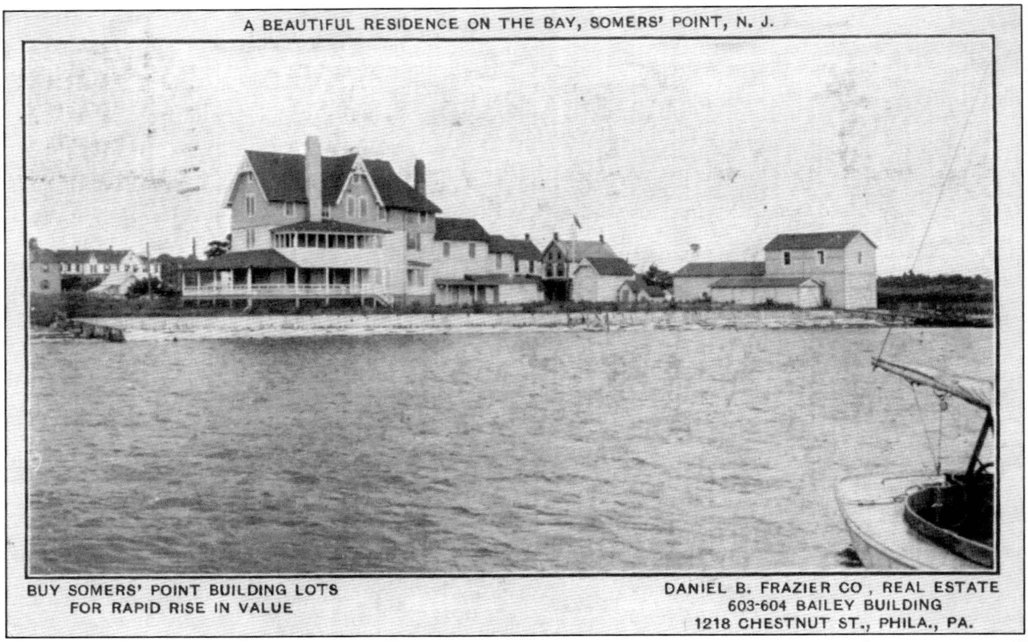

Built in 1884 as a private residence, this house was owned, as a second home, by Burr Powell Noland in the 1880s. Research shows that Noland was not only a prominent Virginia attorney but also a major in the Confederate army. At the time he owned the property, records show he had 10 black servants in his employ. It could be assumed that these servants may have been freed slaves who chose to stay on and work for the family. It cannot be confirmed that they arrived in Somers Point with the family when they came to stay at this home on the bay.

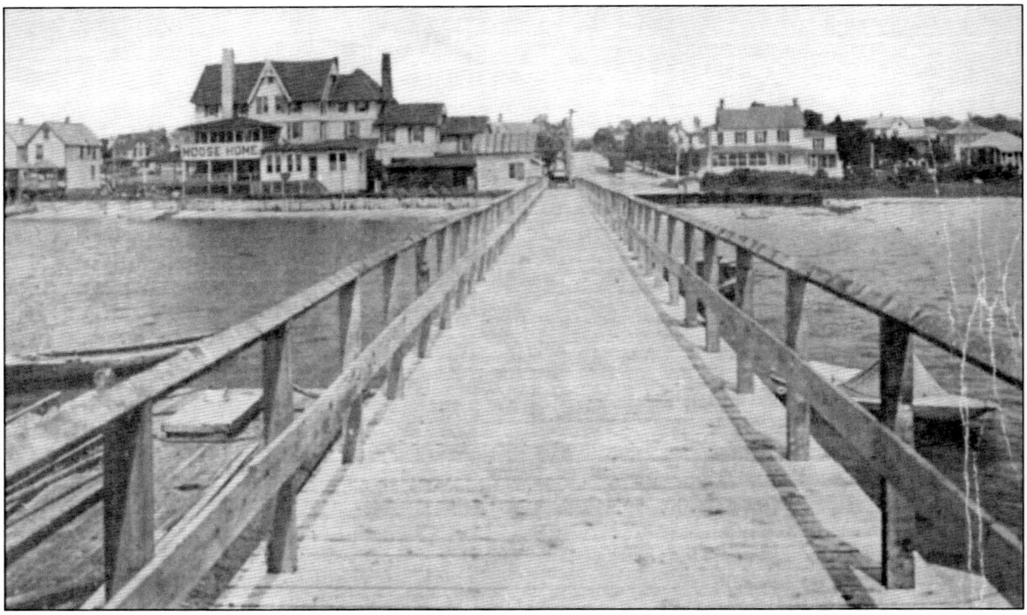

As shown in this c. 1916 photograph, the house owned by Burr Powell Noland was later acquired by a men's club out of Philadelphia, presumably a Moose lodge. During that time, the building served as its summer getaway and was known as the Moose Home.

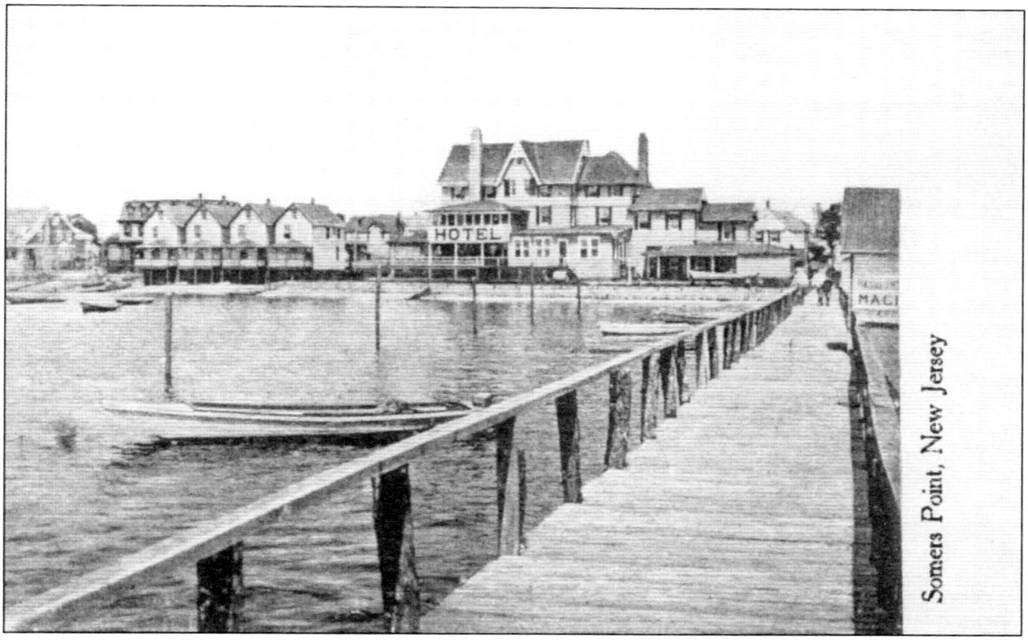

This c. 1910 postcard shows the old Somers Point pier at the beach, as well as the Grandview Hotel. The property later housed the Point Tavern, a popular restaurant and hotel.

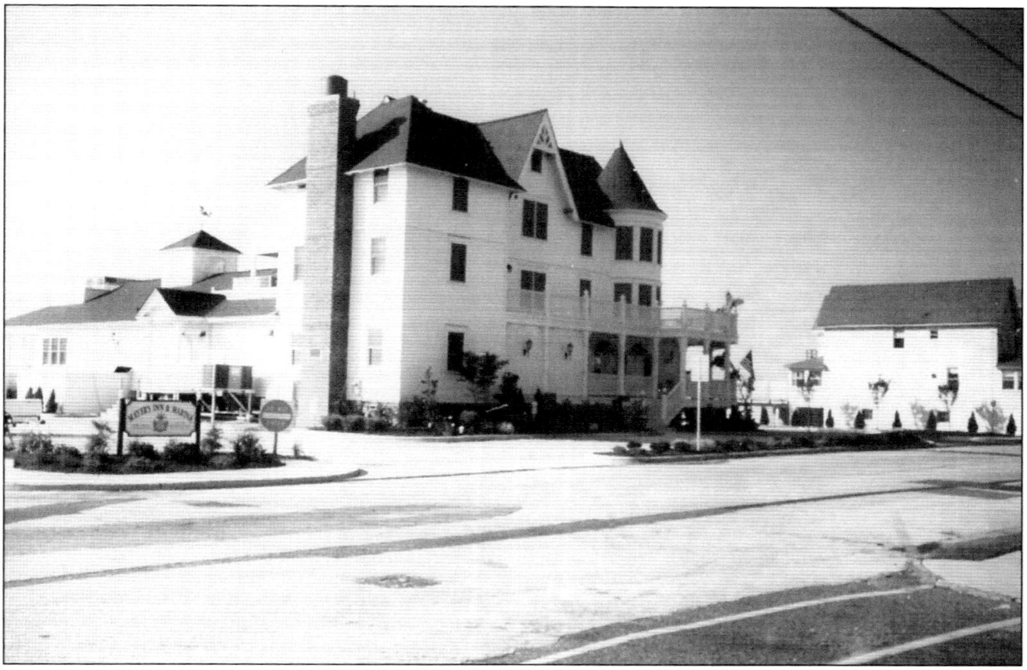

After some tender loving care and rehabilitation in the late 1990s, the former Noland property was raised off its foundation and gutted. The foundation was then replaced and the building was lowered to rest on it. At the end of the restoration, the structure once again stood proud and strong and became a centerpiece of Bay Avenue. This photograph shows the building from the Bay Avenue side. (Courtesy Joan Bird Wilson.)

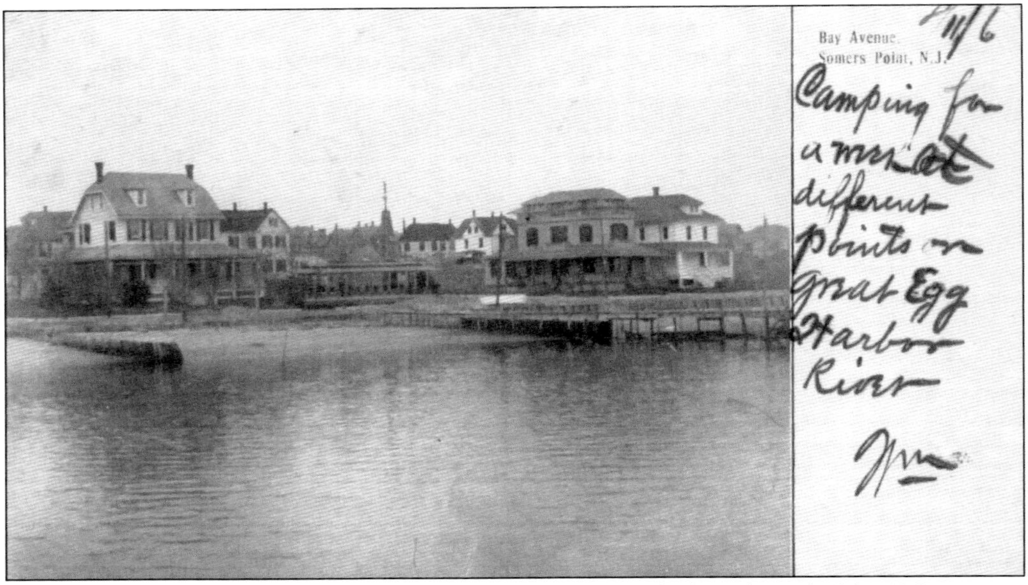

The stately Bay Avenue residence on the left in this image was built at the end of the 19th century. The property was owned by Adolf Kappella, who had been married to Anna Somers. In 1874, Adolf and Anna had a son, Somers Kappella, and Anna Somers Kappella died of typhoid fever soon after the birth. Adolf later married Anna Stinble in 1877. Because both wives were named Anna, it has long been thought that both Annas were one and the same, when in fact they were two different Annas who both married Adolf.

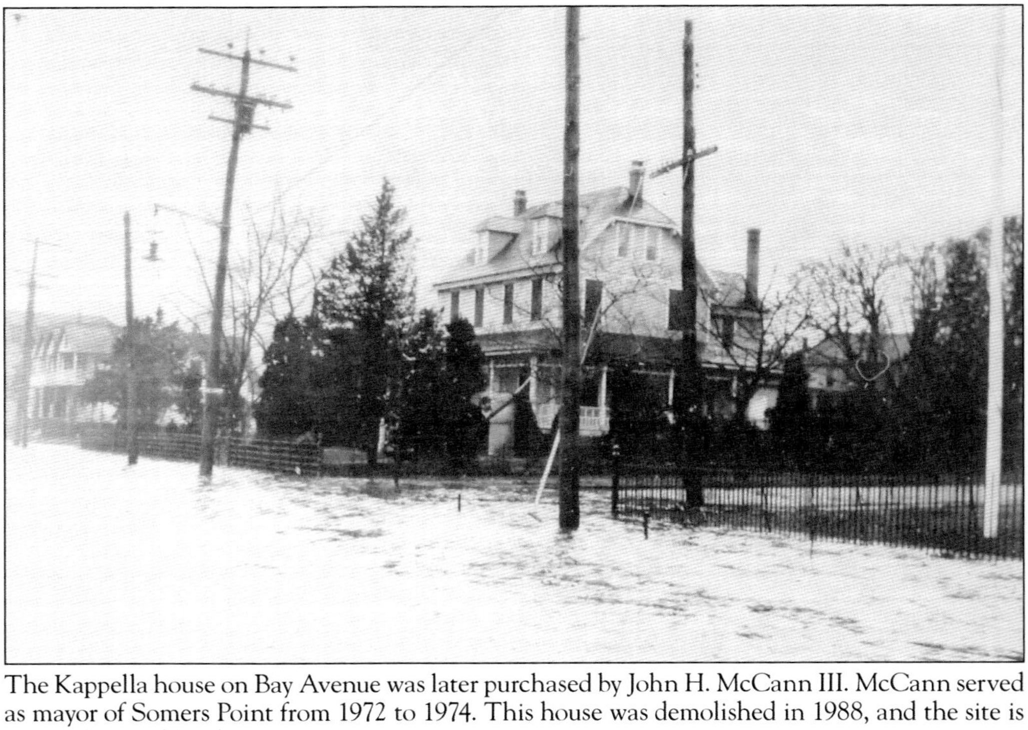

The Kappella house on Bay Avenue was later purchased by John H. McCann III. McCann served as mayor of Somers Point from 1972 to 1974. This house was demolished in 1988, and the site is currently a parking lot.

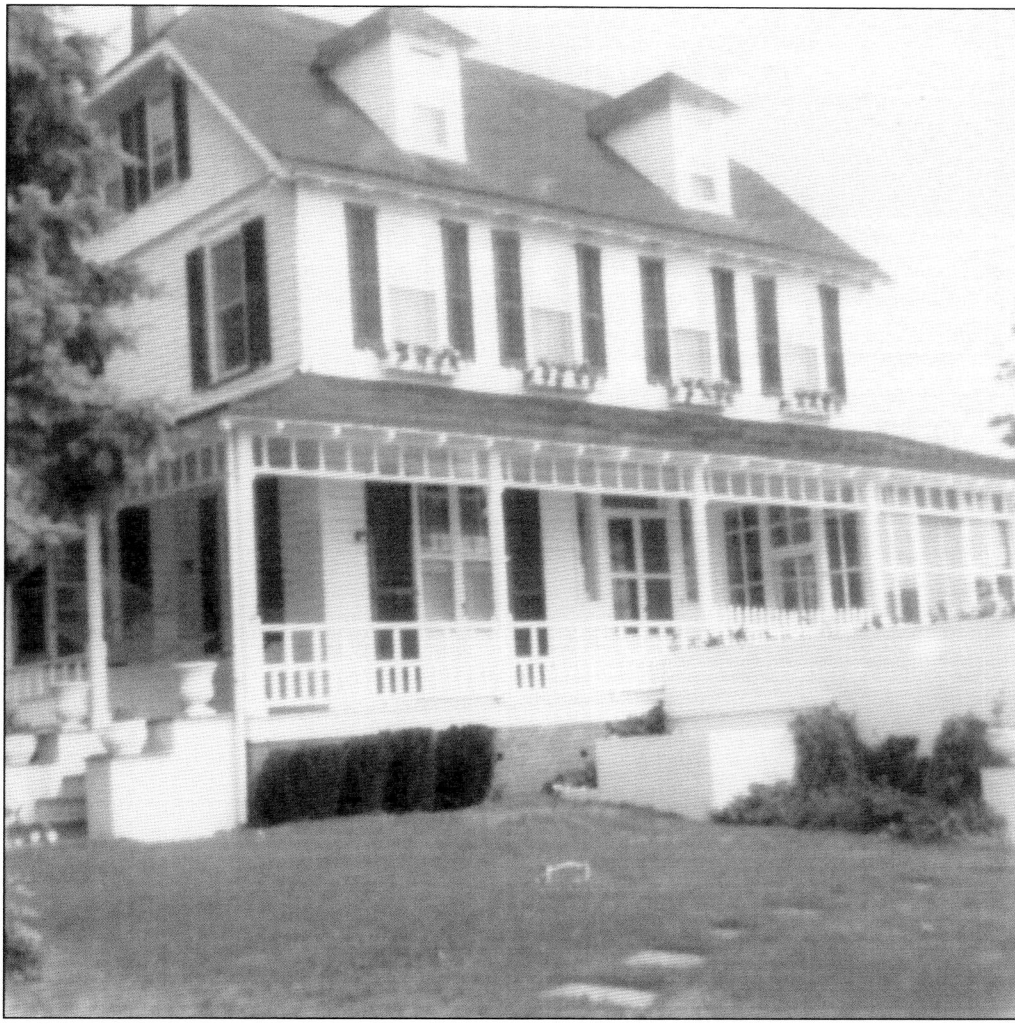

A close-up view of 905 Bay Avenue offers an idea of what a beautiful home it once was. Demolished to make way for new construction that never transpired, it was truly a historic piece of Somers Point that will never be replaced.

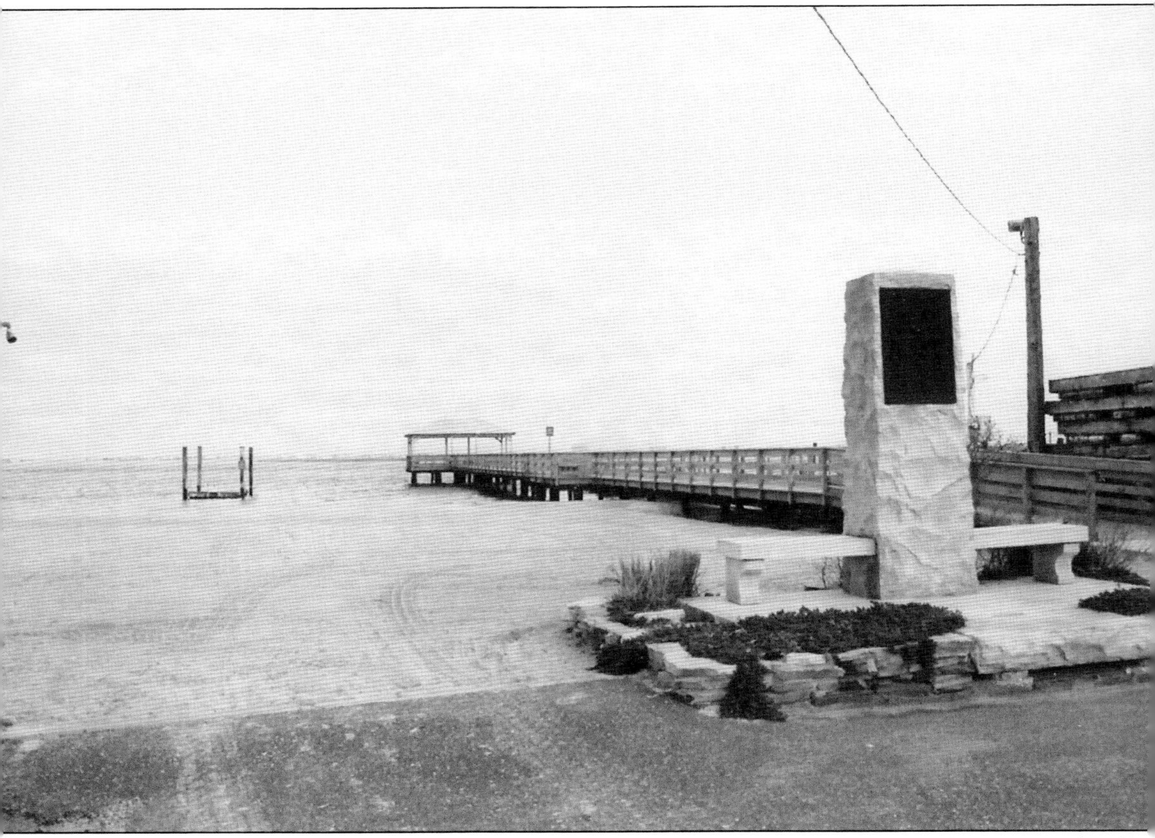

This War of 1812 Monument, located at the beach, was dedicated in the early 1920s and still stands today. A close look at the monument shows the names of the brave men from Somers Point who served in the war. (Courtesy Ruth Mulford Newsome.)

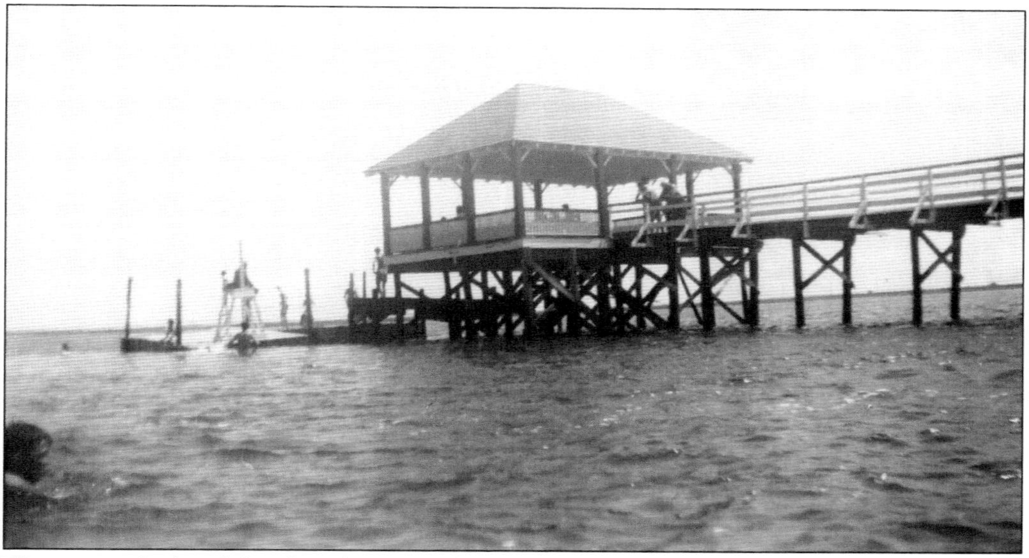

The pier at the beach has long been a gathering place. The picture above shows the pier when the bay was much deeper. The water was deep enough to swim off of the floating pier at the end, and the pier once sported a diving board. The image below shows a more recent version of the pier. The floating piers at the end of the dock and much of the water are long gone. At low tide, one can now walk out to the end of the pier and stand in water that is not even waist-deep. The entire pier was picked up and tossed off of its pilings during Hurricane Sandy in October 2012 and has since been rebuilt. (Above, courtesy Ruth Mulford Newsome; below, courtesy Joan Bird Wilson.)

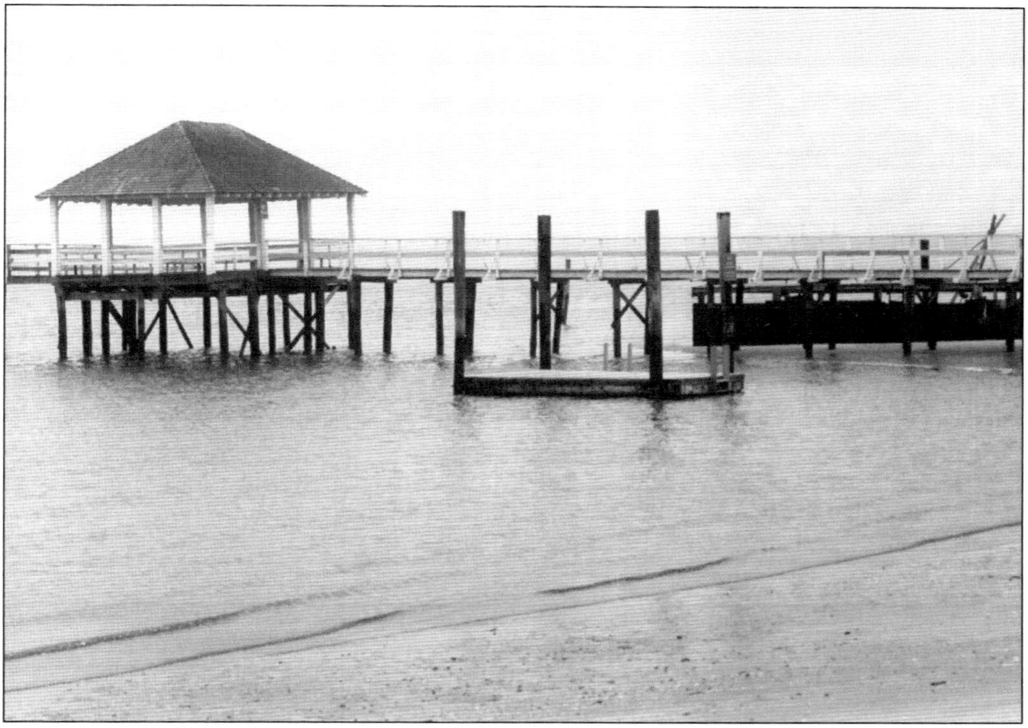

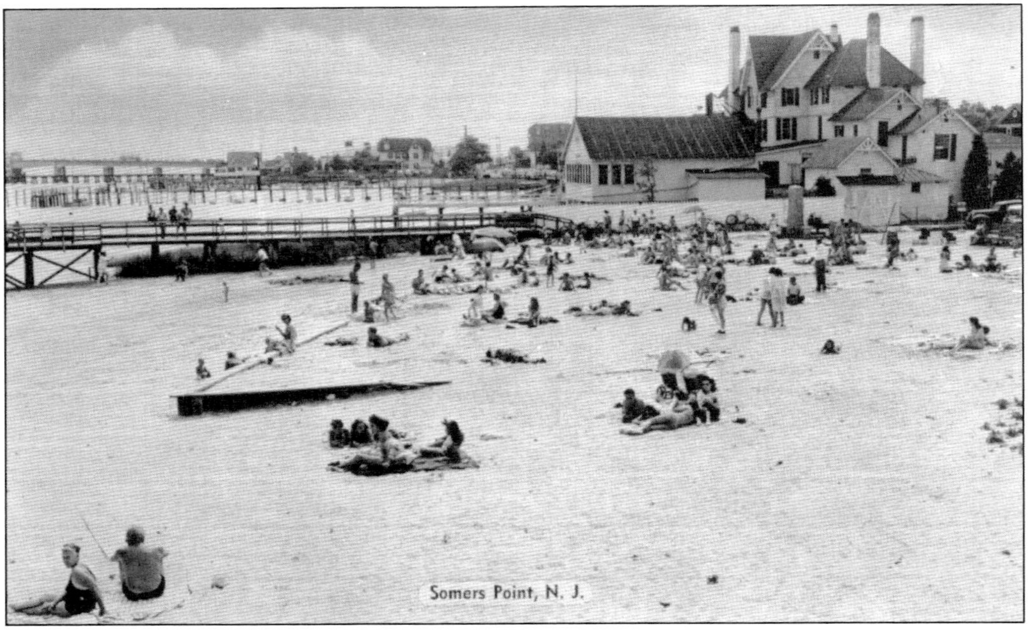

Though small, the Somers Point beach is a popular place to spend a warm summer day. The postcard above shows the bulkhead that once helped to hold back the sand during high tides and storms. Below, a young Bob Loper enjoys a day at the beach during the summer of 1957. In the background, on the right, is the Seaside Theatre (later the Gateway Playhouse), which is currently in the process of being restored and reopened. (Below, courtesy Bob Loper.)

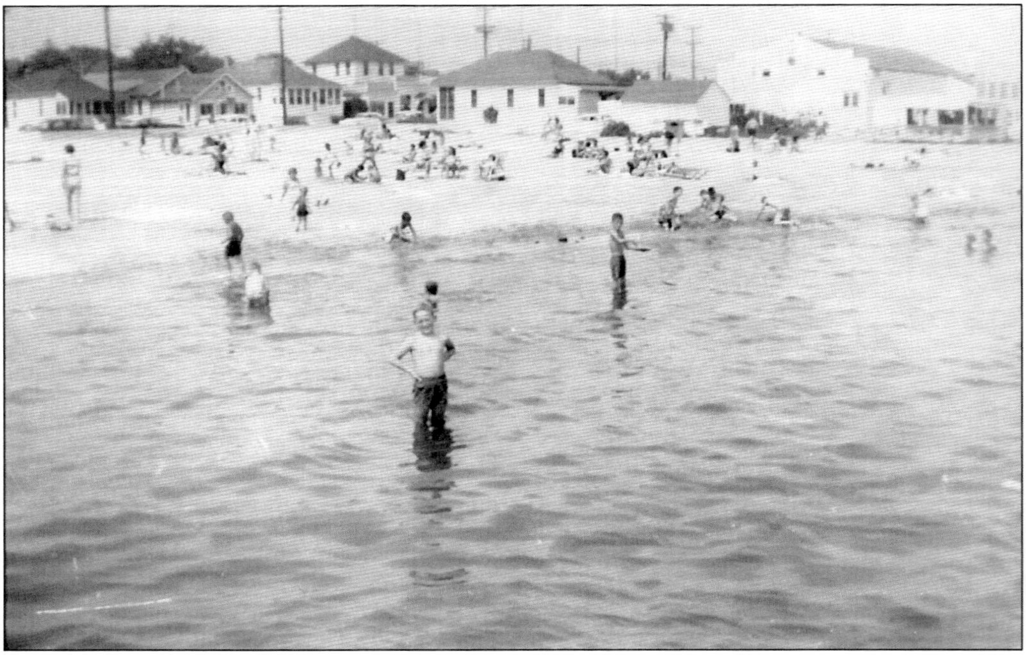

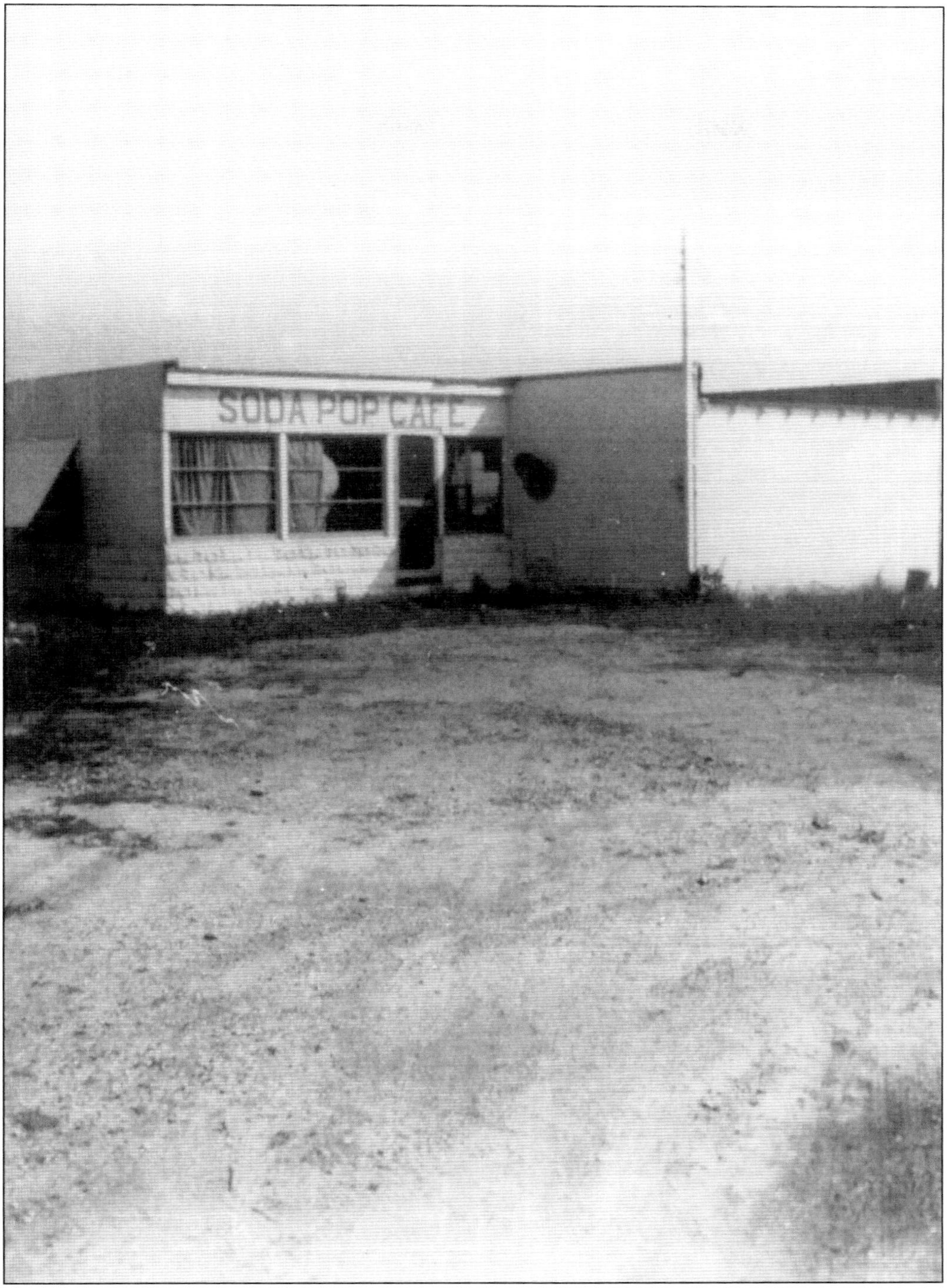

The Soda Pop Cafe was located on the Somers Point beach during the 1940s and 1950s. A popular local hangout, the Soda Pop was the place to go for a snack or a cool drink while spending a day on the beach, or for a bite to eat while meeting friends after seeing a movie at the Seaside Theatre across the street. (Courtesy Kirk Gerety.)

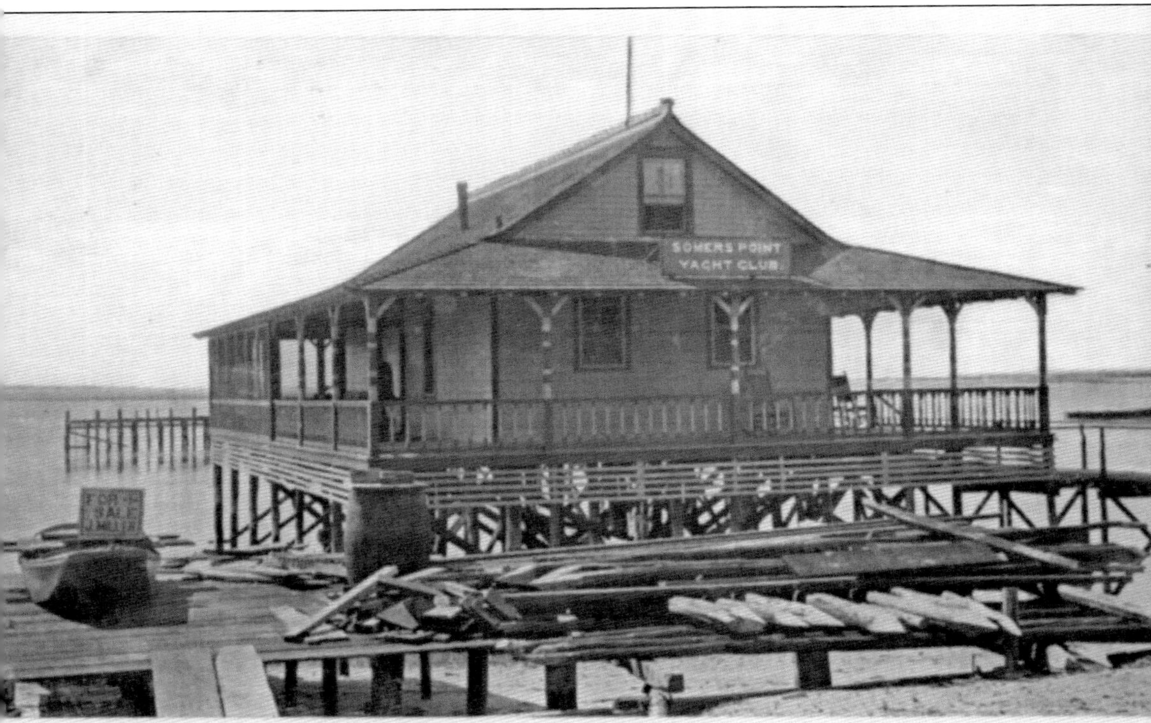

SOMERS POINT YACHT CLUB, Somers Point, N. J. "Pub. for Oscar Nichols."

This postcard shows the former Somers Point Yacht Club. The club was located on Miller's Pier at the foot of Miller Lane on Bay Avenue. It is said that this building was lifted off its pilings during an ice storm and carried north to Bass Harbor by the bay.

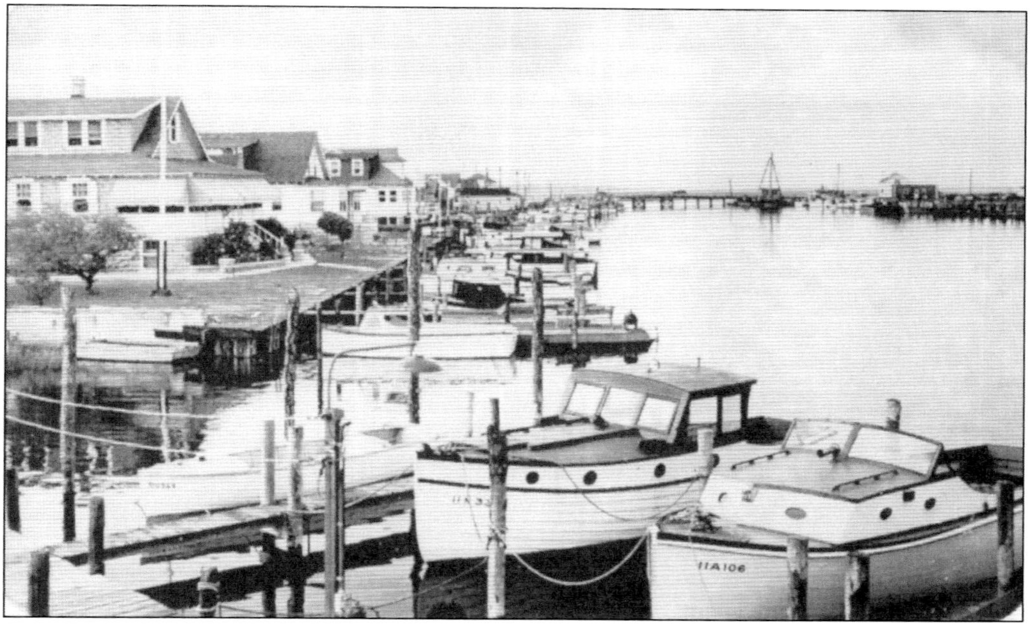

Long home to local fishermen and clammers, parts of Bass Harbor look much the same today as they did decades ago. Although some of the buildings are gone and these boats have been replaced by newer versions, many local residents still call the cottages home.

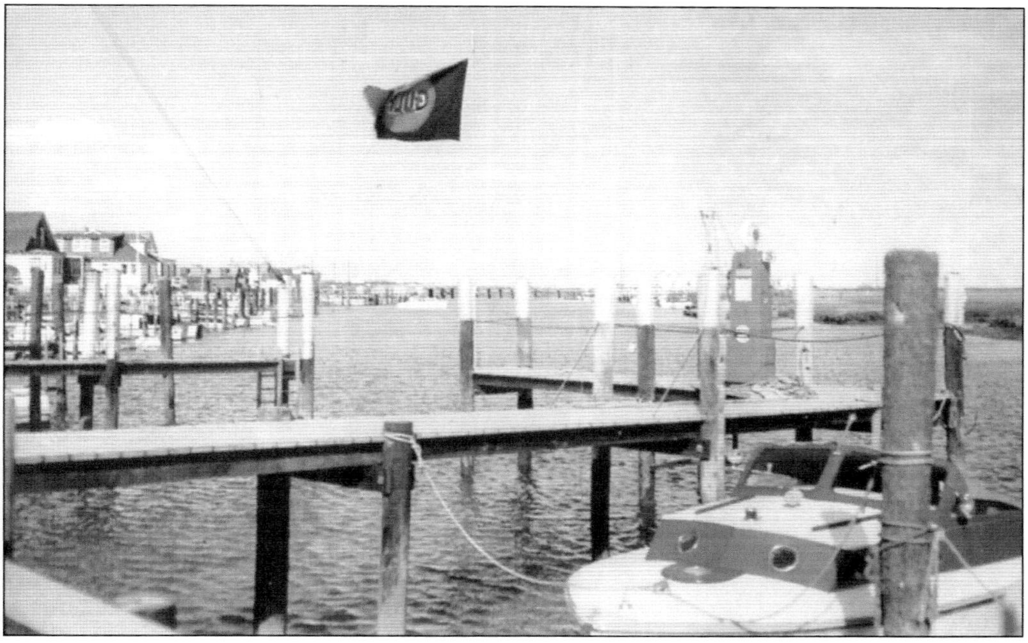

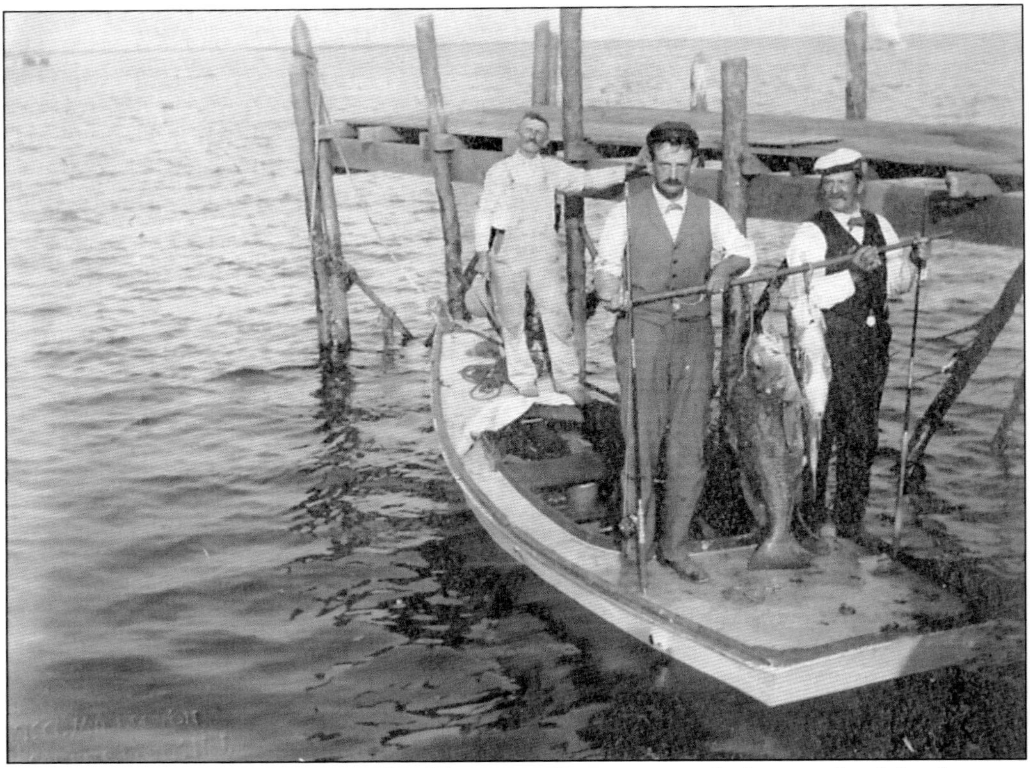

There is a stark contrast between the fishermen of yesteryear with their catch of the day seen above and the more recent fishermen shown below. The boats may have changed—and the present-day fisherman's outfit seems much more comfortable—but the result was the same, and the sport of fishing is still popular today in Somers Point.

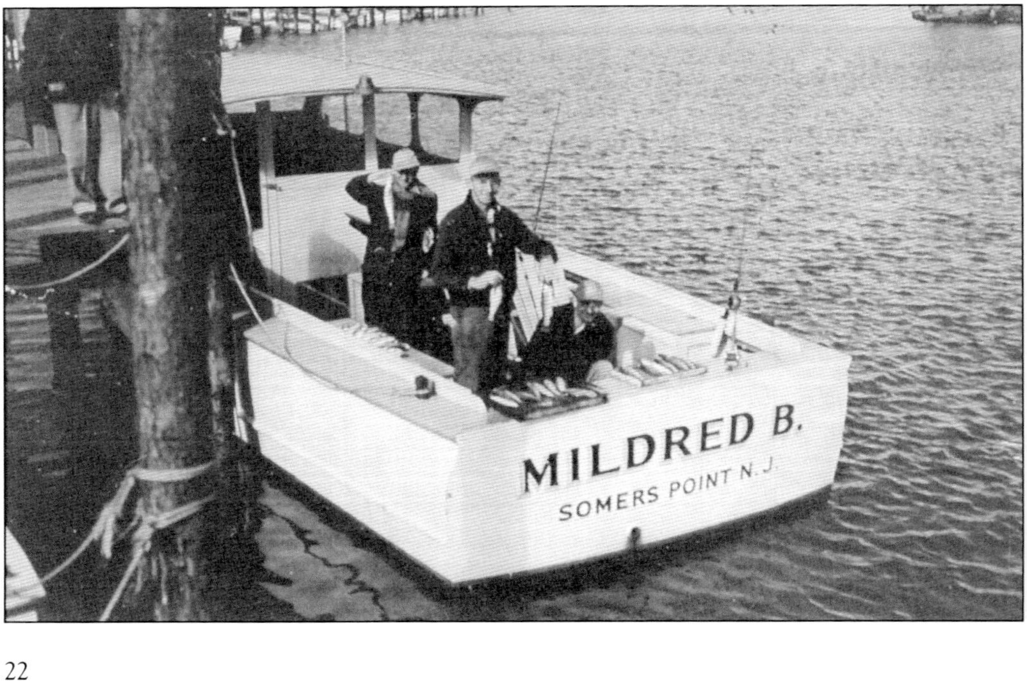

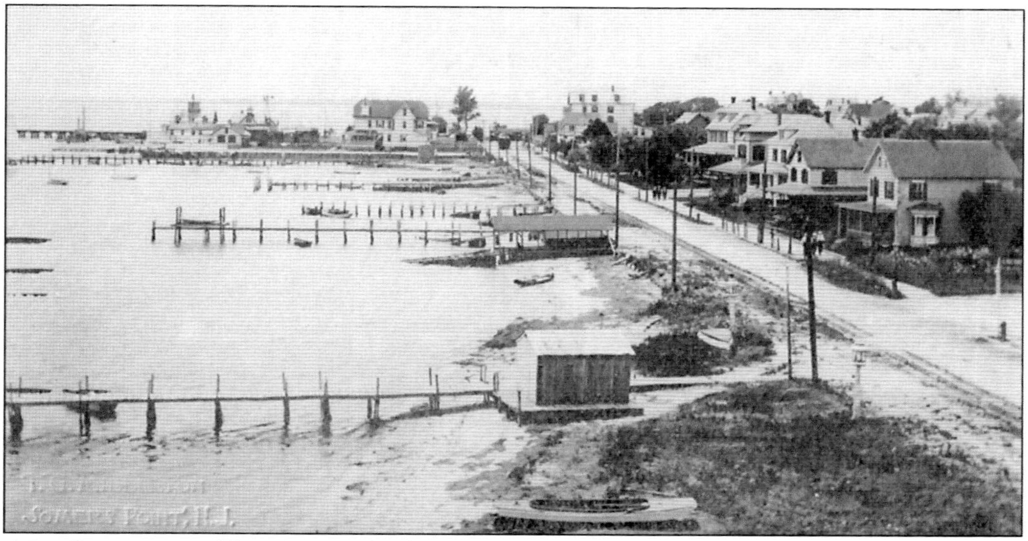

A bird's-eye view of Bay Avenue looking south shows many houses that are still there today along with several buildings in the distance that are now gone. In the background to the left is the building that became Bay Shores. To its right is the house that became Dick's Dock. Across the street in the background is the tall building that was Schick's Tavern and later became Tony Mart's. These three iconic structures have since been demolished.

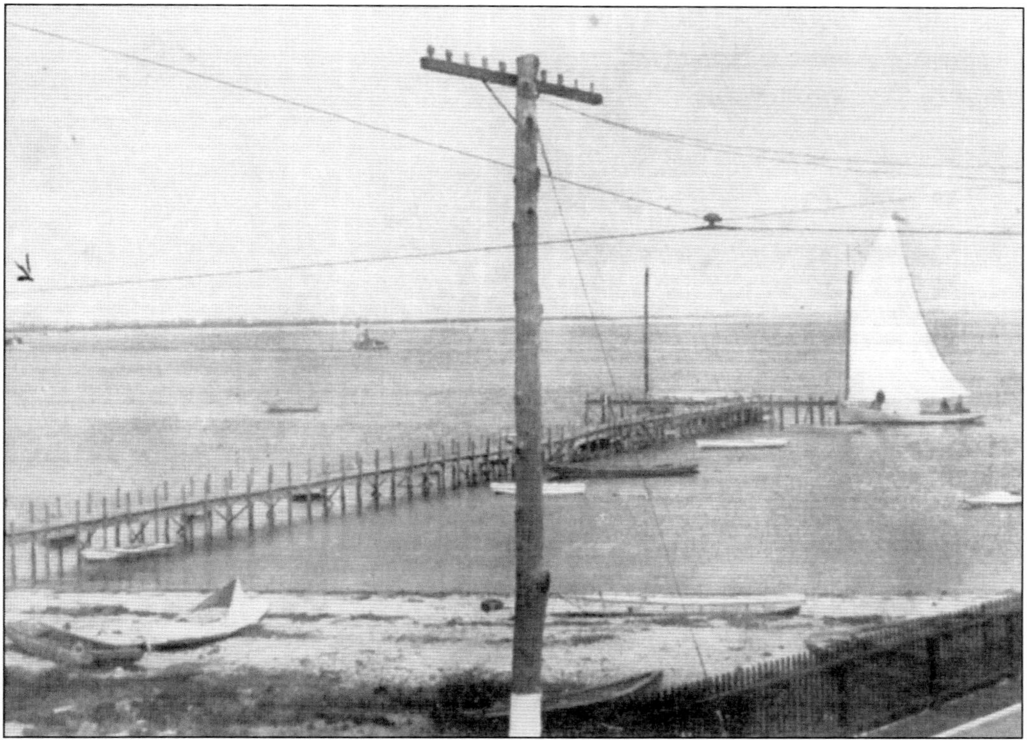

Shipbuilding was once a large part of life by the bay. Though much smaller than the ships that were once built here, this sailboat offers a pretty picture of what spending a day on the bay is all about.

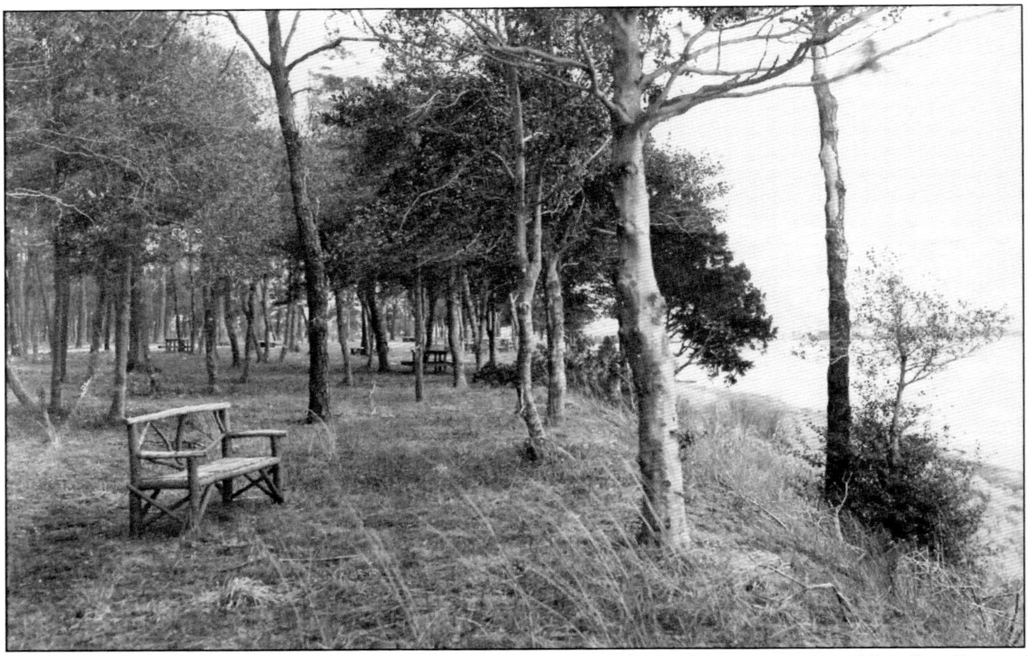

In the late 1930s, High Banks Park (now John F. Kennedy Park) was acquired by the City of Somers Point from the Scull family. The park used to be more wooded than it is today; over time, the trees have been thinned out, and the space now includes a road and parking areas for those who want to spend some time enjoying the bay breezes. (Courtesy Genevieve DeVito—The Don Balsley Collection.)

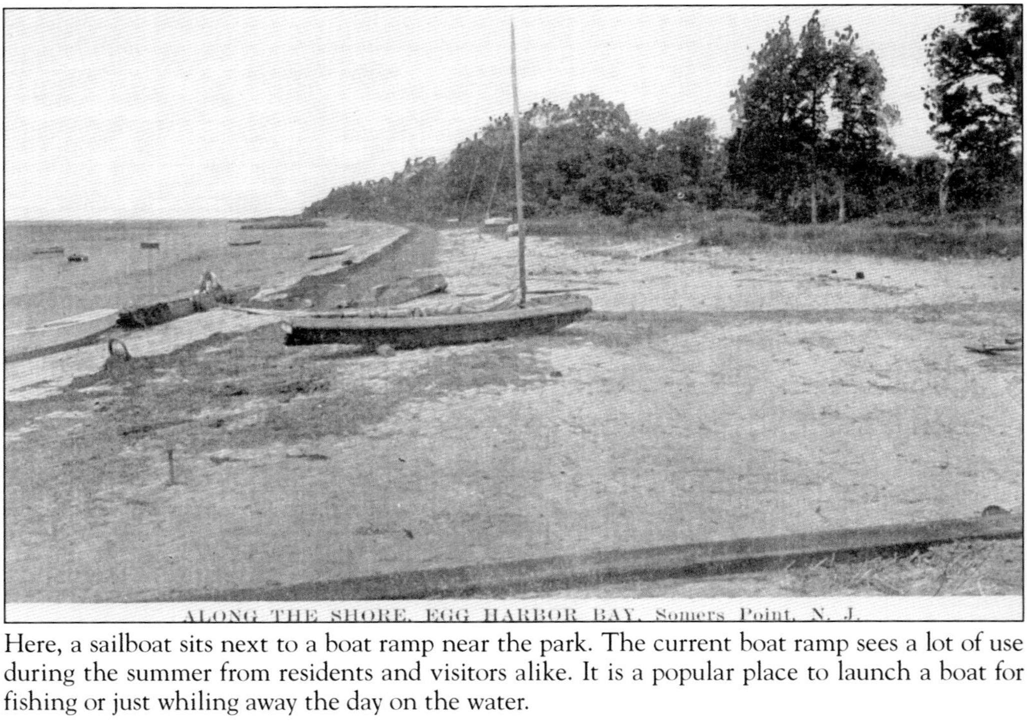

Here, a sailboat sits next to a boat ramp near the park. The current boat ramp sees a lot of use during the summer from residents and visitors alike. It is a popular place to launch a boat for fishing or just whiling away the day on the water.

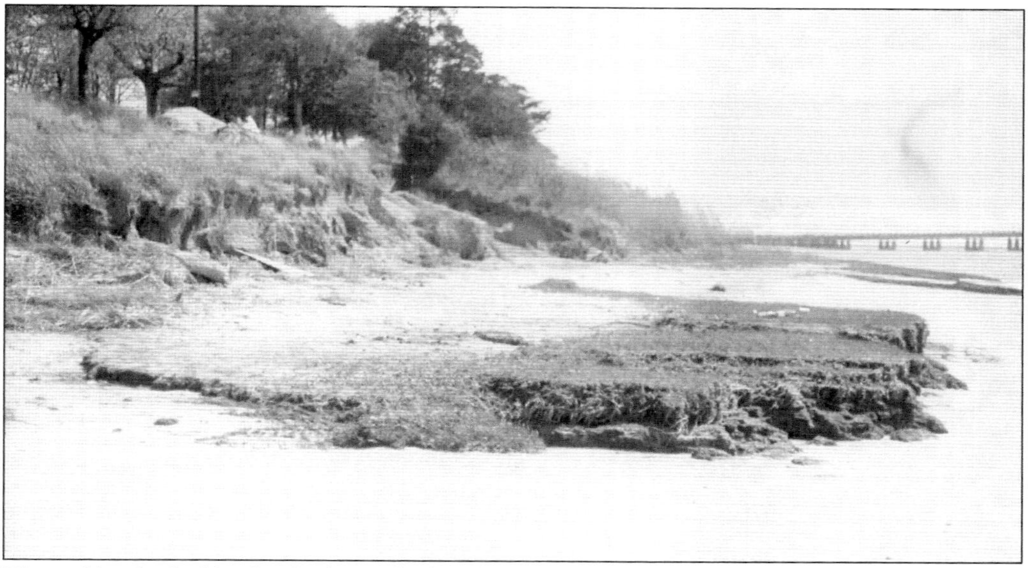

The sod banks, hidden by the bay at high tide, become more visible as the tide recedes. The sod banks are an important part of the ecosystem of the bay, serving as home to many of the small creatures that live there as well as providing food to the sea creatures. (Courtesy Kirk Gerety.)

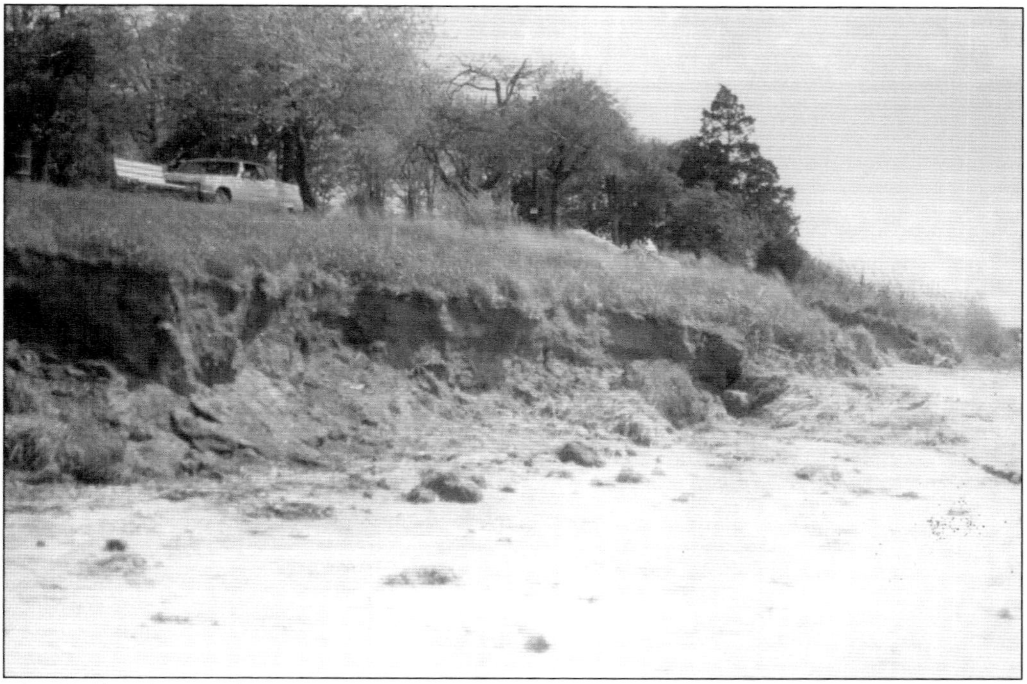

The bluff at the park has taken quite a beating over the years. This image shows how the high tides, especially during a storm, can damage and cut into the land below. For years, locals told legends of Capt. William Kidd burying his pirate treasure in Somers Point. Although damage from passing storms could often uncover an assortment of shells, arrowheads, remnants of Indian encampments, and even old bottles buried by the bay, no treasure has ever been recovered at the park. (Courtesy Kirk Gerety.)

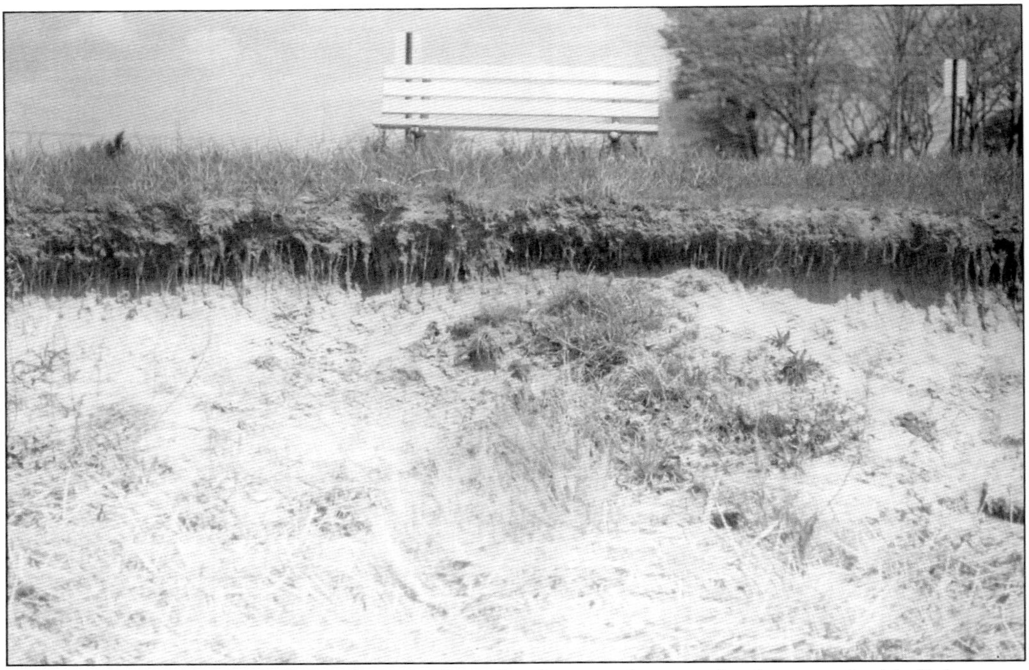

These two photographs offer a closer look at the damage that can be done to the bluff during a storm. The bluff at High Banks is one of only two bluffs in New Jersey. Over the years, precautions have been taken to protect the bluff from further erosion. A local school group ran a "Save the Bluff" campaign to help in this effort. (Both, courtesy Kirk Gerety.)

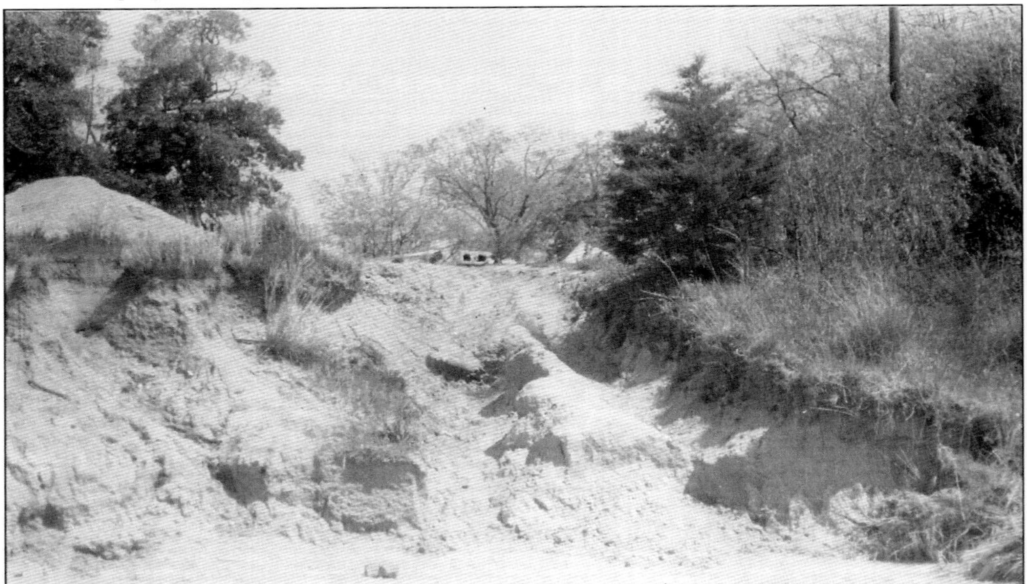

Two

AROUND THE CIRCLE

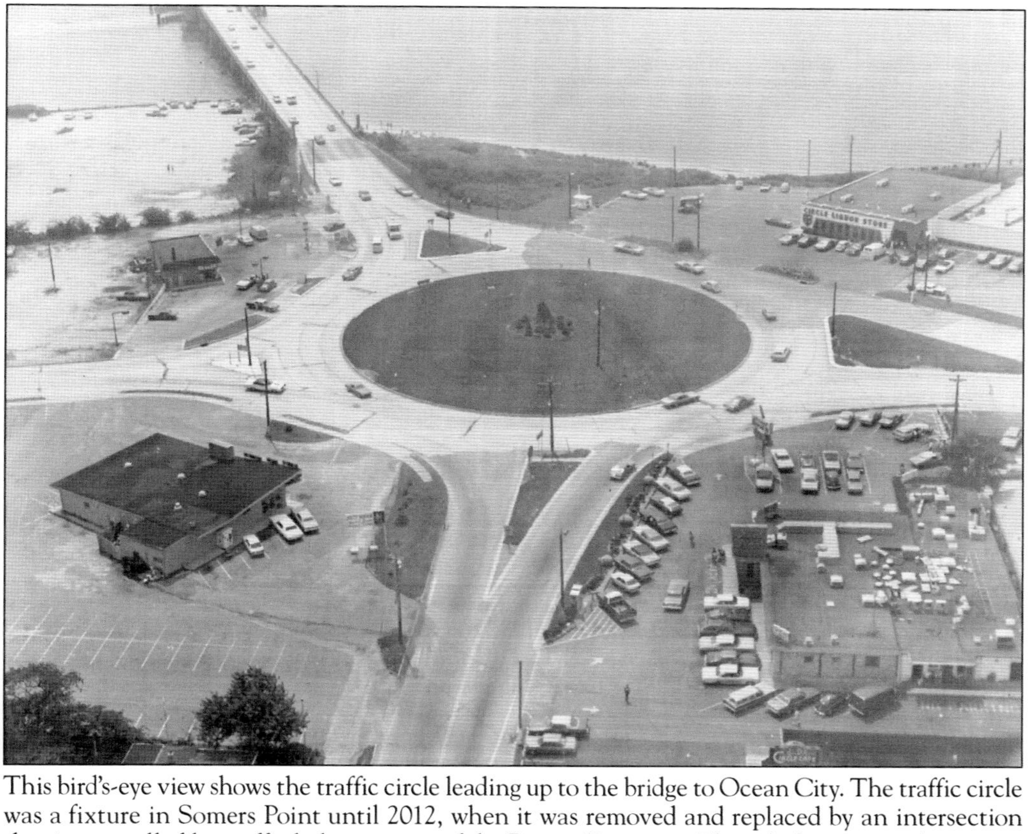

This bird's-eye view shows the traffic circle leading up to the bridge to Ocean City. The traffic circle was a fixture in Somers Point until 2012, when it was removed and replaced by an intersection that is controlled by traffic lights, as part of the Route 52 project. Thought by many to be a more efficient way to get around the intersection, the circle will be missed by many longtime residents for many years to come. (Courtesy William E. Swain.)

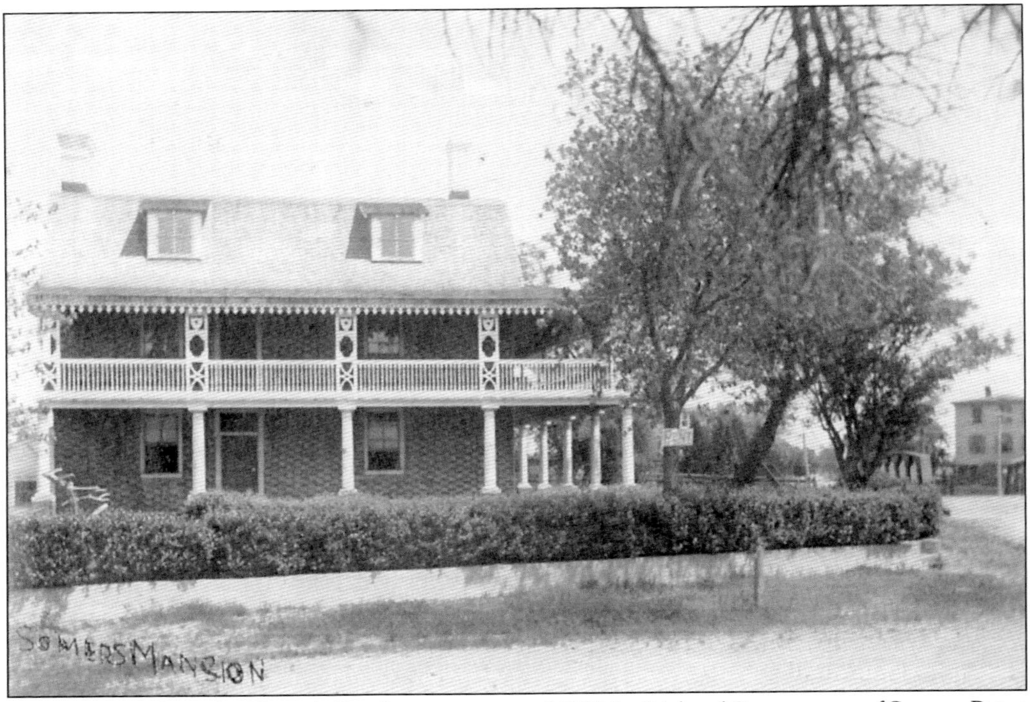

Built from brick in the Flemish Bond pattern around 1725 by Richard Somers, son of Somers Point founder John Somers, Somers Mansion still stands today. The picture above shows the mansion after renovations done around 1860 gave it a more Victorian look that was popular at the time. The picture below shows the results of the restoration done by the Work Projects Administration (WPA). This restoration brought the mansion back to its original appearance. On September 26, 1944, Mayor Fred Chapman declared a public holiday and a dedication ceremony was held for the Somers Mansion.

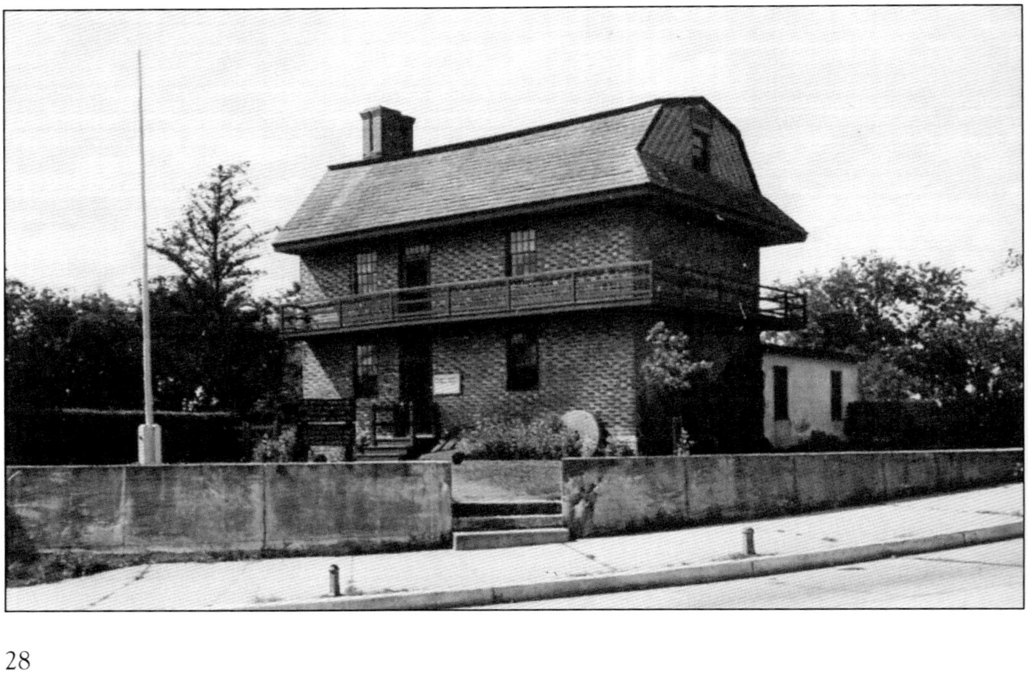

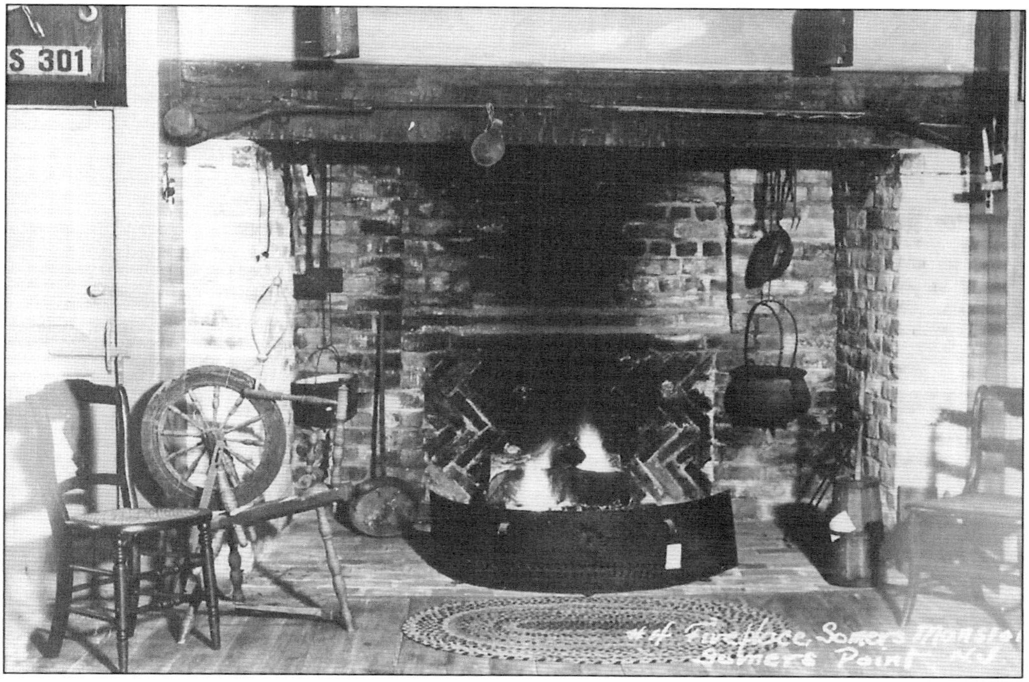

Interior views from Somers Mansion show the downstairs fireplace (above), used for cooking and heat, and many of the period furnishings and artifacts (below) that were once part of the public tour of the mansion. Somers Mansion is the former home of the Atlantic County Historical Society and is currently owned by the New Jersey Department of Environmental Protection. (Both, courtesy Ruth Mulford Newsome.)

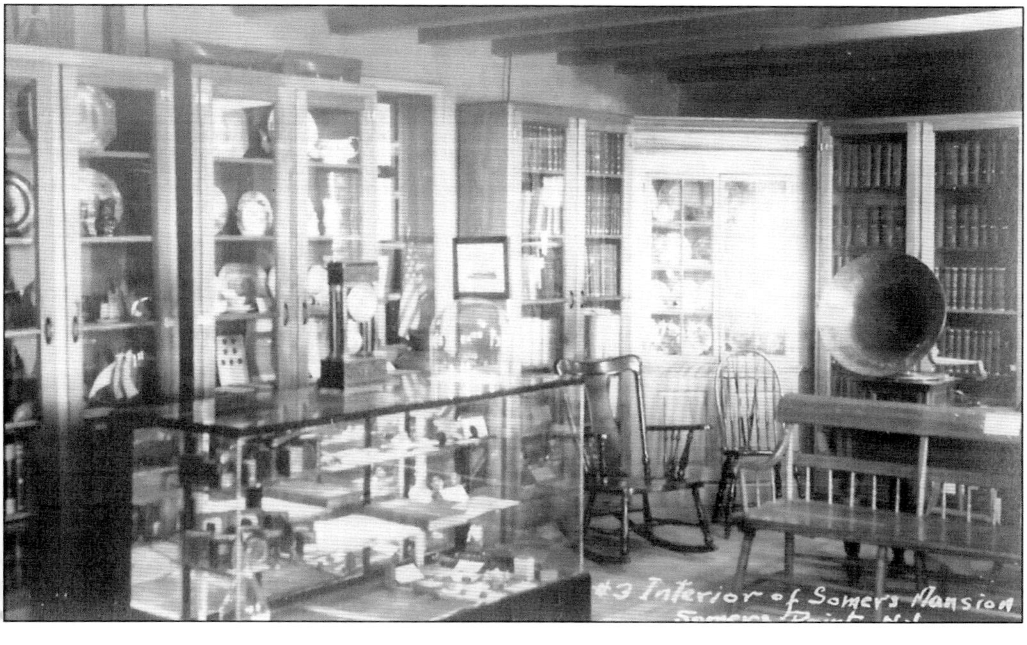

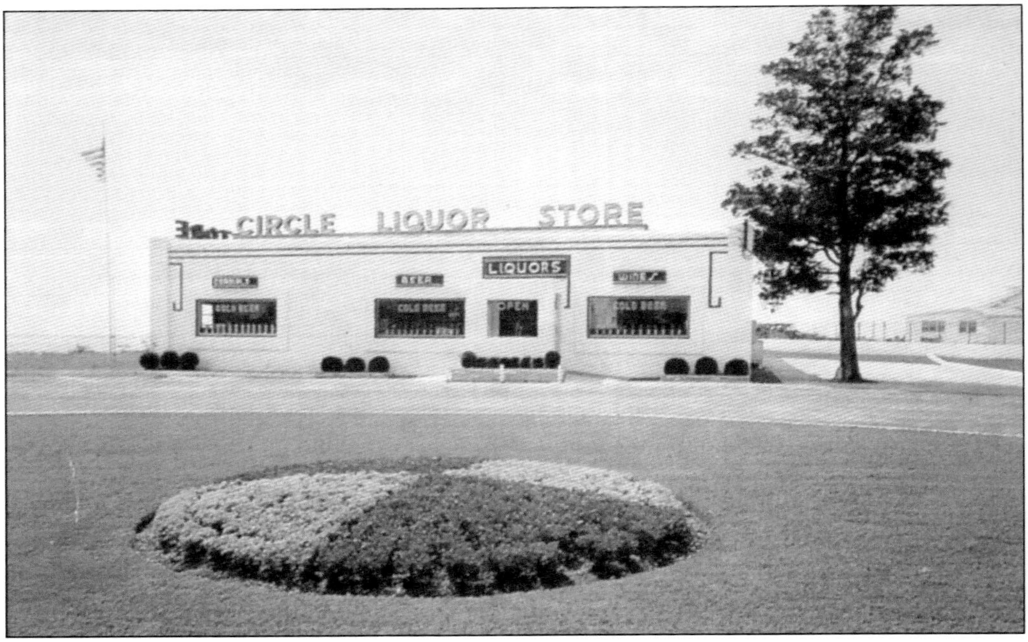

The Circle Liquor Store opened on the traffic circle in 1938. Although the circle may now be gone, the Circle Liquor Store is celebrating its 75th anniversary in 2013.

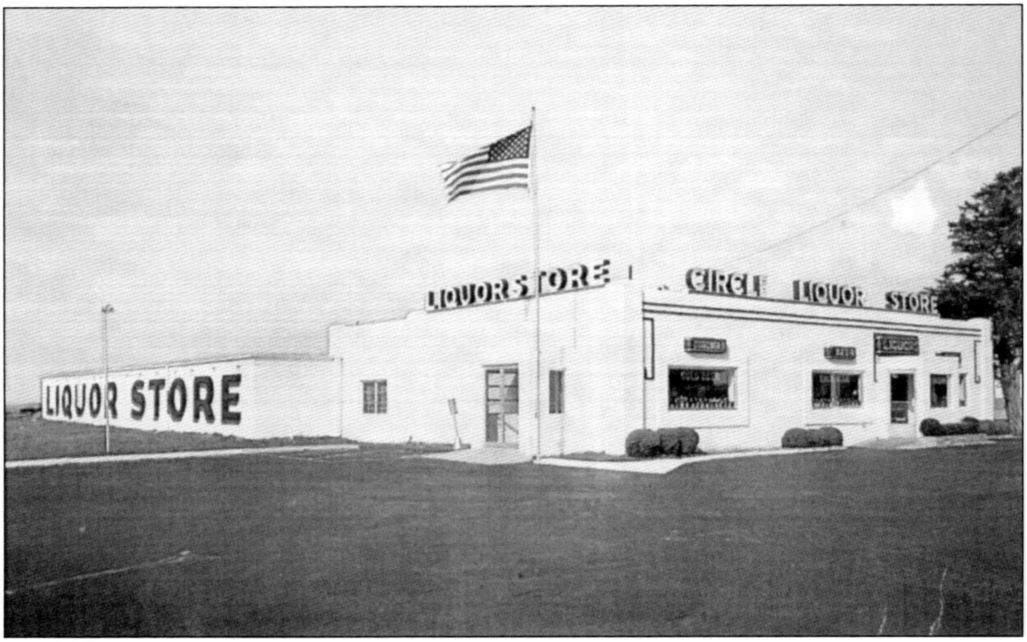

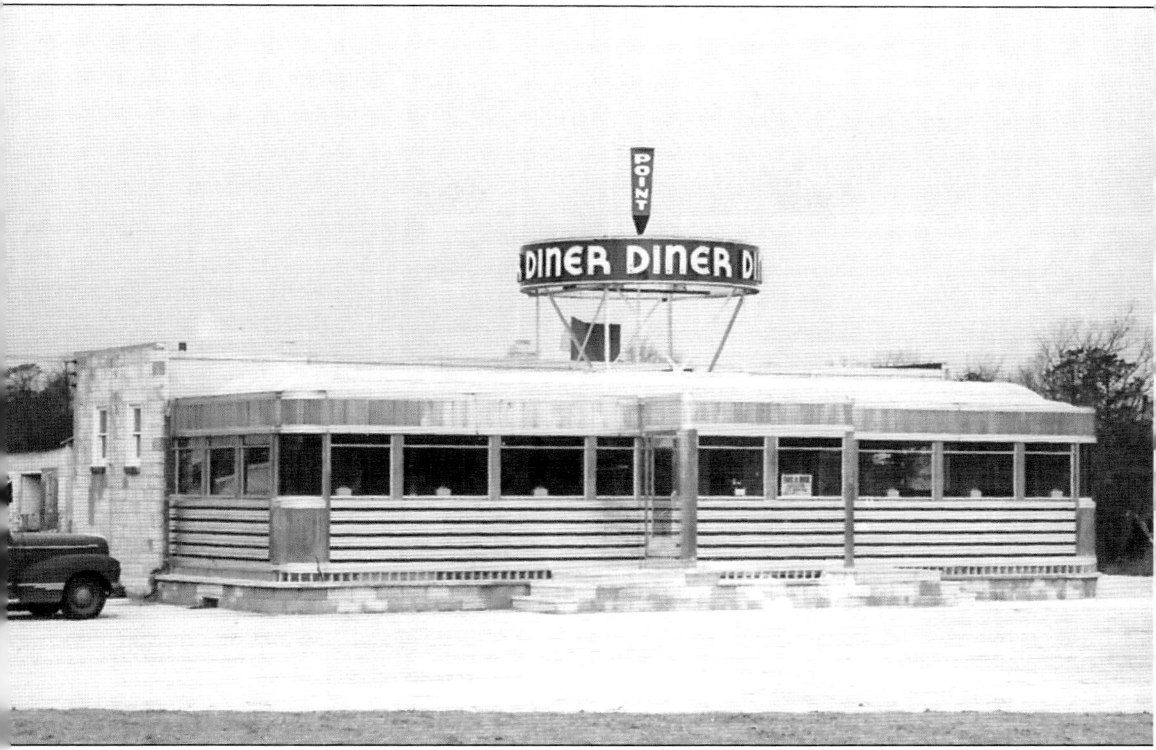

An early photograph of the Point Diner, located on the circle, shows a 1950s-style diner. In more recent years, the building has undergone updating and expansion. Just as it did in the 1950s, the diner continues to serve locals and visitors. Young people can still be found here, grabbing a bite to eat after a night on the town, just as their predecessors did decades ago.

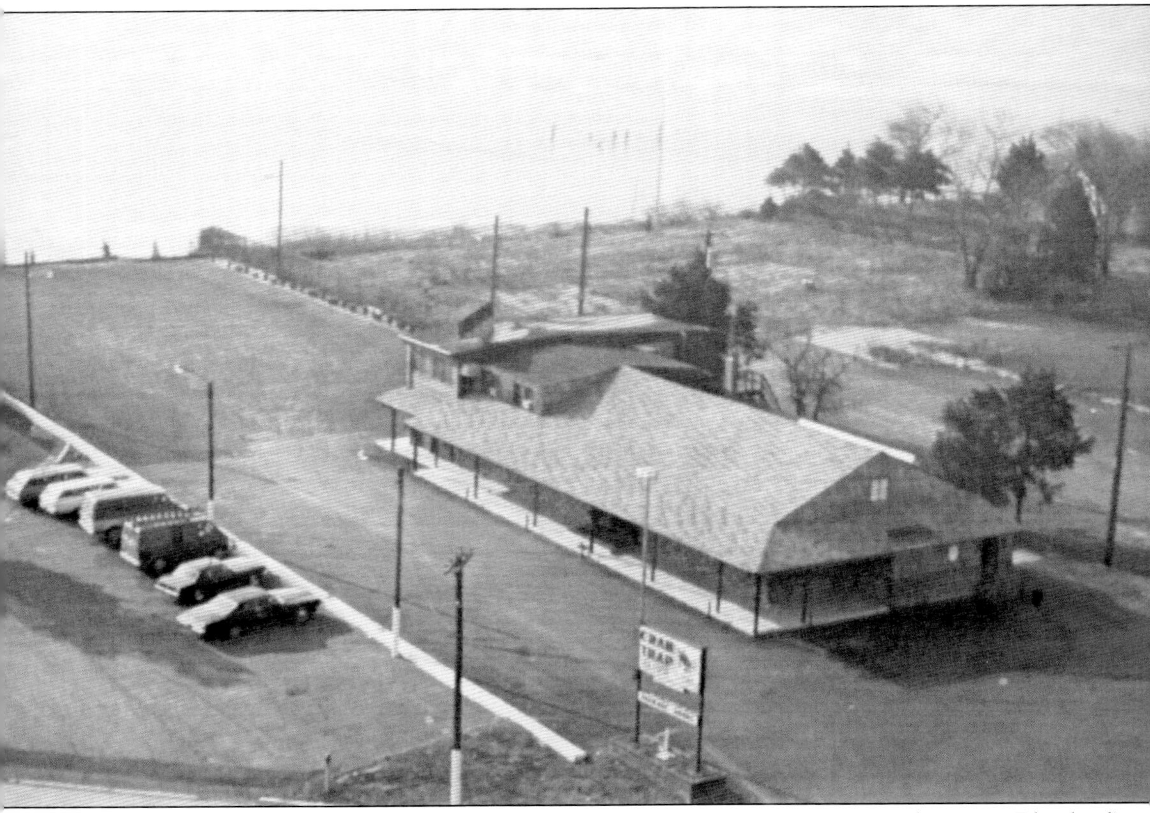

The Crab Trap Restaurant was established in 1967 at the former Maenner's location. This bird's-eye view, taken in the 1970s, shows how little development was in that area of town at the time. Since then, the Crab Trap has seen expansion and renovations, as well as the addition of Crabby Jack's to the rear of the property on the bay. The area has seen development as well, with the Pier 4 Hotel next door to the Crab Trap and residential housing on Broadway. The Crab Trap remains a popular fine dining establishment in Somers Point.

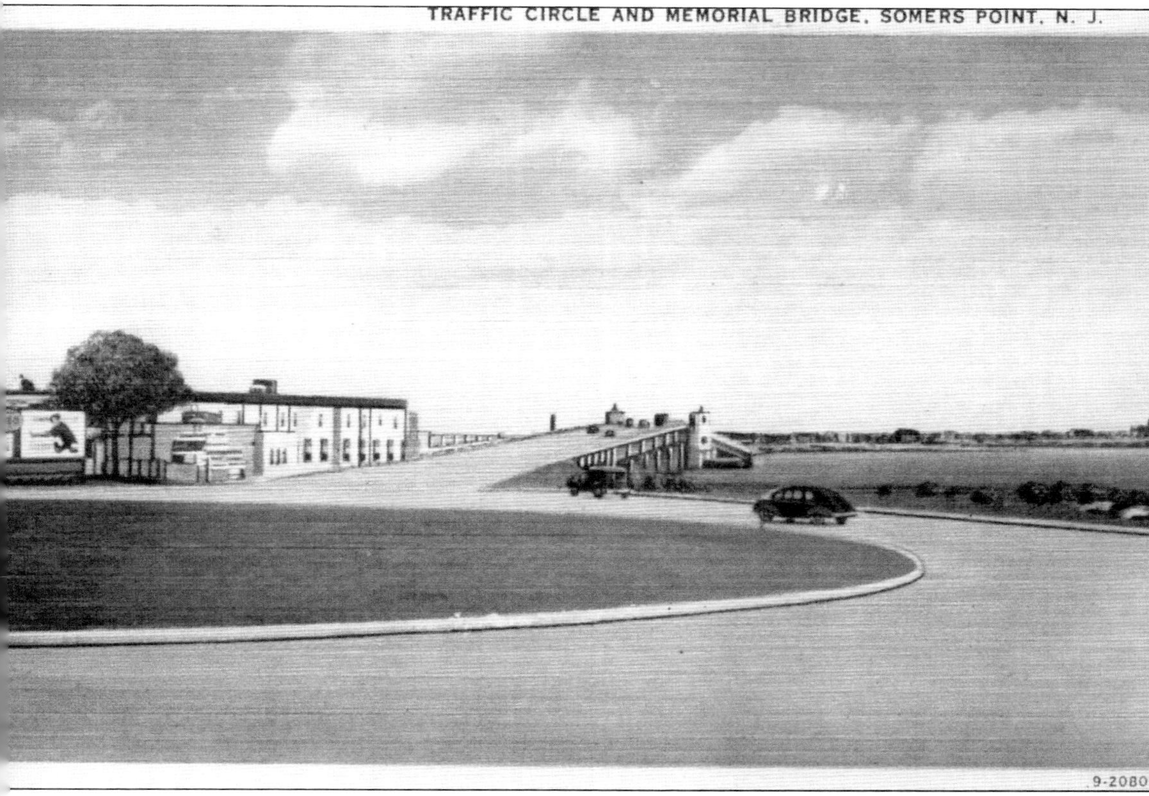

This is an early view of the Somers Point traffic circle (completed in 1935) approaching the Somers Point–Ocean City Bridge (built in 1932). At left is the former Gateway Casino building. Constructed in 1926, the Gateway Casino saw good times and bad, including the stock market crash of 1929, Prohibition, and foreclosure. From 1952 to 1957, the building served as the Gateway Playhouse. In 1957, it was occupied by the Prudential Insurance Company and the playhouse moved down Bay Avenue to the Seaside Theatre at the corner of Bay and Higbee Avenues.

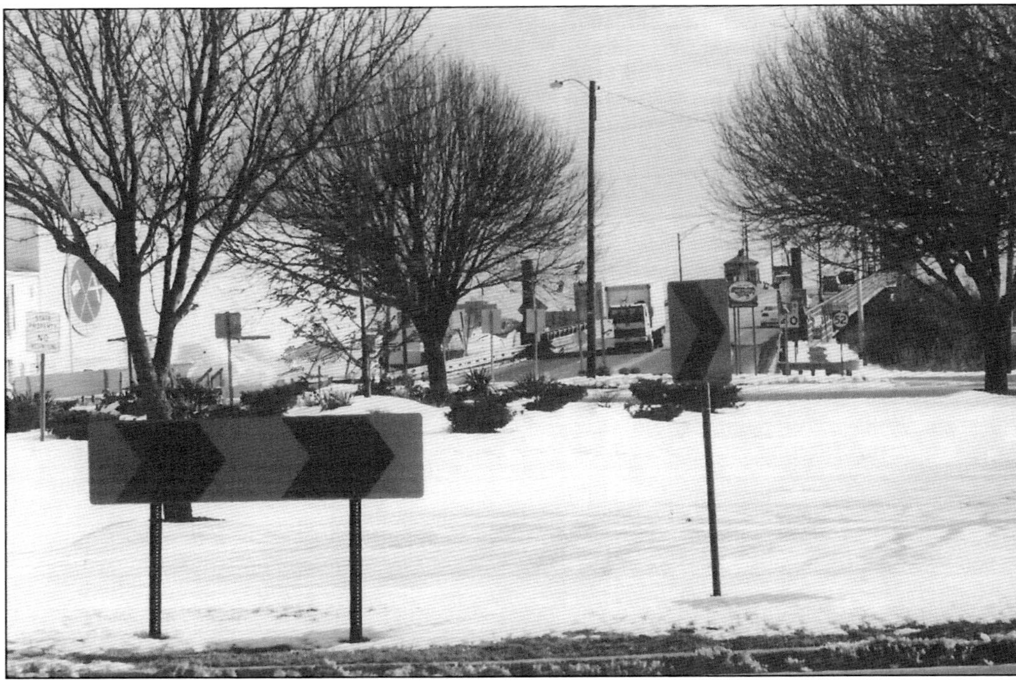

These two photographs offer a driver's view of the Somers Point circle. With the increase in traffic over the years, the department of transportation added arrow signs pointing in the direction drivers needed to follow to navigate the circle. This is not to say that people, on occasion, would not go the wrong way. (Both, courtesy Joan Bird Wilson.)

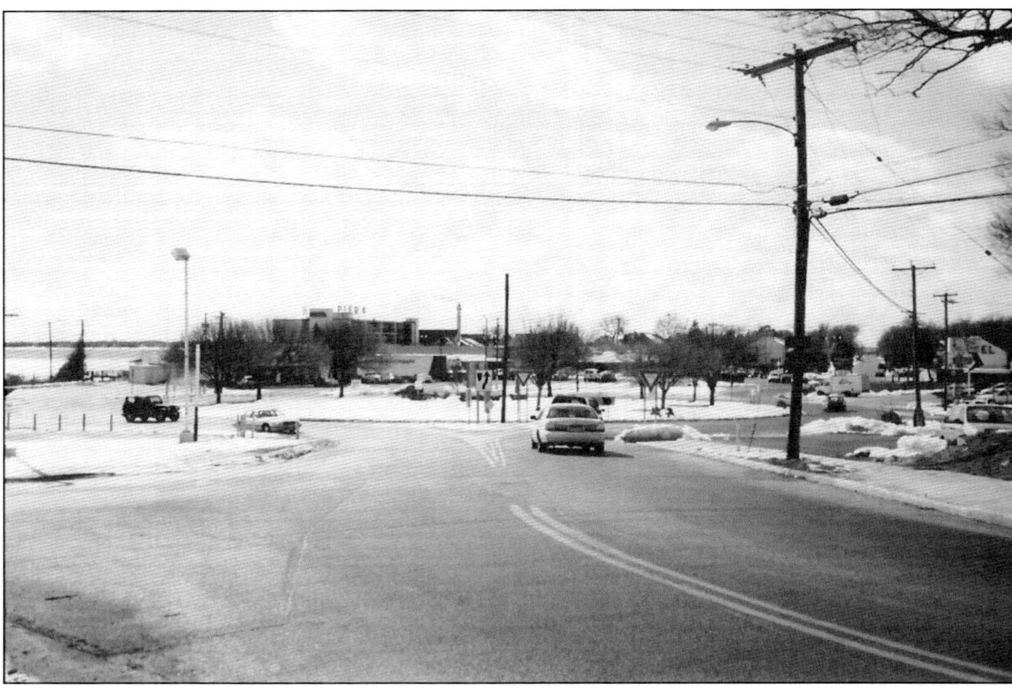

Three

TRANSPORTATION

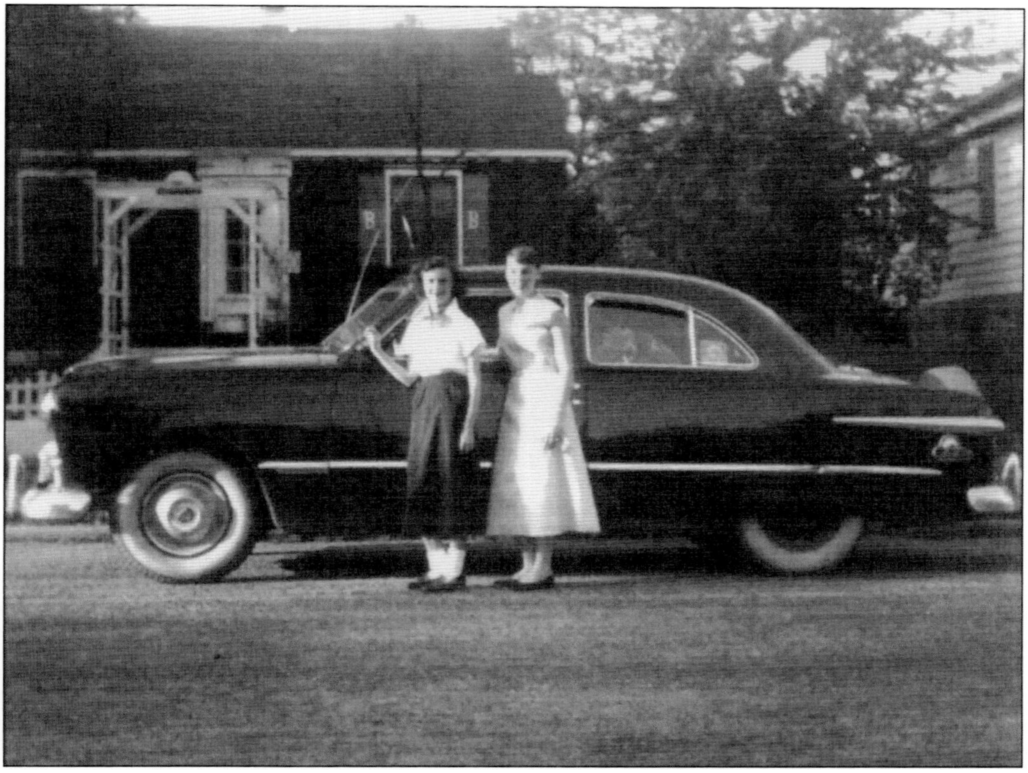

Ruth Mulford Newsome (left) and Joan Bird Wilson stand beside Joan's brother Ronnie's 1949 Ford. With Ronnie away serving in the Navy and Joan getting her driver's license, this car soon became Ruth and Joan's main form of transportation. (Courtesy Ruth Mulford Newsome.)

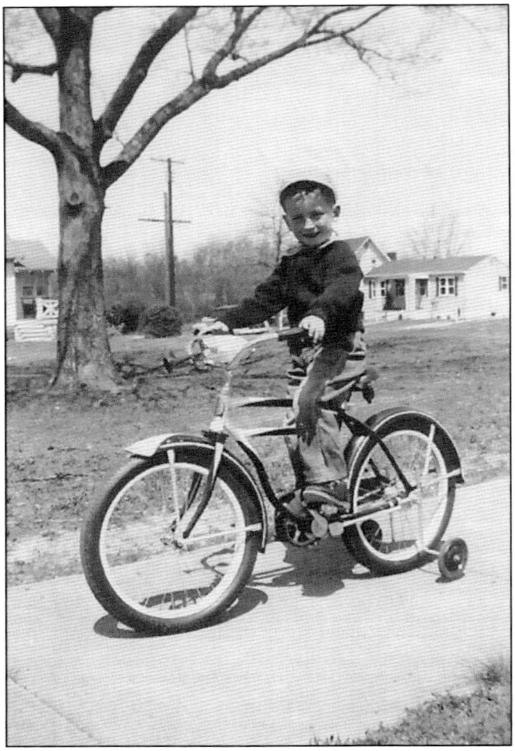

Transportation does not always have to be motorized. Here, young Bob Loper enjoys a bike ride on Easter Sunday in 1954. As in most towns, a bike was often a young person's main source of transportation. (Courtesy Bob Loper.)

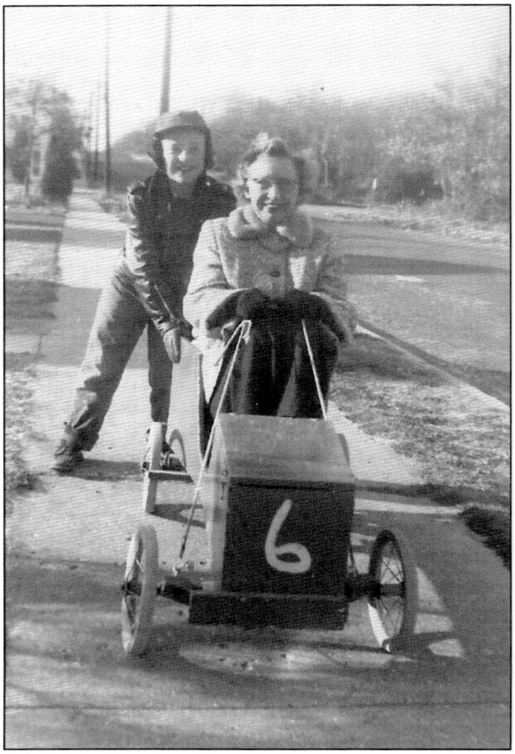

Bob Loper pushes his mother Ruth Greis Loper in the soapbox derby car built for him by his uncle Bill Greis. Soapbox derby races were held on Goll Avenue, where racers would begin at the top of the hill at Shore Road and race to the bottom of the hill at Bay Avenue. In 1956, Bob, driving this car, came in second to Billy Shaffer's first-place win. Once a popular pastime for kids, soapbox derby races are now mostly a thing of the past. (Courtesy Bob Loper.)

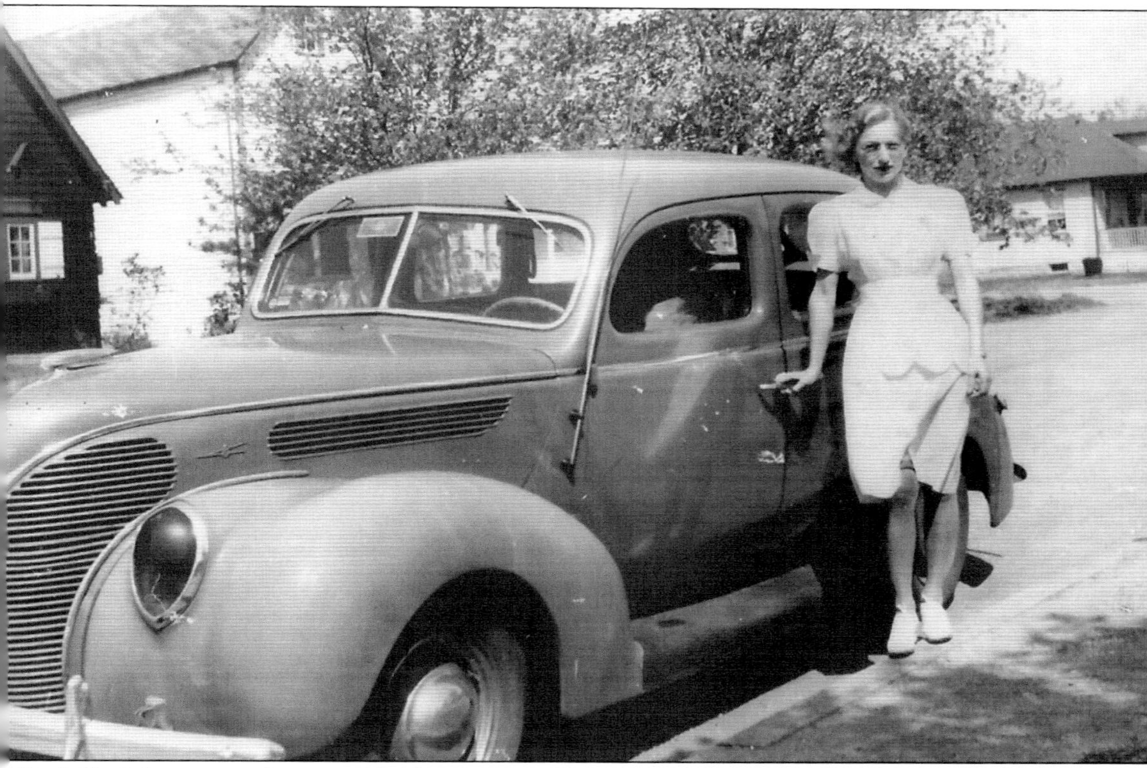

Ruth Greis Loper stands next to the family car on Pennsylvania Avenue in the 1940s as she gets ready to head to work for the day. Wearing her uniform, she is headed to her shift as a waitress at Mac's Restaurant. (Courtesy Bob Loper.)

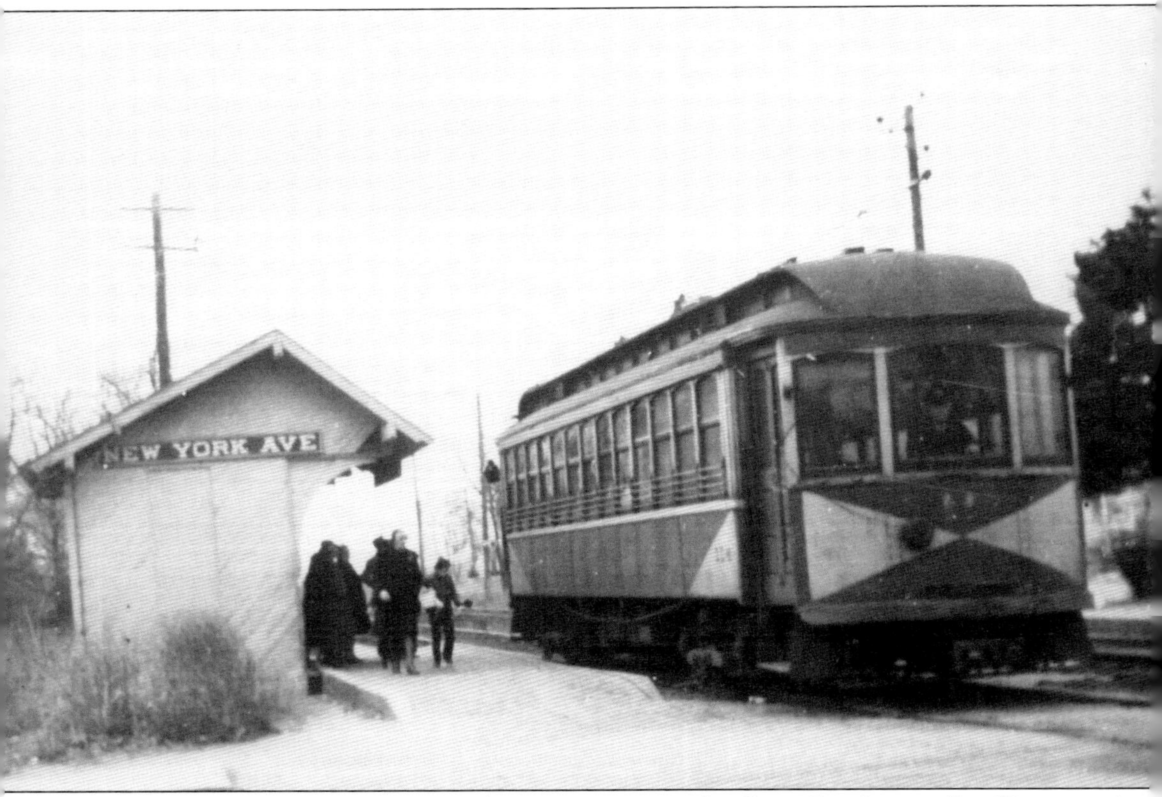

A popular form of transportation for many years was the Shore Fast Line trolley. Here, people board the trolley to head north toward Atlantic City. (Courtesy Ruth Mulford Newsome.)

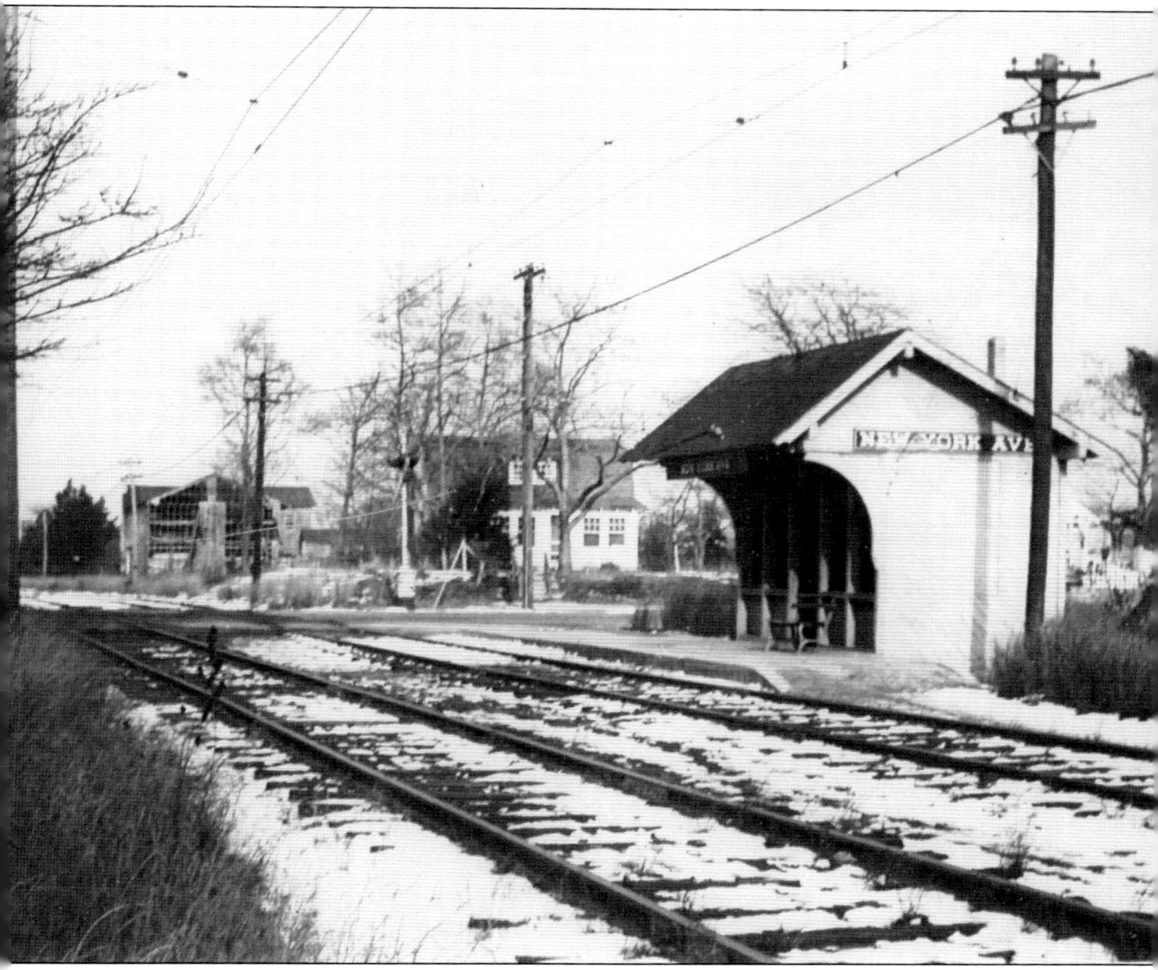

The New York Avenue trolley stop was located at the southeast corner of New York Avenue and First Street. The first Smith Lumber building is visible in the distance on the left. At 11:20 p.m. on February 18, 1949, the building burned to the ground. (Courtesy John Dunn.)

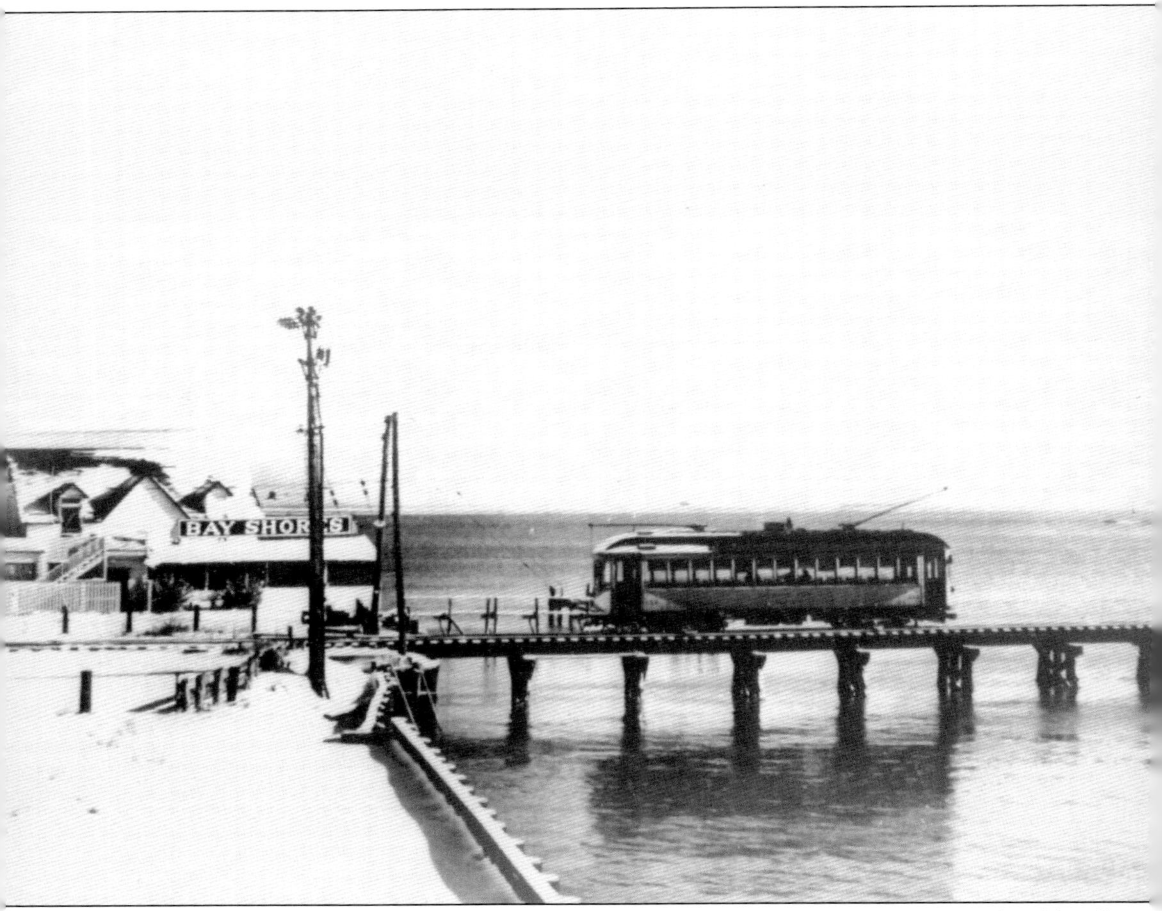

This Shore Fast Line trolley is on its way back from Ocean City to Somers Point on the old trolley bridge. After trolley service was stopped and the main portion of the bridge was removed, a section of this bridge remained. Many young people spent many a night sitting on that remaining portion of the trolley bridge and listening to bands playing at Bay Shores. The last part of bridge was removed in May 1989. (Courtesy Bob Loper.)

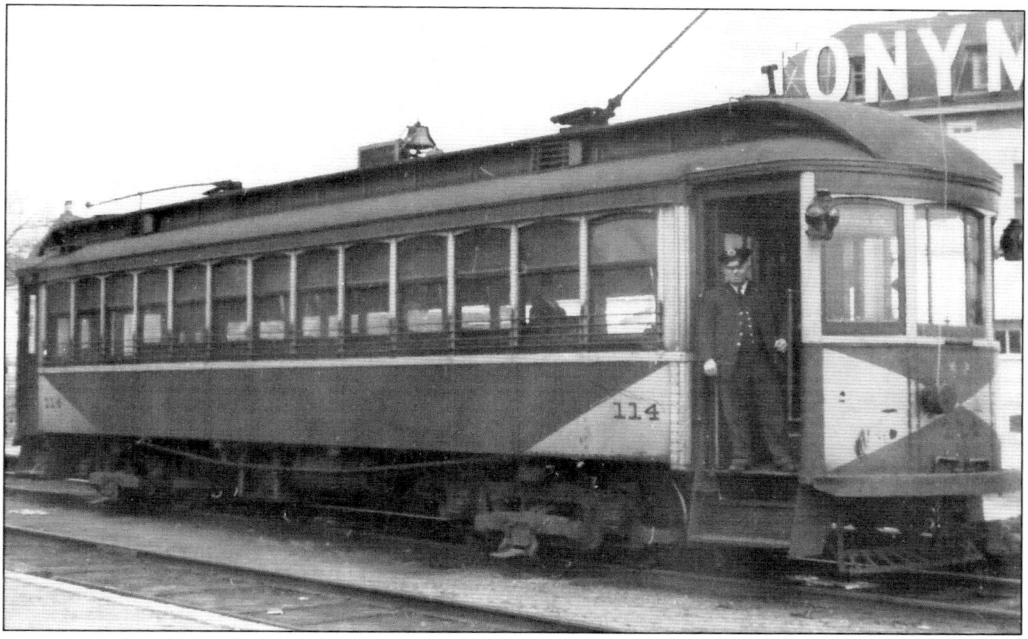

Trolley No. 114 and its conductor wait for passengers, with Tony Mart's in the background. The Shore Fast Line ran between Atlantic City and Ocean City beginning on August 25, 1906. Service was ended on January 18, 1948.

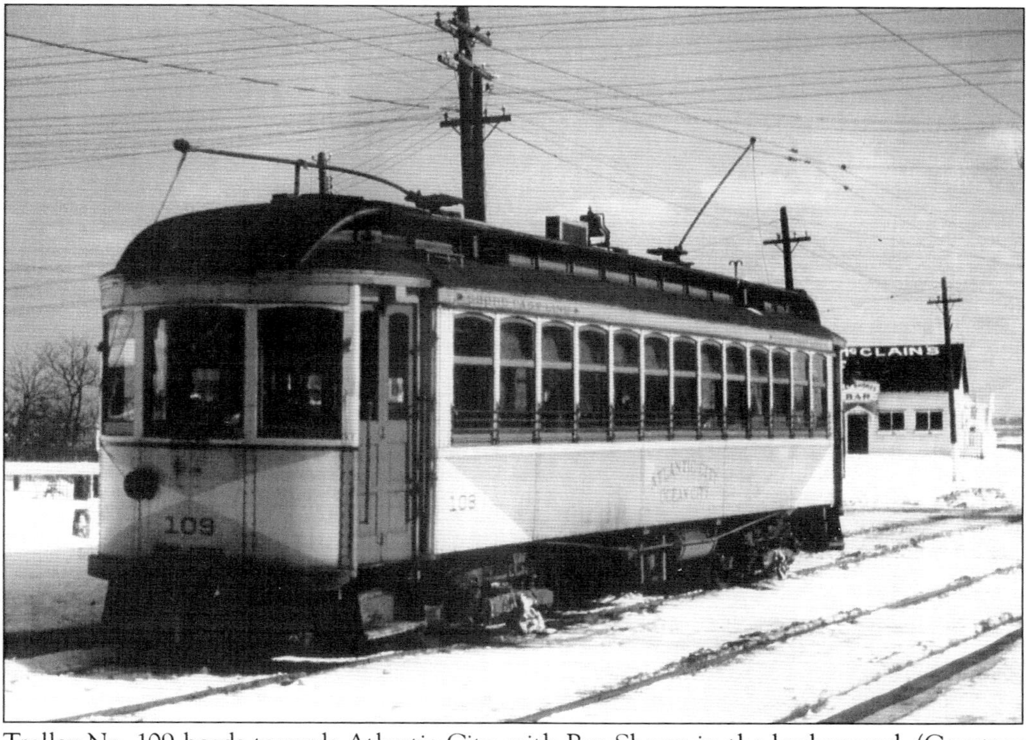

Trolley No. 109 heads towards Atlantic City, with Bay Shores in the background. (Courtesy John Dunn.)

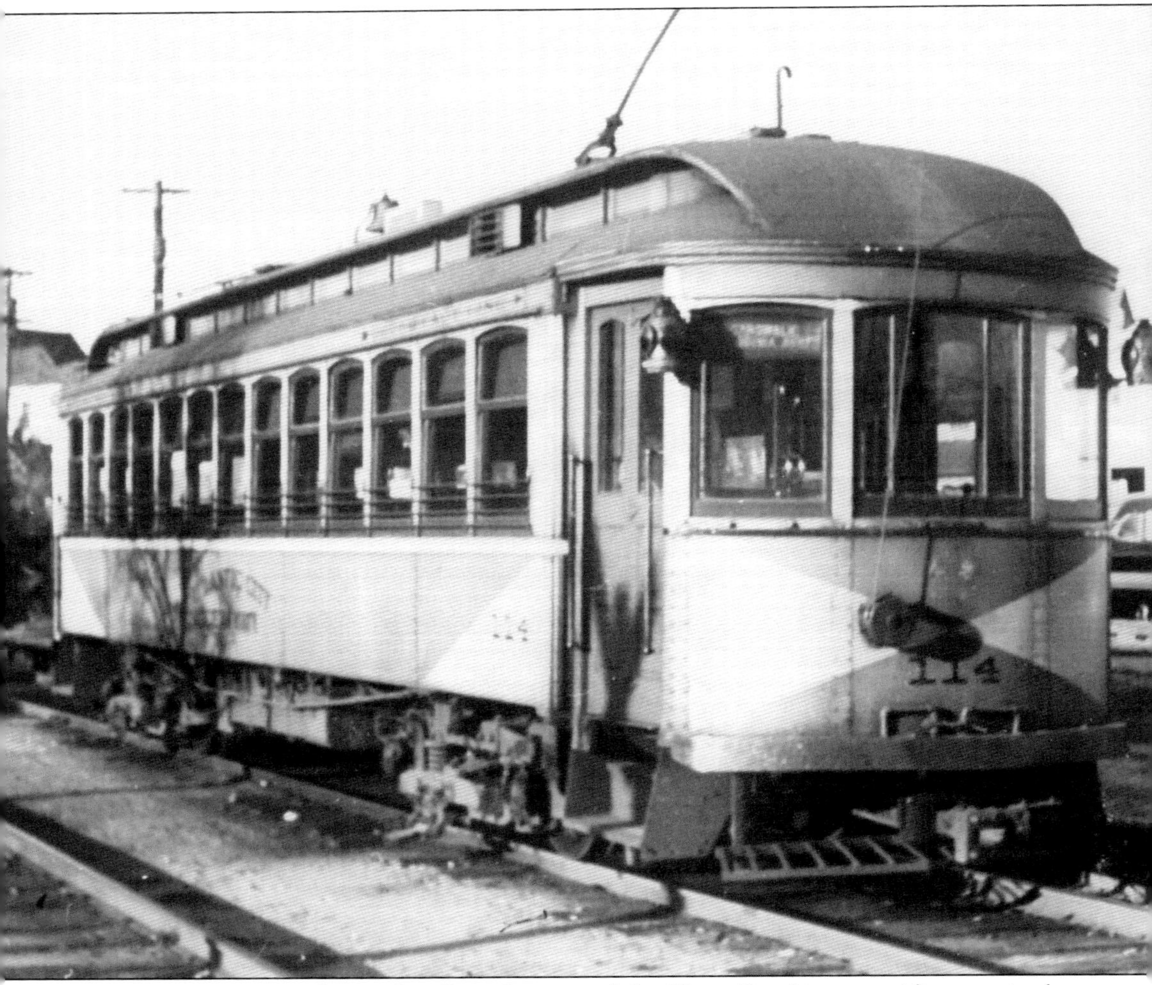

No. 114 was one of several trolleys that served the Shore Fast Line, providing service between Atlantic City and Ocean City. (Courtesy John Dunn.)

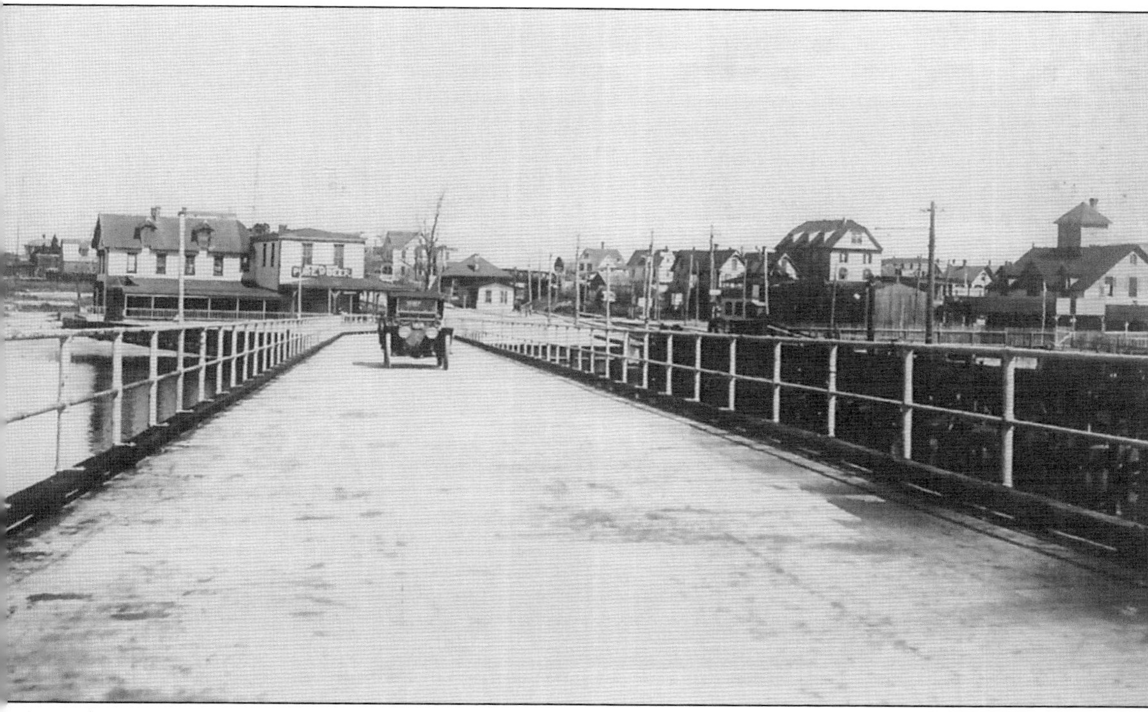

A car leaving Somers Point heads towards Ocean City on the first automobile-accessible bridge to link the two communities. In the background at left is the Bayview House. To the immediate right of the bridge is the trolley station, and farther to the right is the tall building that was Schick's Hotel and, later, Tony Mart's.

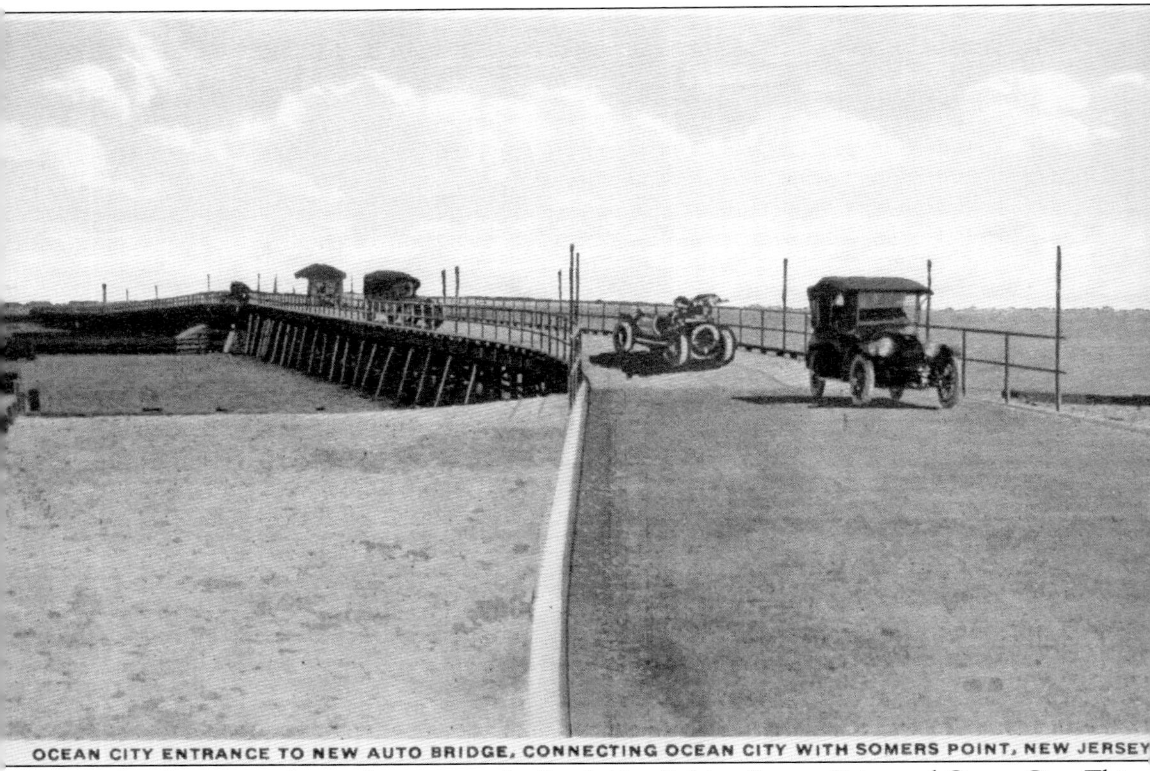

On this postcard, cars drive across the first bridge linking Somers Point and Ocean City. This was a private toll bridge until it was acquired by the Highway Department of New Jersey in 1922. The toll tender's building is visible about halfway along the span.

Four

Around Town

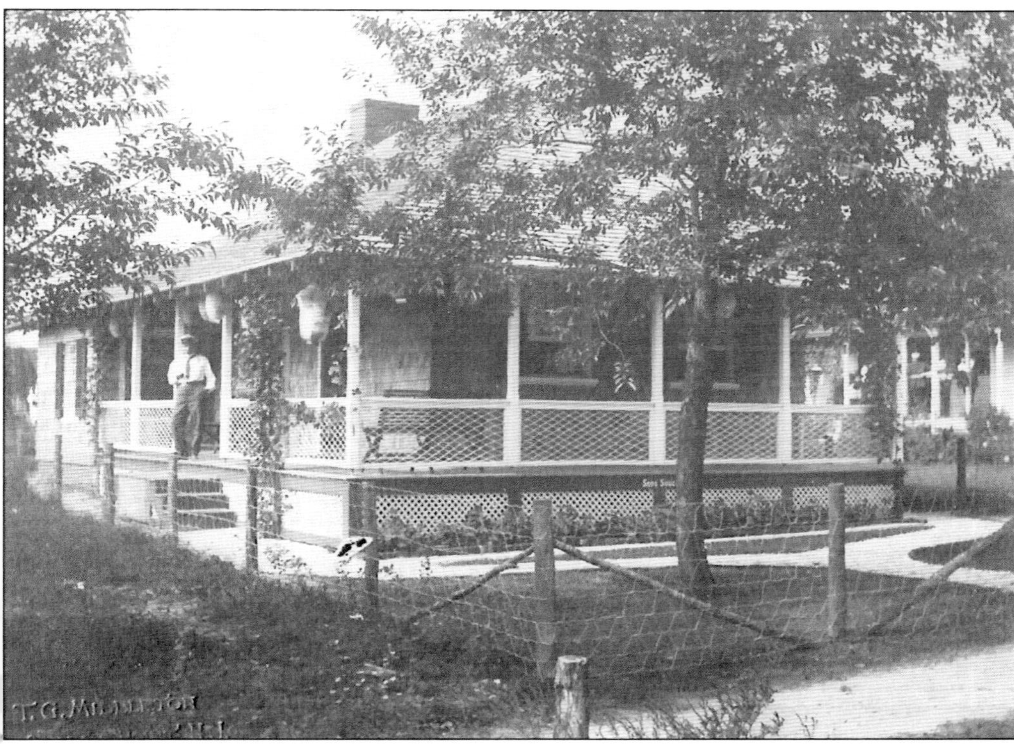

C.T. Murray stands on his Annie Avenue porch in 1908. According to writings by Murray, the lanterns hanging on the porch were from a ball held at the house; in his words, "the lanterns looked gay at night."

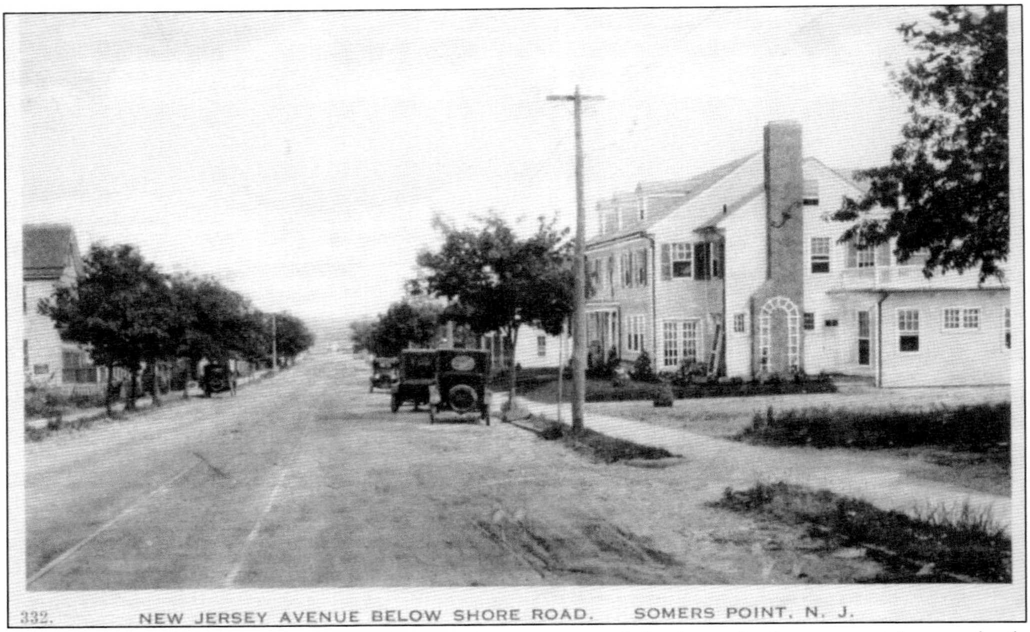

In this image looking east on New Jersey Avenue toward the bay, the home at right was built in two sections and has always been two residences. The left side of the house was constructed around 1886 by Jobwin Steelman, who had been commissioned to build it for John Townsend. Townsend had been a sea captain and was a councilman on the first council of Somers Point. The original home was sold to postmaster Capt. Walter Sooy in the 1890s. In 1919, Arthur Chenoweth and his wife, Mary North Chenoweth, purchased the home. During the Depression, Naomi Craighead, a friend of Mary Chenoweth, added onto the right side of the building to create her residence—having lost her husband, she sold their property, Craig Hall, in Atlantic City, and moved to Somers Point.

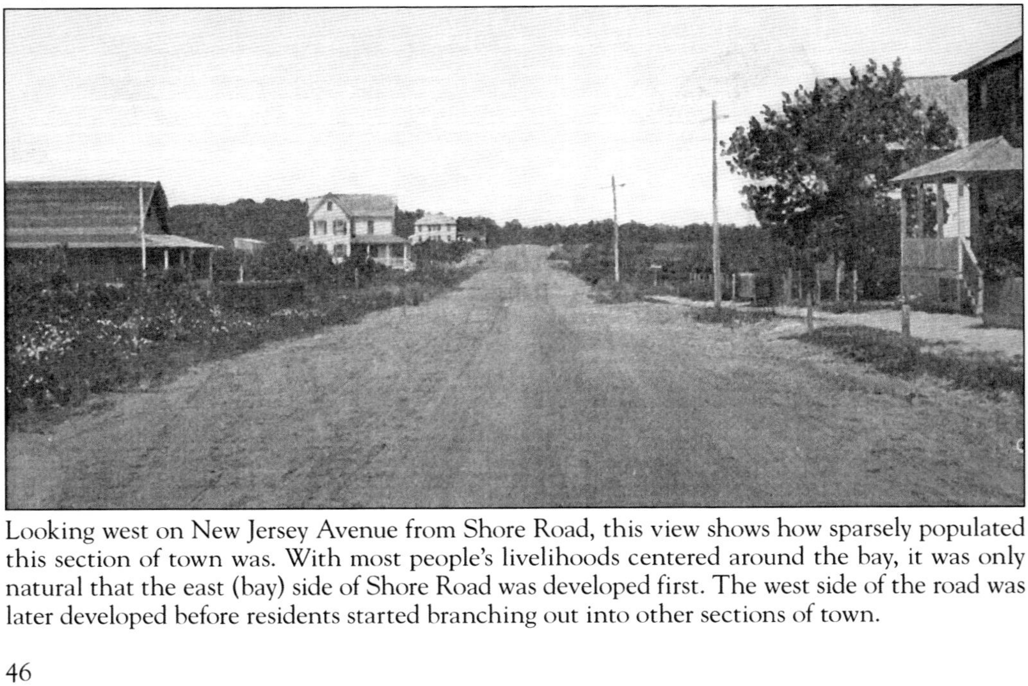

Looking west on New Jersey Avenue from Shore Road, this view shows how sparsely populated this section of town was. With most people's livelihoods centered around the bay, it was only natural that the east (bay) side of Shore Road was developed first. The west side of the road was later developed before residents started branching out into other sections of town.

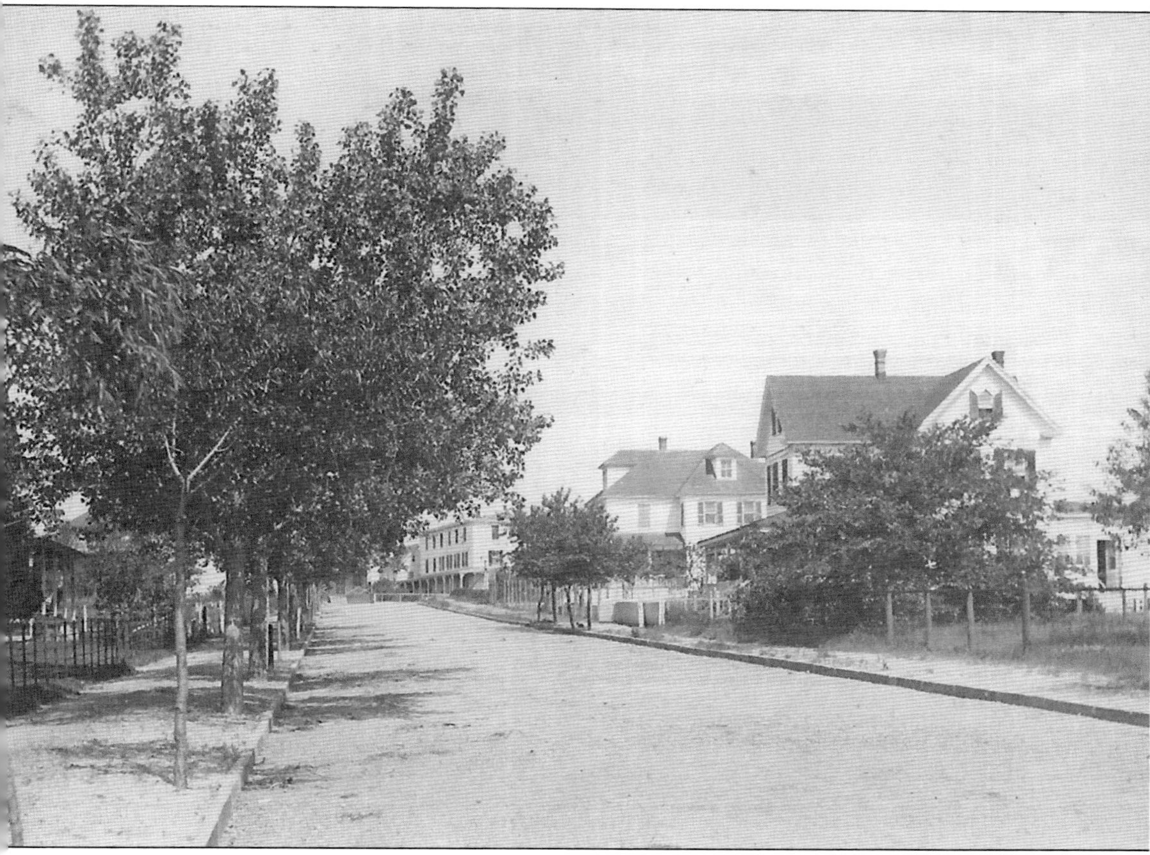

This view looking up Somers Avenue from Bay Avenue shows buildings that are still there today. At the top of the street, to the right, is the Waverly Hotel. It was located on the southwest corner of Somers Avenue and Shore Road. This structure has since been torn down, and the site is now a parking lot.

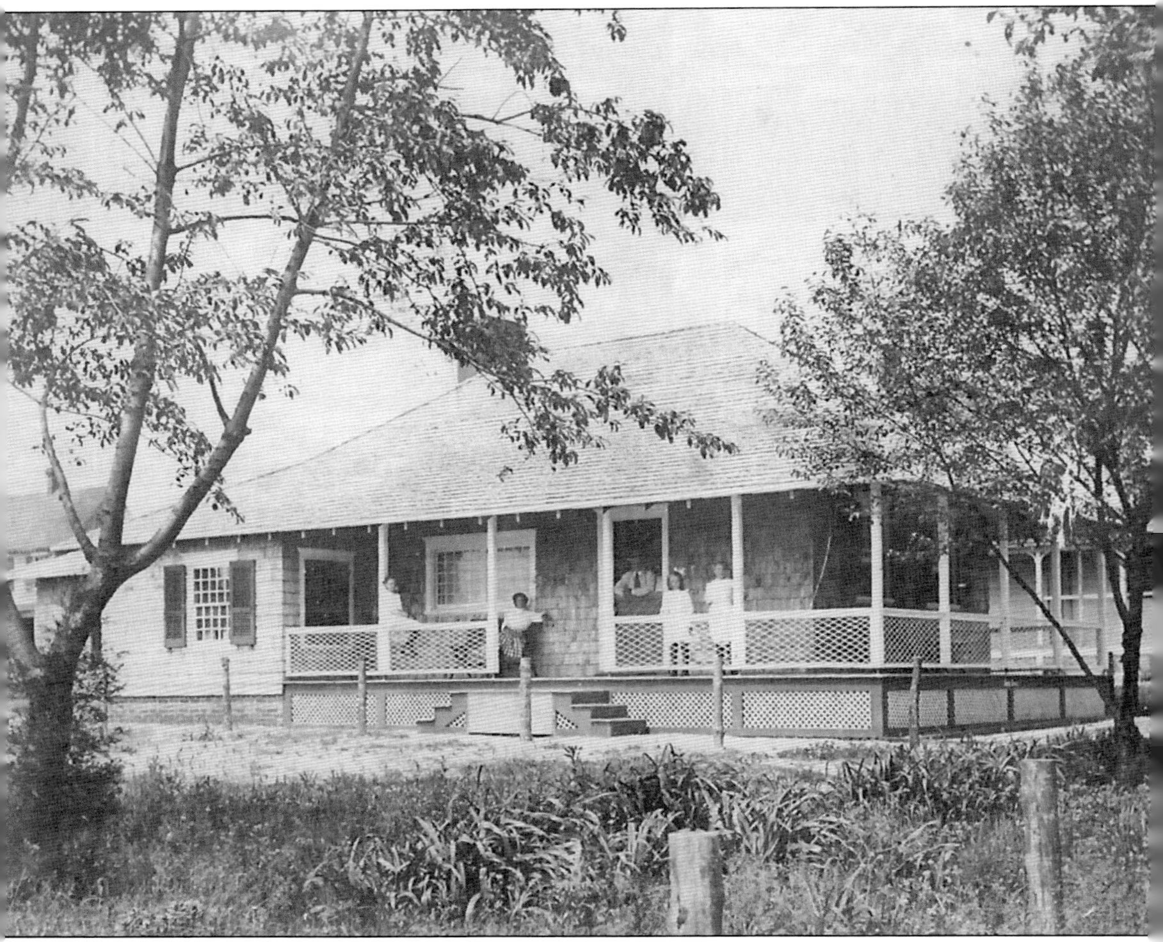

In this 1908 photograph, C.T. Murray stands in the doorway of his Annie Avenue home as his wife, Cora, sits on the bench on the porch. C.T.'s writings state that the front of the house faces Annie Avenue and the "salt water is just below."

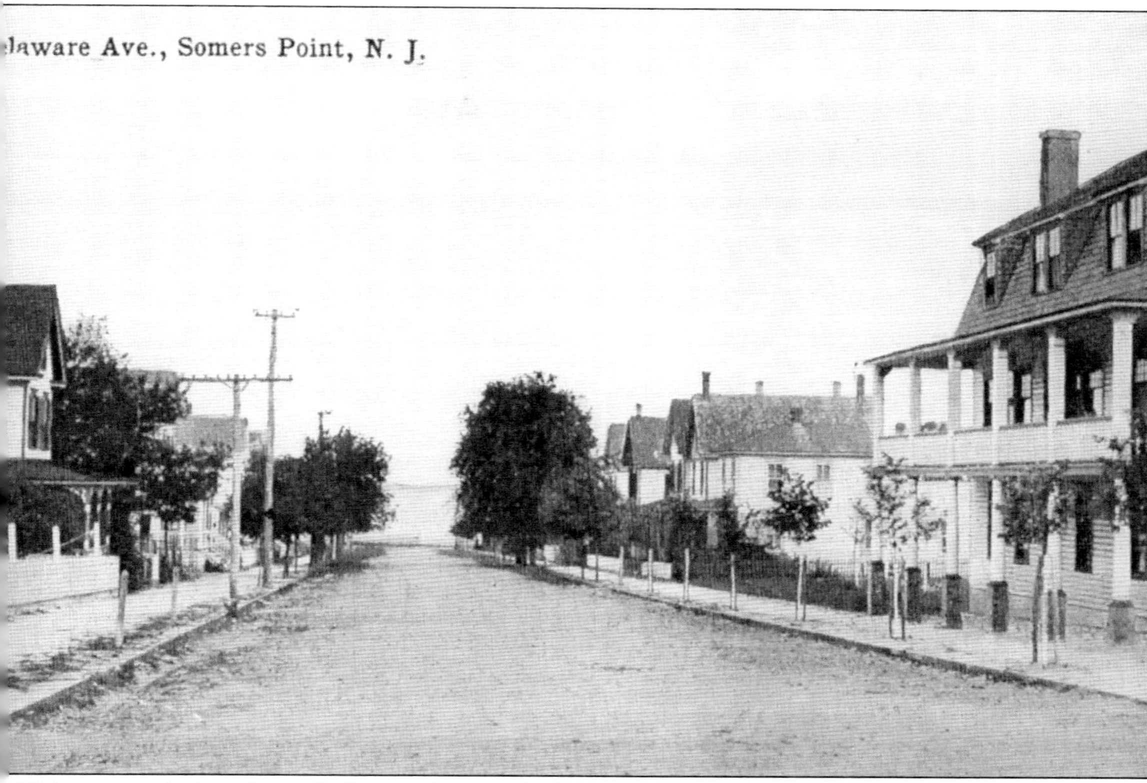

This postcard view shows Delaware Avenue looking east from Shore Road toward the bay. Delaware Avenue has not changed much over the years, and many of the older homes still stand there today. The building in the right foreground was originally a private home and dry goods store. It later housed the Piercy Hotel, the Hotel Boulevard, and the Davis Hotel, and is currently home to Gregory's Restaurant and Bar.

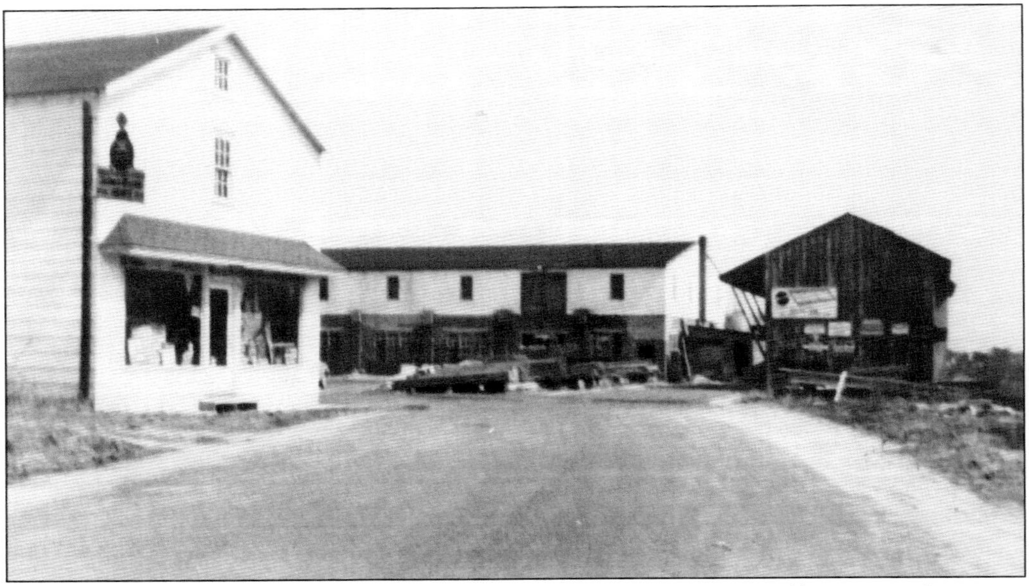

This photograph shows the Raymond Smith Lumber Company at its second location at the corner of Groveland Avenue and the railroad. Smith Lumber was a Somers Point staple for many years prior to the fire that destroyed the first mill property at the corner of Connecticut Avenue and the railroad. As with many businesses of the day, Smith Lumber was very community-oriented. The second floor of the mill housed a basketball court and hosted many community basketball games starting in the early 1940s. (Courtesy Ruth Mulford Newsome.)

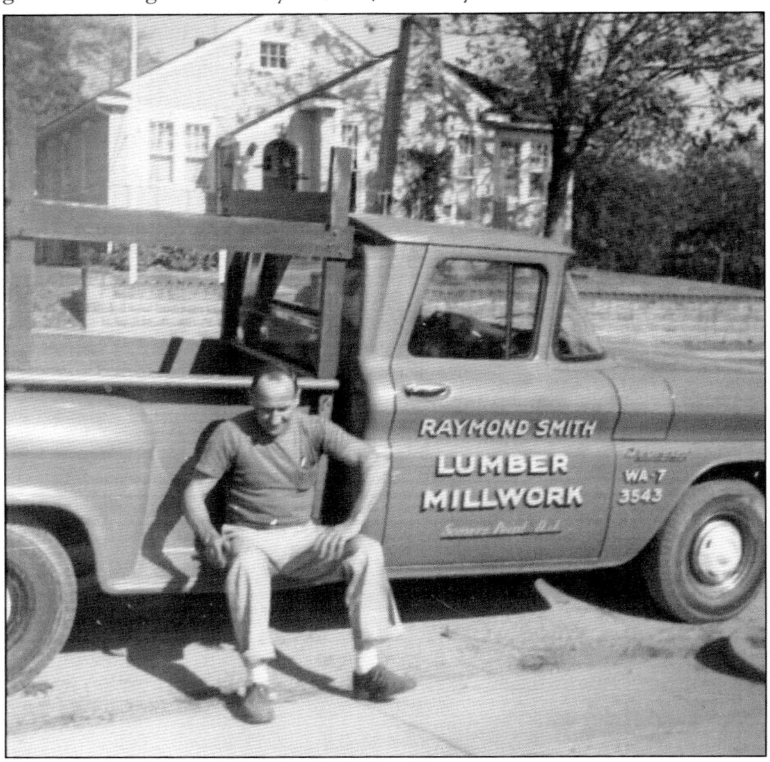

Arthur E. Elwell Sr.—better known as Autsie—sits on the running board of his work truck on New Jersey Avenue. Autsie was a longtime employee and foreman at the Raymond Smith Lumber Company. After starting there as young man, he worked for the company for more than 35 years. (Courtesy Ruth Mulford Newsome.)

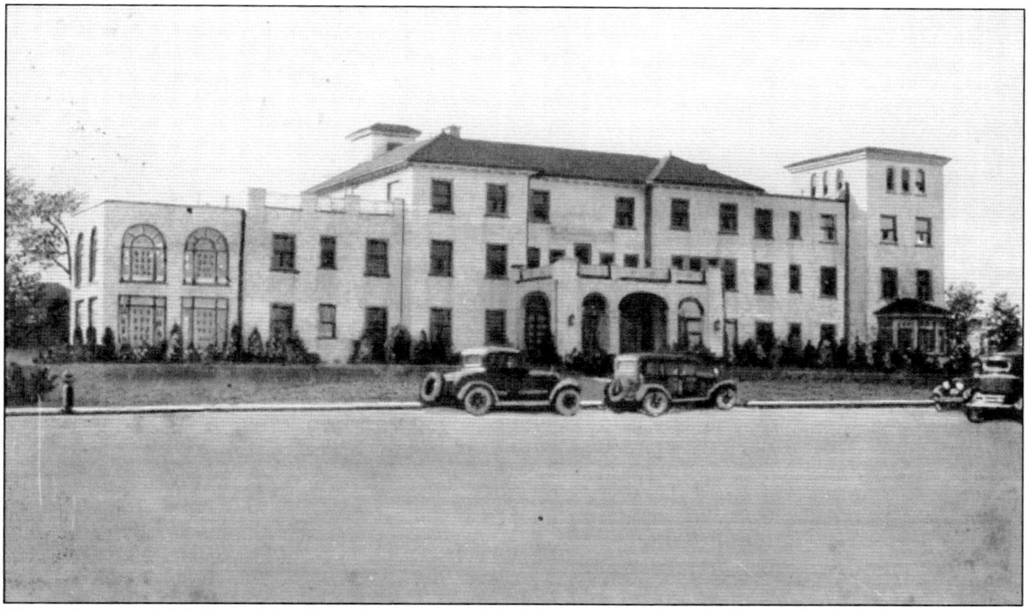

Shore Memorial Hospital, which was incorporated in 1940, was originally an alcohol and drug treatment facility that opened in 1928 as Atlantic Shores Hospital and Sanatorium (later known as Atlantic Shores Hospital). The hospital has undergone numerous changes over the years and is no longer recognizable as the building it once was. In 2012, Shore Memorial Hospital became Shore Medical Center.

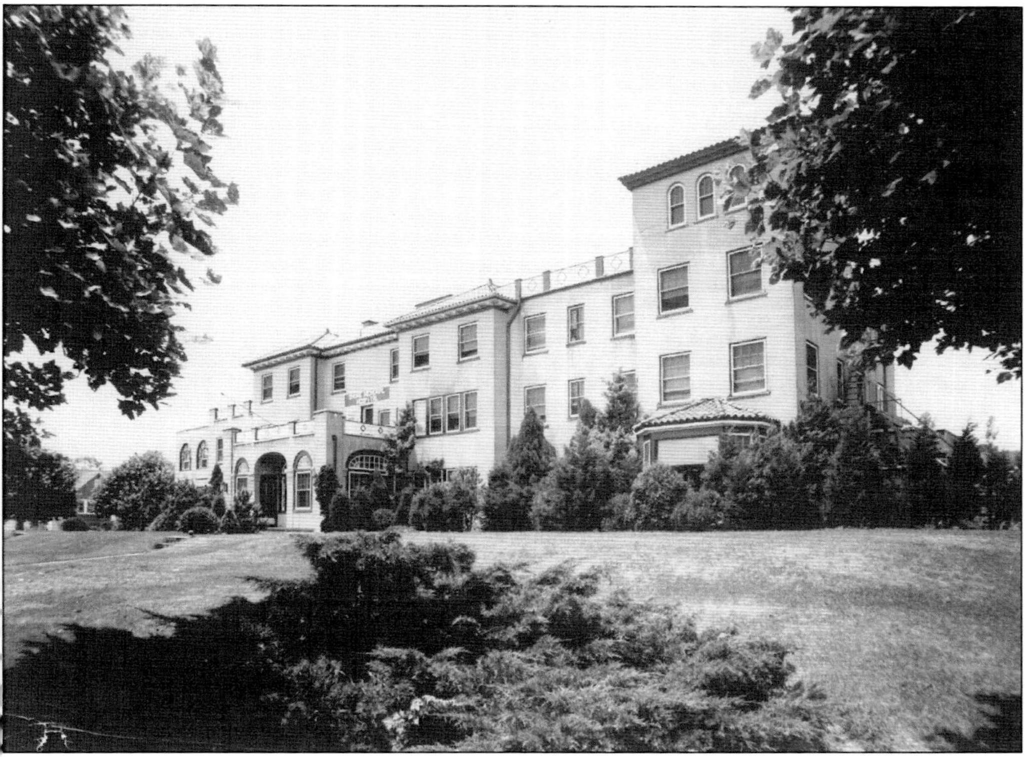

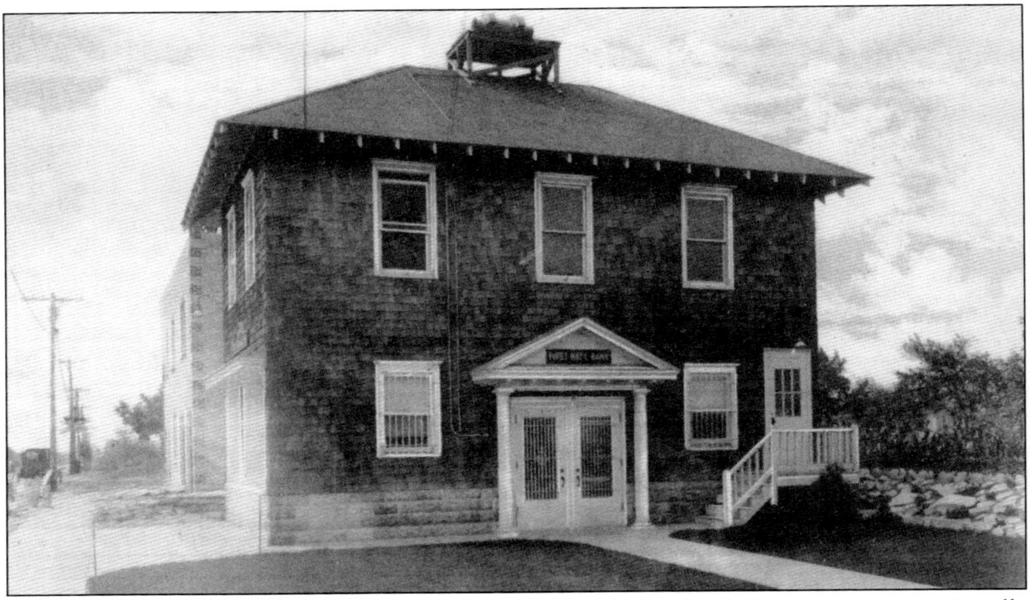

Located on the northwest corner of New York Avenue and Shore Road, this structure was originally built as a firehouse before becoming the First National Bank of Somers Point. The bank opened on July 15, 1924, with Charles P. Robinson as president, Mayor George Goll as vice president, and Earl R. Ryne as cashier. After the bank left, the building became the Somers Point Post Office. In 1953, the structure was moved across New York Avenue, where it still stands today.

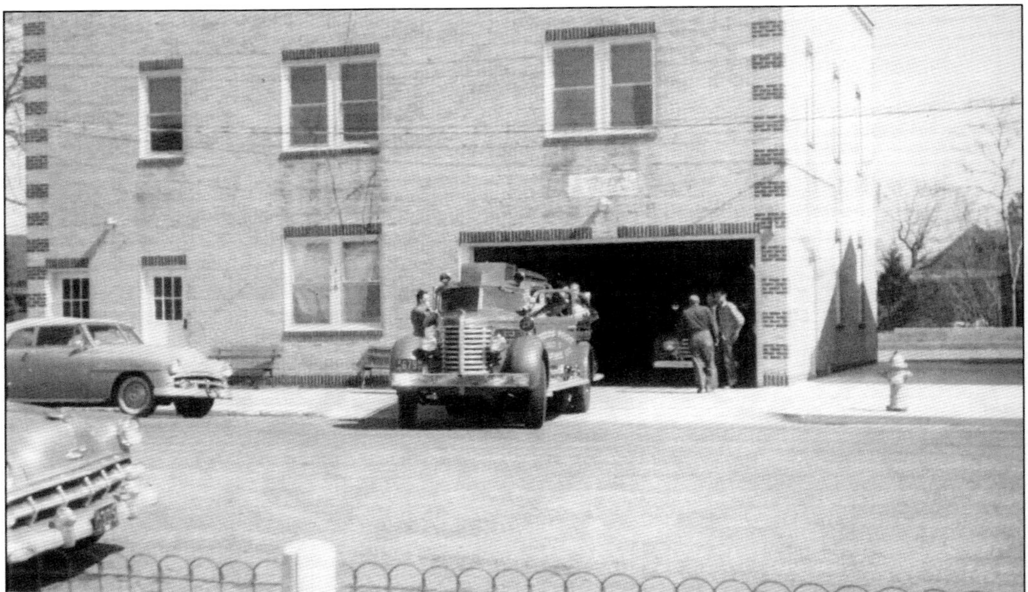

This building, located on New York Avenue, was the home of Somers Point Fire Company No. 1 after it sold its former location to the First National Bank of Somers Point. This building remained the company's home base until it built the current headquarters on Bethel Road, which is still in use today.

Harry Higbee (left) and Bob Loper enjoy some ice cream after riding their bikes to the Dairy Queen on Shore Road on opening day in 1956. (Courtesy Bob Loper.)

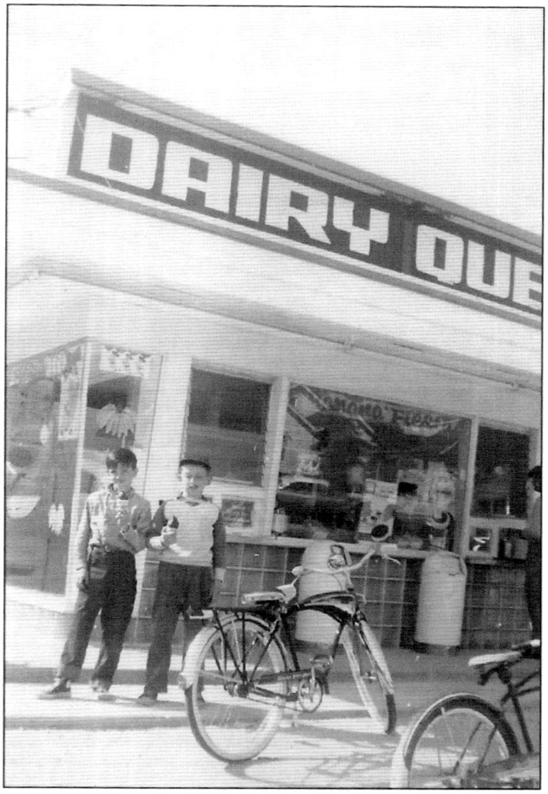

This house, located on Dawes Avenue adjacent to the old Dawes Avenue School, was purchased by the Somers Point Board of Education and used to house its Child Study Team. When the old Dawes Avenue School was razed to make way for the new school, this house was demolished along with it.

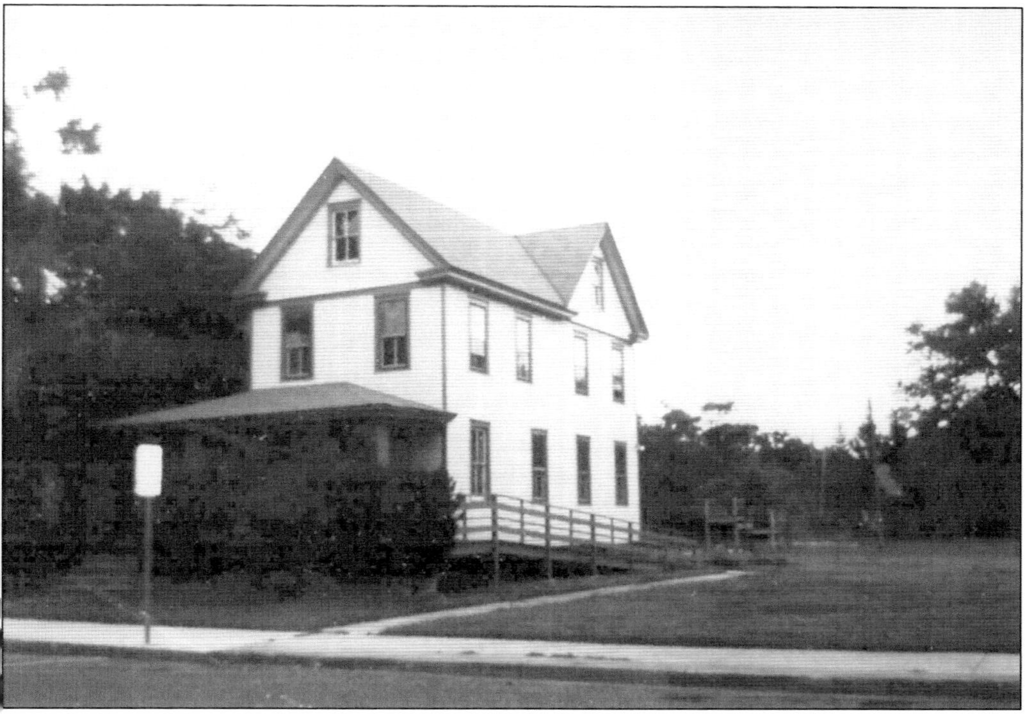

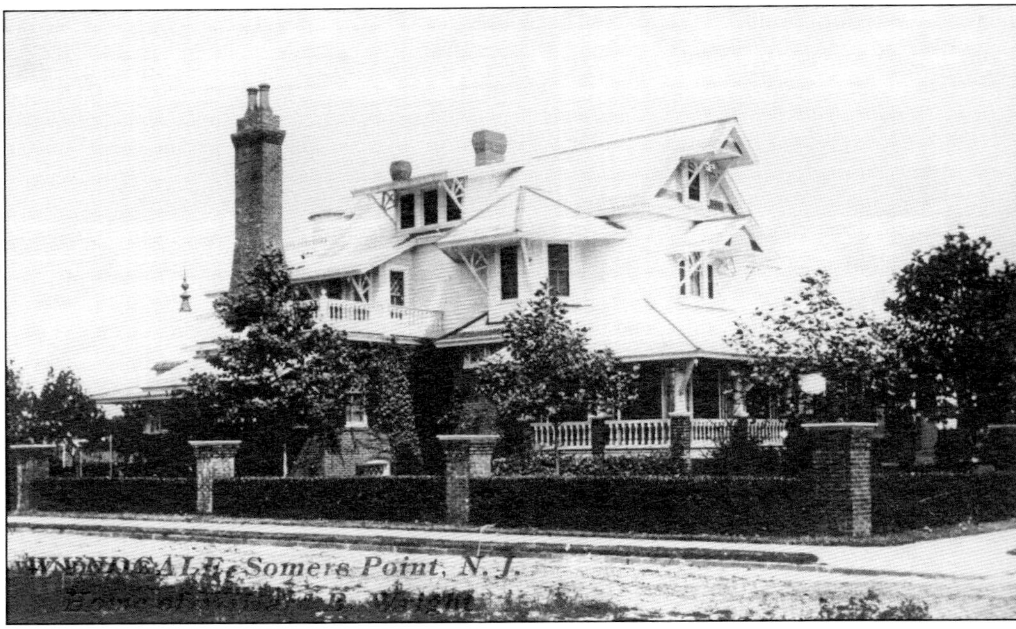

Willard Wright, a prosperous Philadelphia businessman and former Shakespearean actor, built the Wyndgale property pictured here. Once a sprawling estate, the property stretched the entire length of a block from Fourth Street to Fifth Street. An early photograph of the estate shows manicured lawns, ornate statues, and a path leading through the property. The main house pictured above was Wright's home after he moved to Somers Point from Philadelphia. The building in the picture below served as the carriage house for the estate. Though no longer part of a sprawling estate, both buildings still stand today.

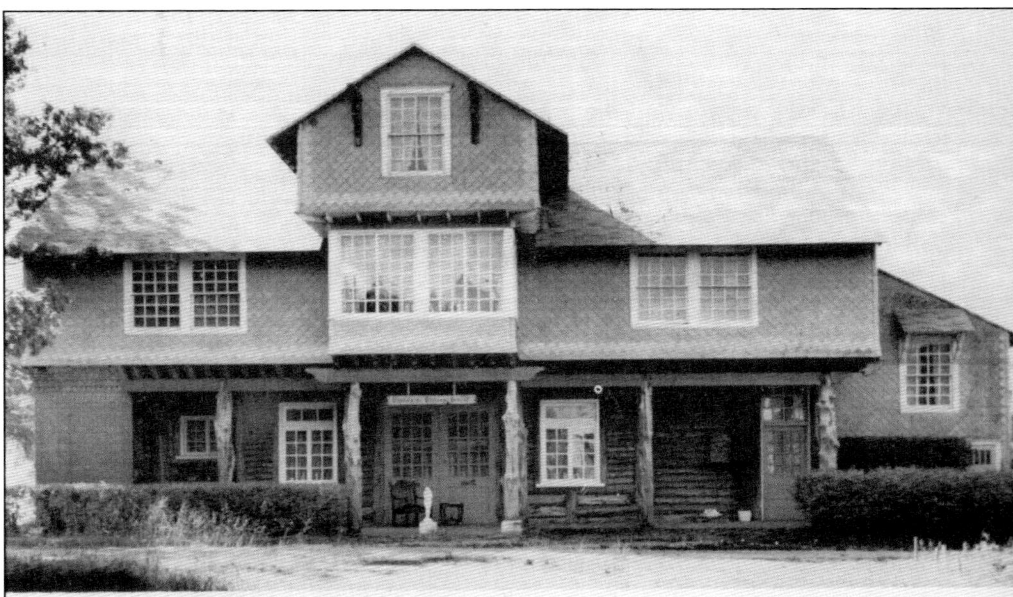

WYNDGALE - Home of Mr. and Mrs. Wm. F. Braden - Somers Point, N. J.

Five

Along Shore Road

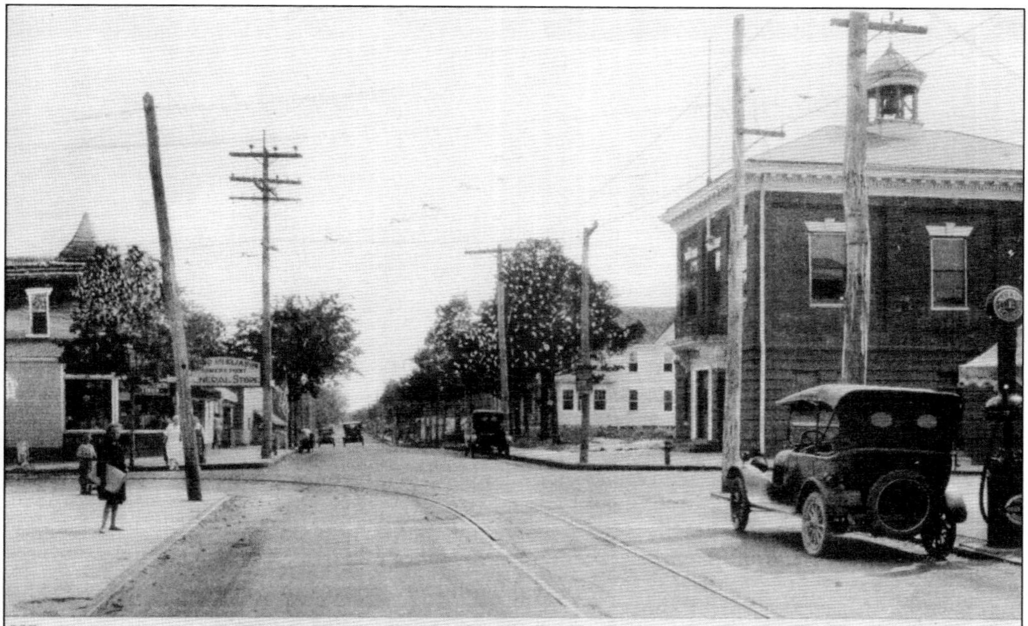

327. CITY HALL, NEW JERSEY AVENUE AND MAIN STREET, SOMERS POINT, N. J.

This view, which looks south on Shore Road, shows the trolley tracks as they travel east down New Jersey Avenue towards Bay Avenue. In the right foreground is the old city hall—at the time the new city hall—built in 1906, complete with a balcony (above the front door) that was used by officials to address the public. On top of the building is the bell tower that is no longer there. This was sounded to summon fire company members when there was an emergency. The firemen would know where the fire was based on the number of times the bell was sounded. Three taps meant the fire was south of New Jersey Avenue, while five taps indicated a fire north of New Jersey Avenue. (Courtesy Michael Bohs.)

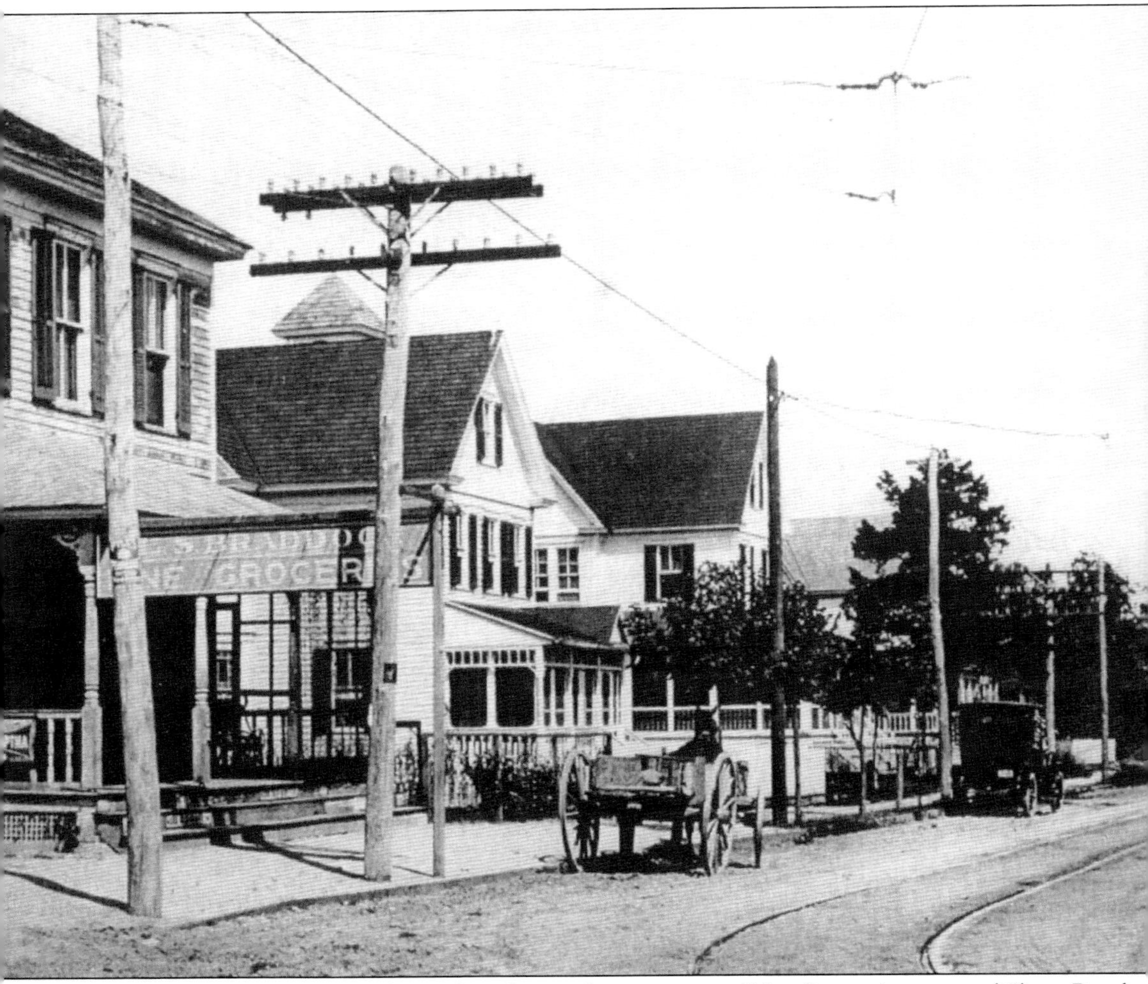

Braddock's Groceries was located on the northwest corner of New Jersey Avenue and Shore Road. The business later became Conover's Market. This is the location of the current city hall.

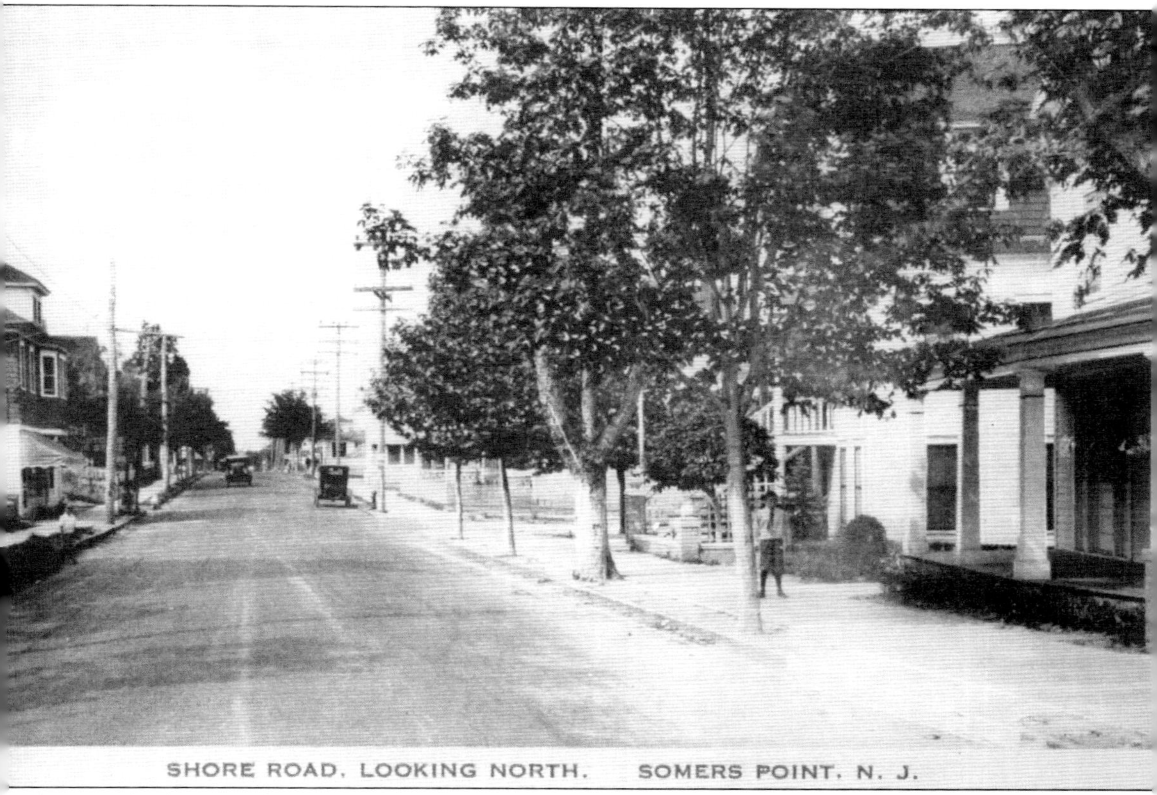

This view looking north on Shore Road from Somers Avenue shows many buildings that are still there and several that are now gone. The structure on the left was Ralston's Pharmacy, at the foot of Delaware Ave and Shore Road. It is still standing today.

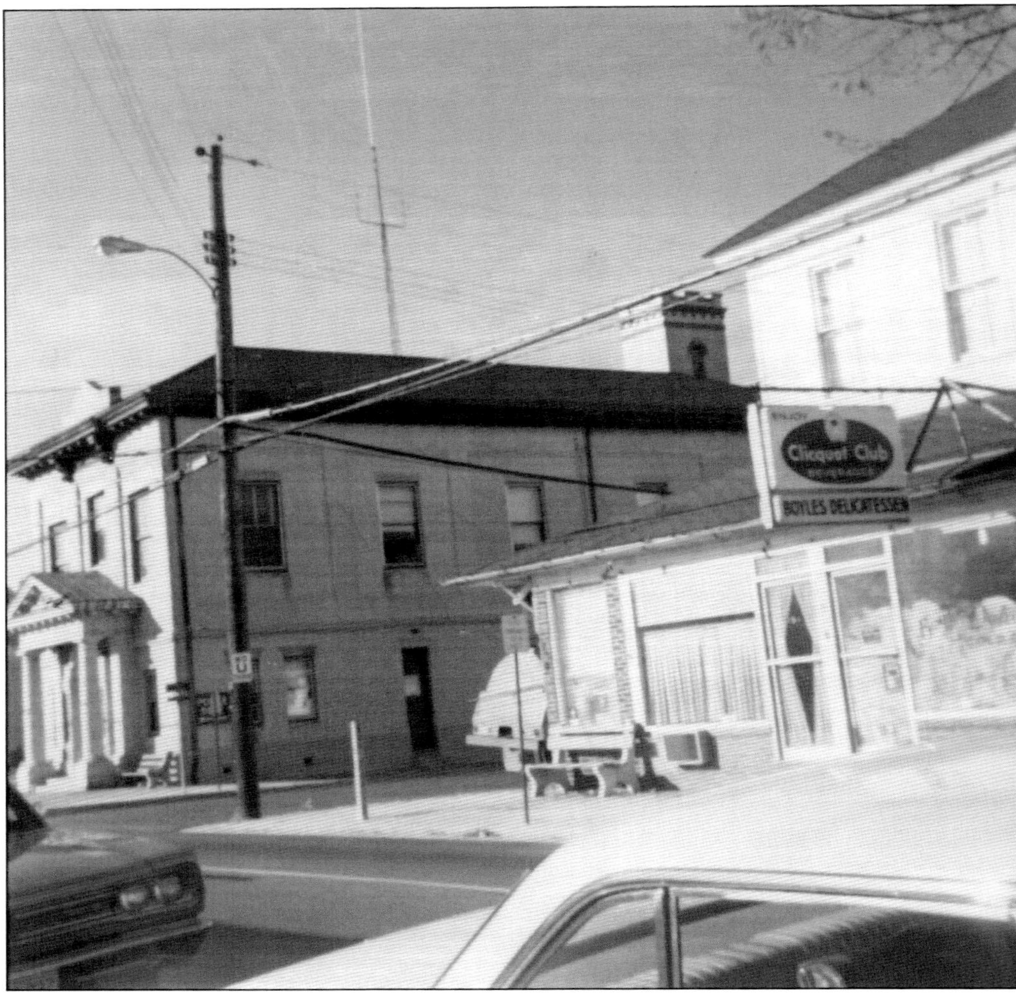

A view of the west corners of Shore Road and New Jersey Avenue shows the old city hall and Boyer's Delicatessen. Next to Boyer's on the left-hand side was a beauty shop. This property was formerly Conover's Market. The building was demolished to make way for the new city hall.

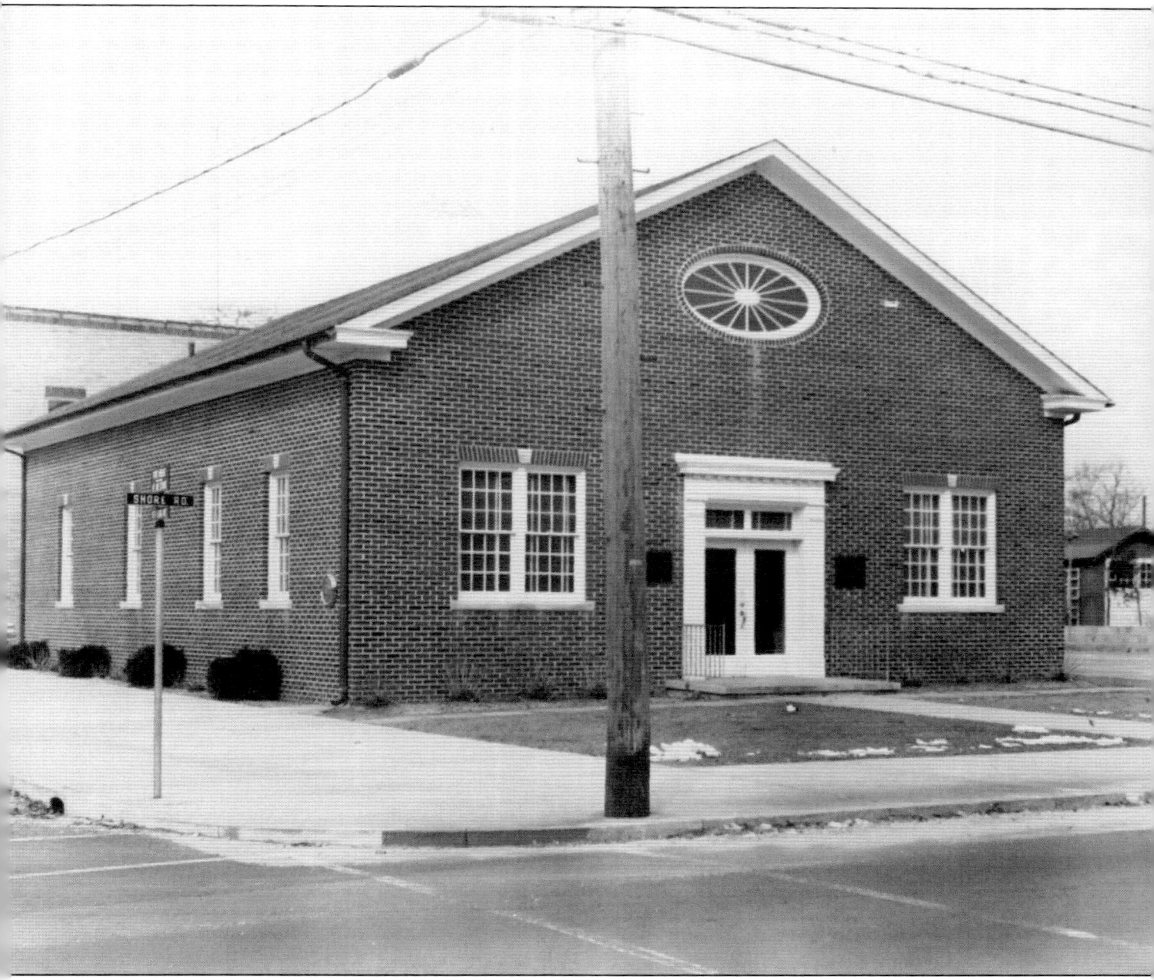

The new Boardwalk National Bank stood on the northwest corner of New York Avenue and Shore Road. The bank changed names several times before being purchased by Shore Memorial Hospital. (Courtesy Kirk Gerety.)

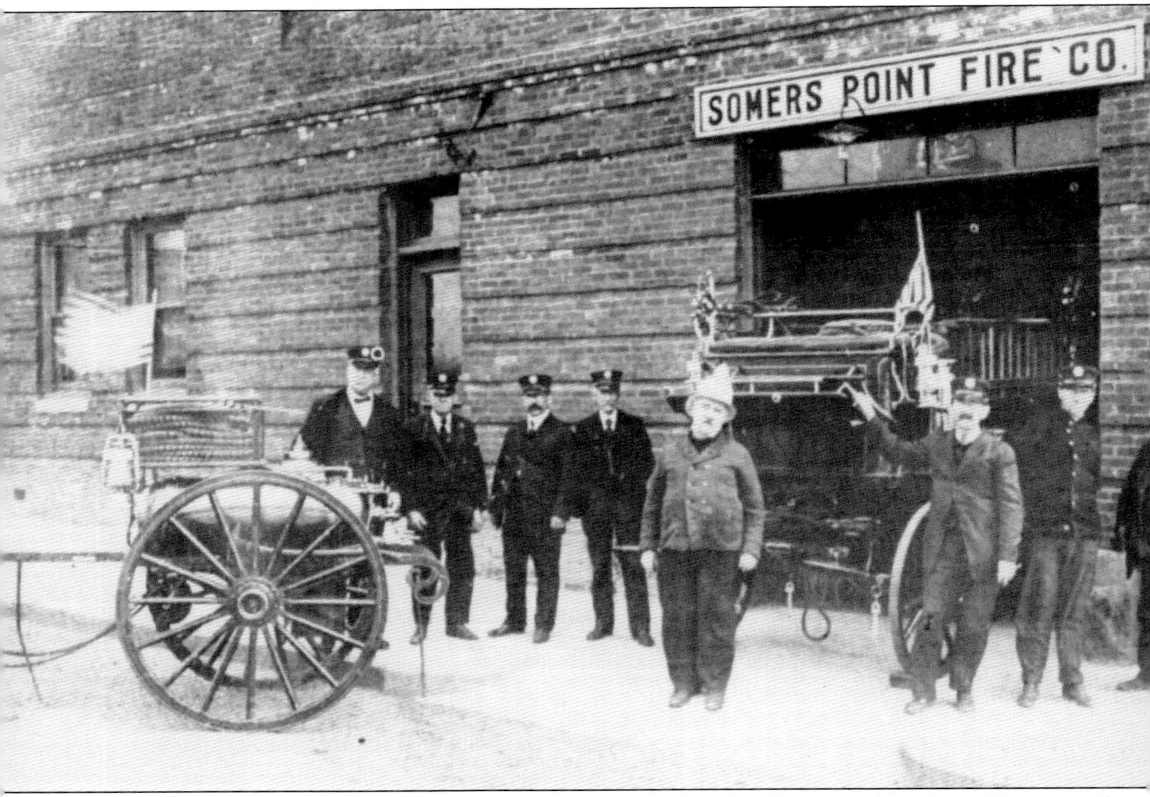

Organized in 1907, the Somers Point Fire Company was headquartered in the addition on the rear of the old city hall. Here, members of the fire department are shown with some of their early nonmotorized apparatus. (Courtesy Kirk Gerety.)

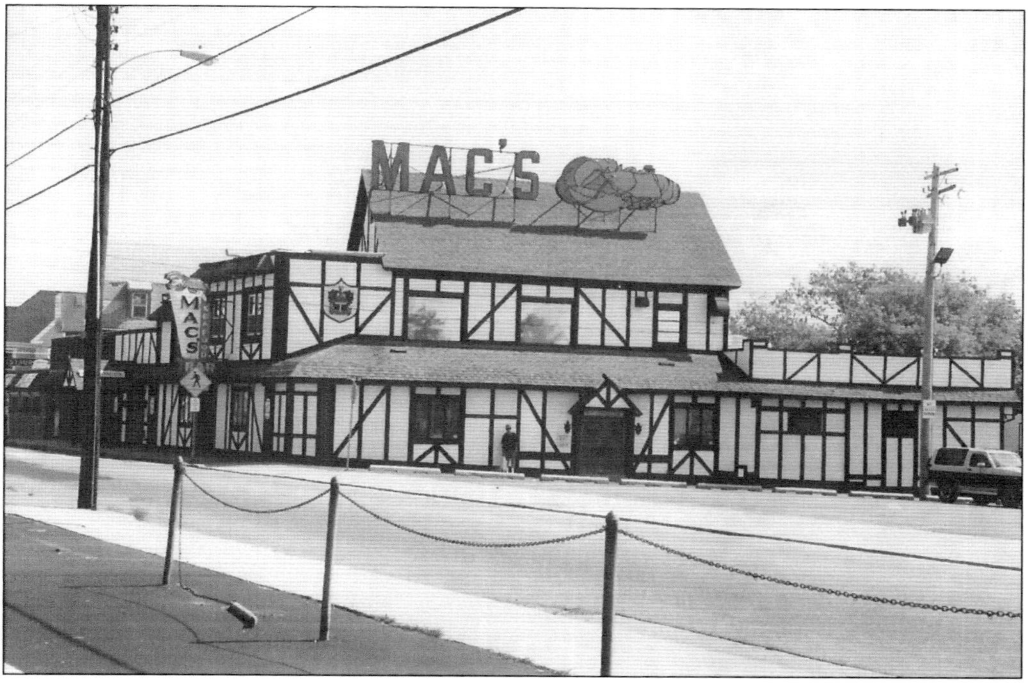

Mac's Restaurant was opened in 1924 by Harold Megronigle. With its Tudor look and medieval decor and offering fine seafood and Italian specialties, Mac's was a longtime landmark enjoyed by many. (Courtesy Joan Bird Wilson.)

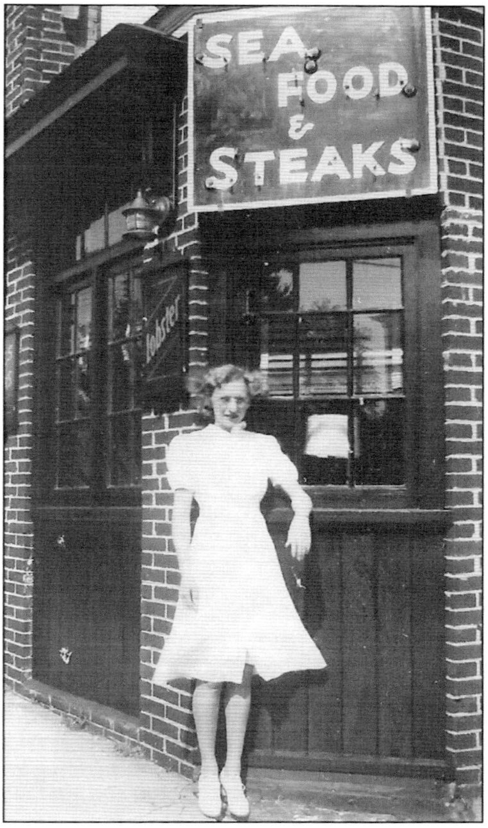

Ruth Greis Loper stands outside Mac's Restaurant, prior to the Tudor exterior, as she waits for her shift to start. She is standing below the "sea food & steaks" sign that hung above the front door on the corner of the building at Miller Lane and Shore Road. (Courtesy Bob Loper.)

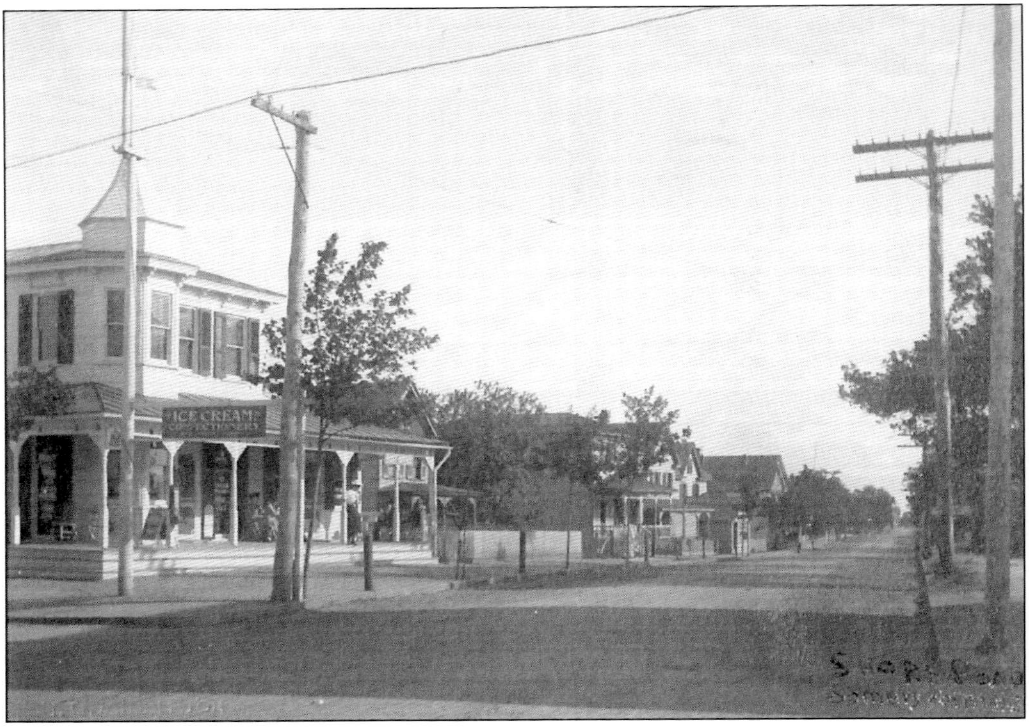

The building on the southeast corner of Shore Road and New Jersey Avenue was home to Oscar Nichols Ice Cream Confectionery and the Somers Point Post Office. With its sprawling porches and cupola, this Victorian structure was a popular place to go for ice cream on a hot summer day. Among his items for sale, Nichols offered many old postcards of Somers Point.

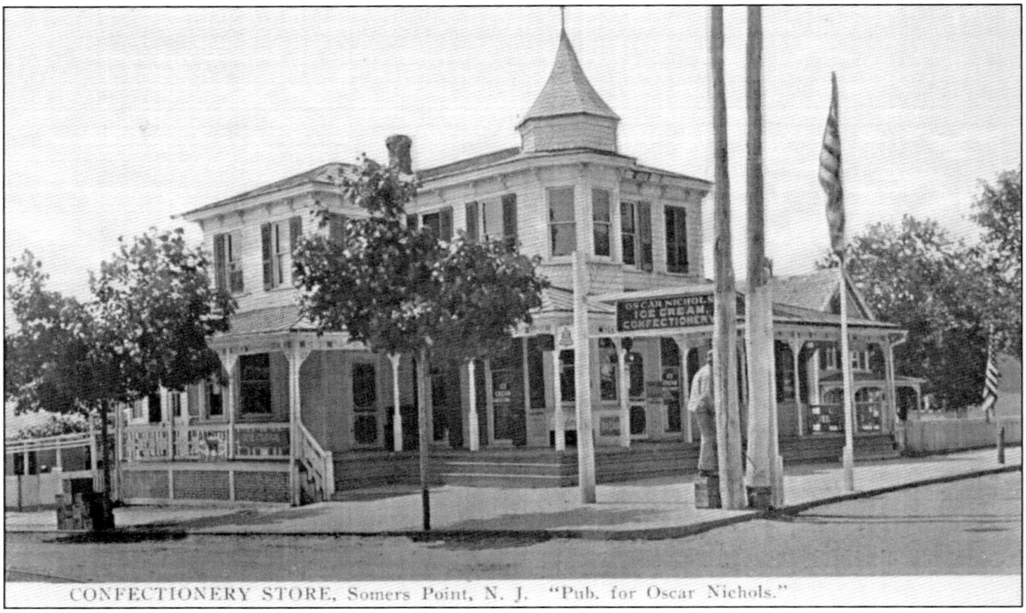

CONFECTIONERY STORE, Somers Point, N. J. "Pub. for Oscar Nichols."

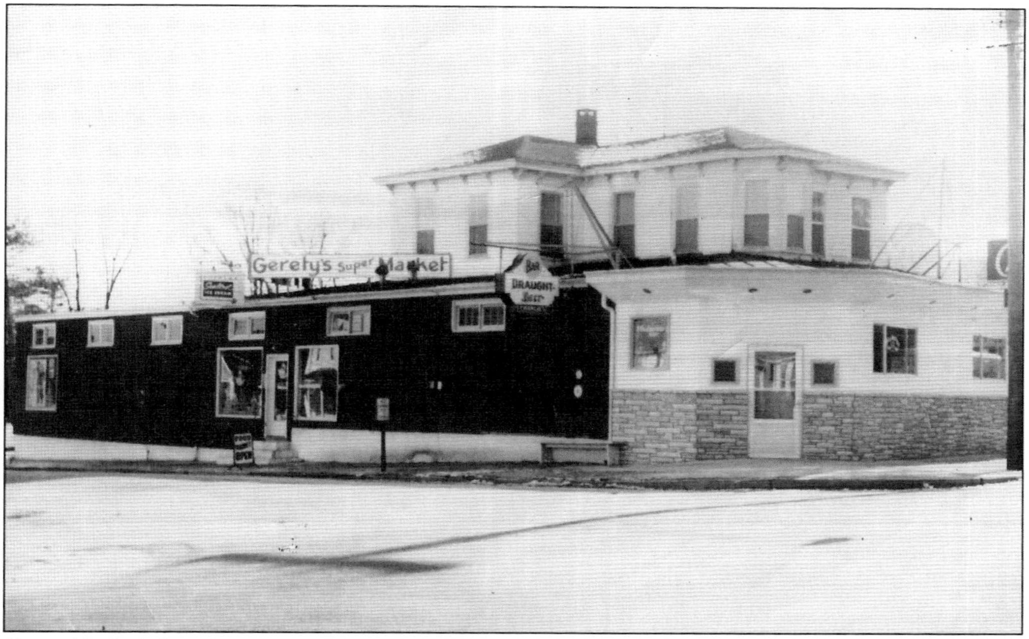

Oscar Nichols Ice Cream Confectionery gave way to Gerety's Super Market, and Gerety's later shared the space with Charlie's Bar. Gerety's eventually moved down Shore Road to a new location. (Courtesy Kirk Gerety.)

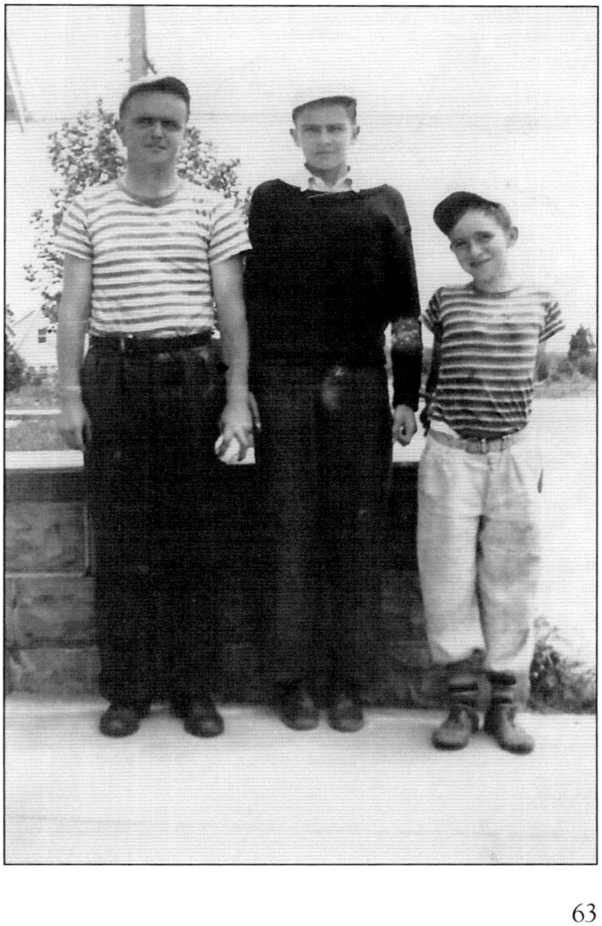

Here, the Gerety brothers—George (left), Joseph (center), and Jack—pose for a picture. Jack later owned Gerety's Super Market at the time when it moved down Shore Road. Many locals have fond memories of George and his fun-loving antics and jovial personality, which he utilized as manager of the Somers Point Bowling Alley. (Courtesy Kirk Gerety.)

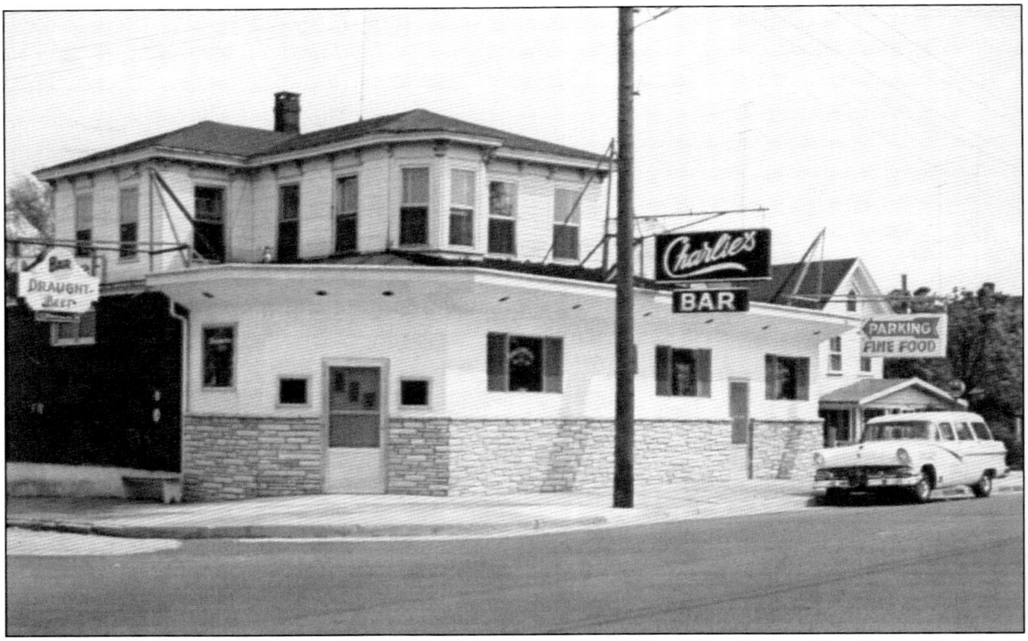

As shown in this image, many changes have occurred at the building located at Shore Road and New Jersey Avenue; gone are the sprawling porches and cupola that gave the building a Victorian feel. Charlie's Bar has been a long-standing, successful business in Somers Point since 1944.

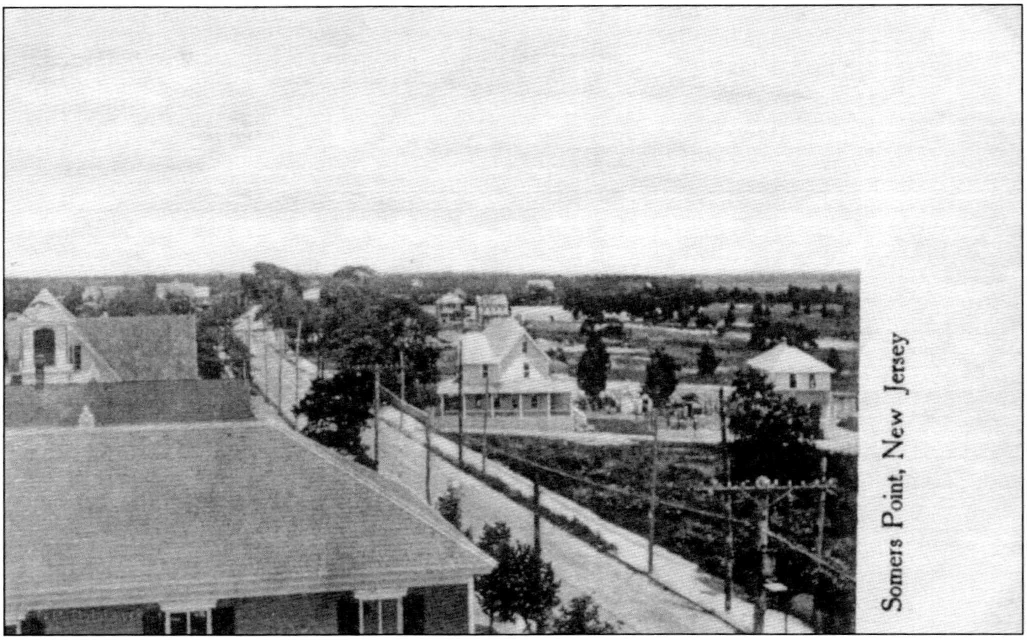

Looking north along Shore Road from the upstairs at old city hall, this view offers an elevated look at the east side of Shore Road and shows how sparsely it was populated.

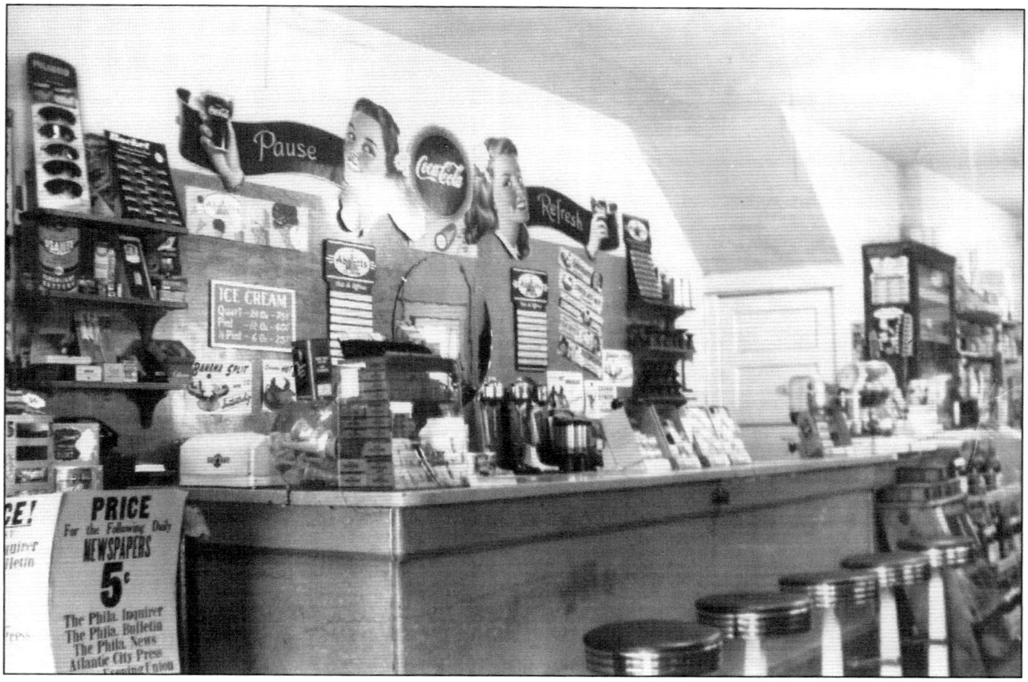

The inside of Pharazan's store shows the soda fountain and booths that were popular with local youths. With the bus stop out front and the movie theater down the street, it was often a popular spot, and longtime locals may recall the store's delicious ice cream. (Both, courtesy Kirk Gerety.)

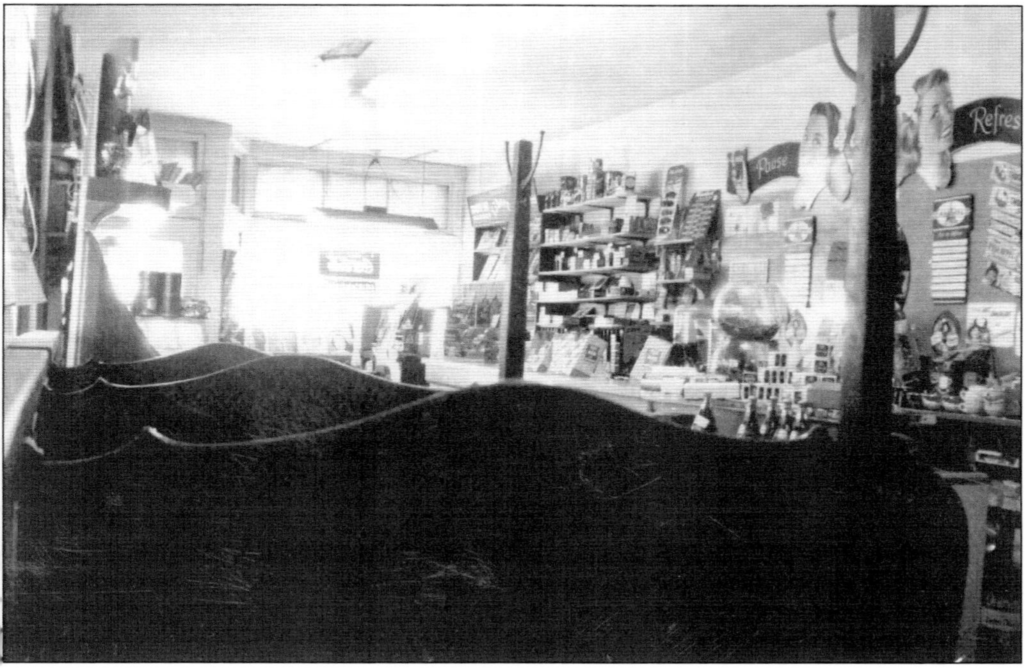

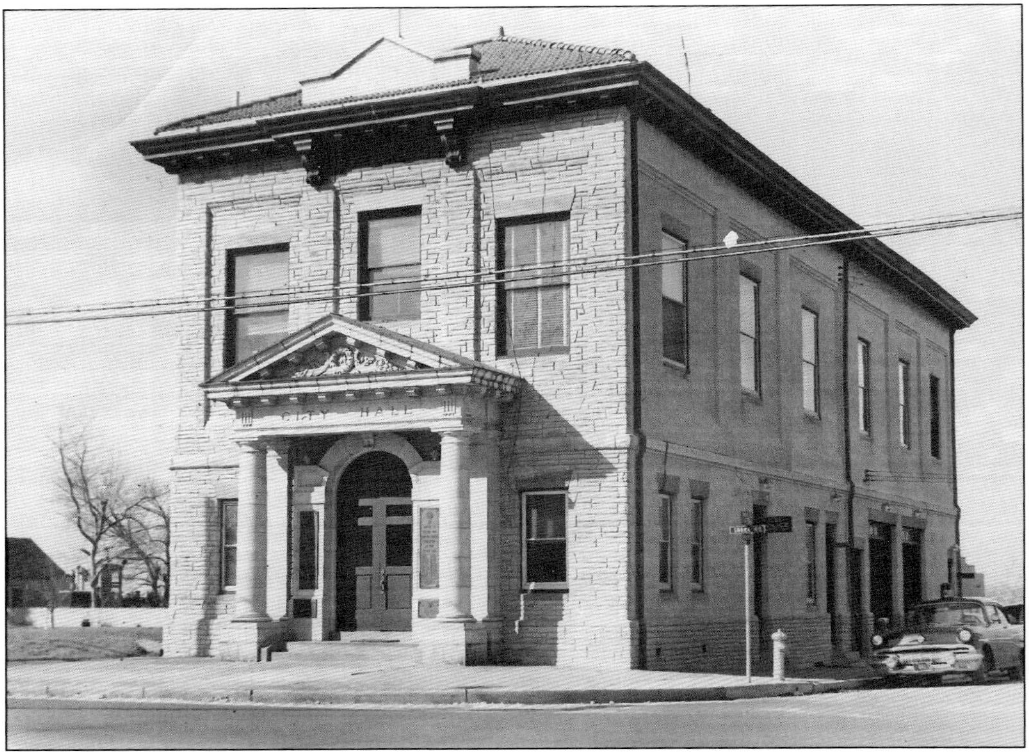

The old city hall is shown here after the addition and the removal of the balcony over the front doors. This was replaced by a more ornate entranceway. Many will remember going here to conduct city business. With the courtroom upstairs and the jail cells on the main floor, as well as many city offices, this was a hub of activity in the town. (Courtesy Ruth Mulford Newsome.)

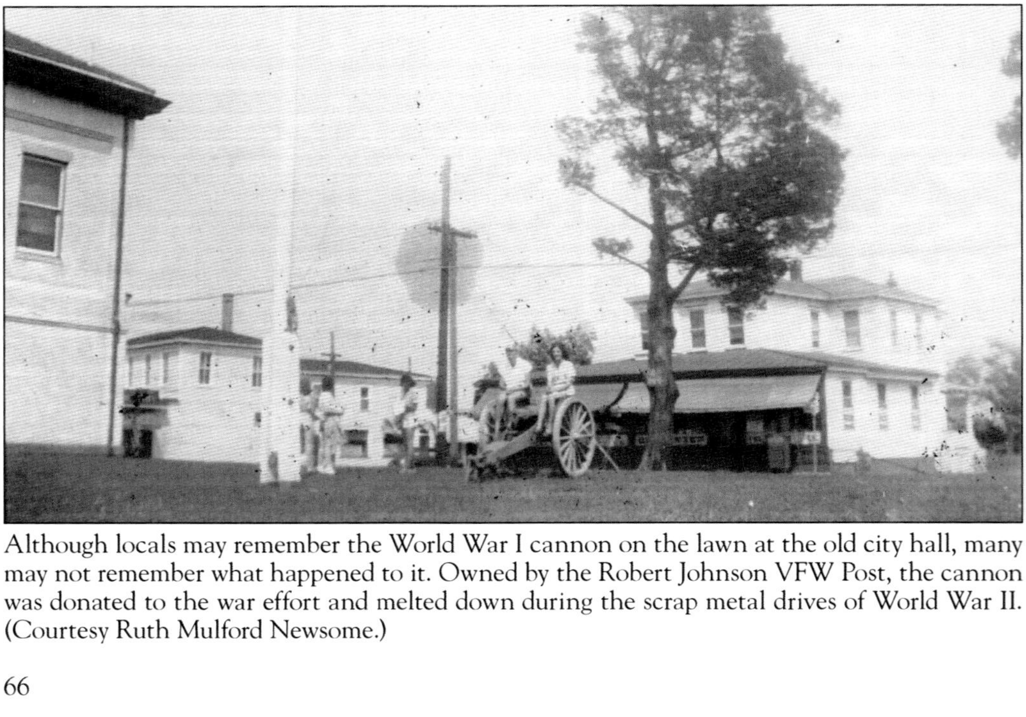

Although locals may remember the World War I cannon on the lawn at the old city hall, many may not remember what happened to it. Owned by the Robert Johnson VFW Post, the cannon was donated to the war effort and melted down during the scrap metal drives of World War II. (Courtesy Ruth Mulford Newsome.)

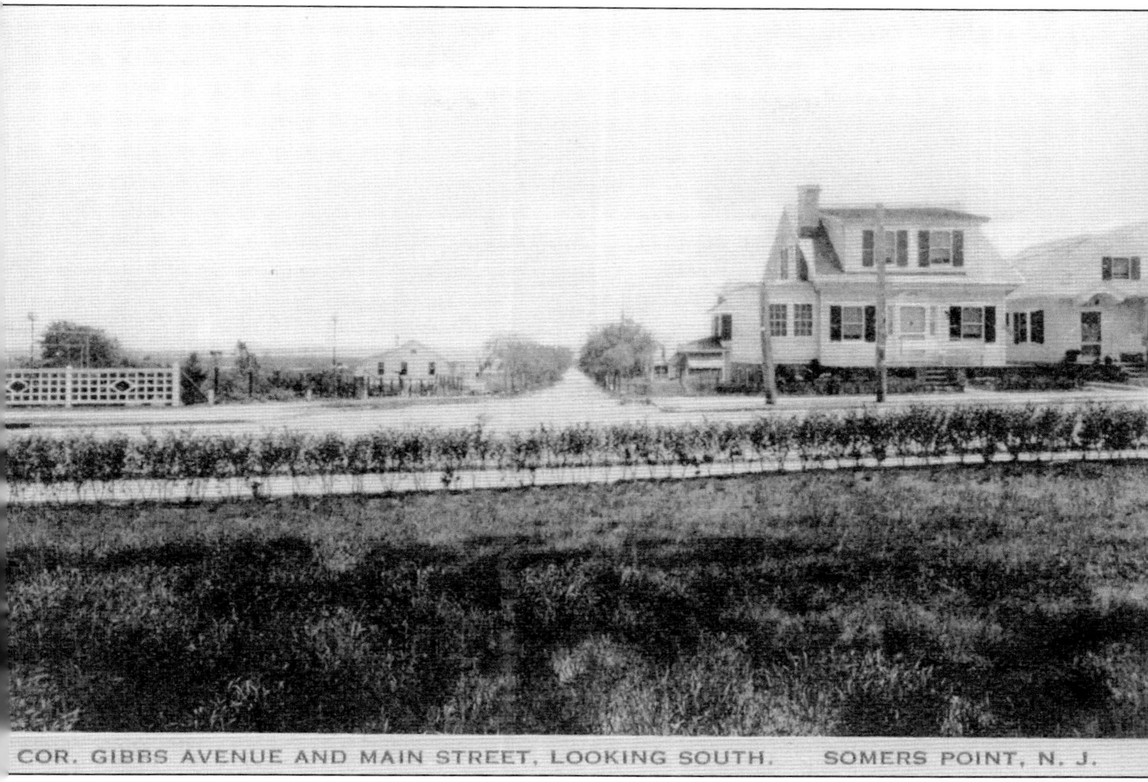

Looking east from Shore Road toward the bay on Gibbs Avenue, this view shows how little development had taken place in that area in the early 1900s. The house on the right still stands today and is currently a doctor's office.

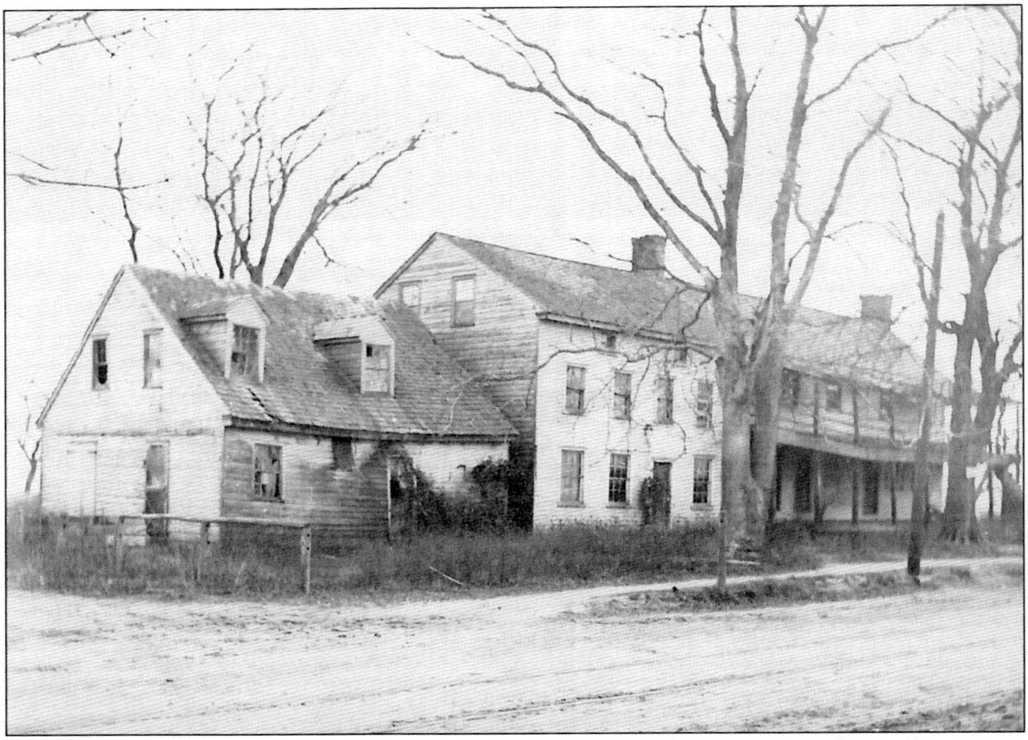

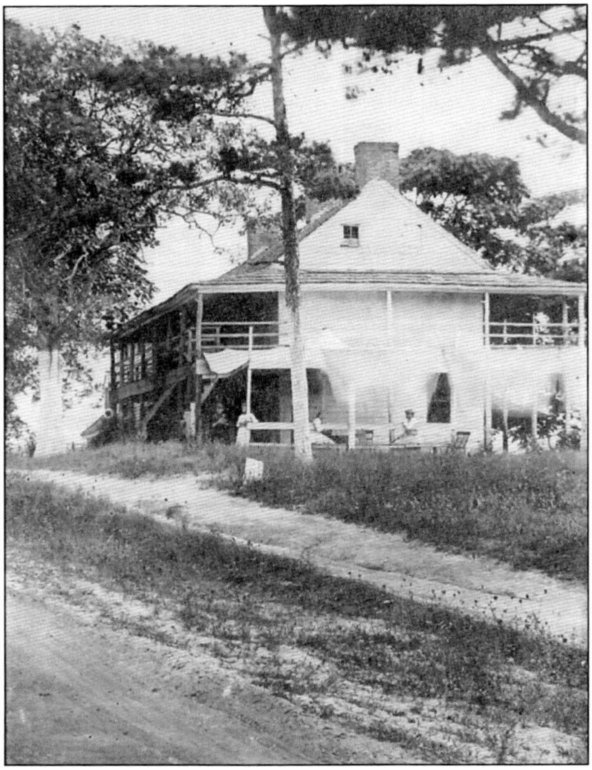

Dolphin House was located on Shore Road between New York and Brighton Avenues. In 1872, the proprietor was W. E. Braddock. According to Harold Lee's book, *History of Ocean City, New Jersey*, it was here that the first four streets of Ocean City were named, while people were sitting around the dinner table on February 10, 1880. (Left, courtesy Genevieve DeVito—The Don Balsley Collection.)

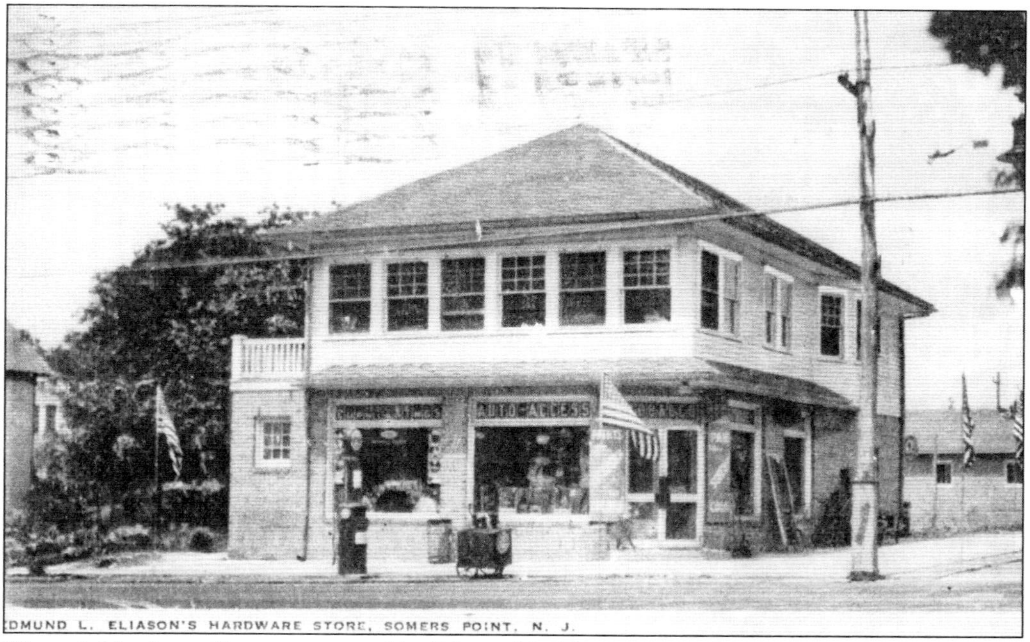

Eliason's Hardware Store was owned by Edmund L. Eliason Sr. and provided the town's citizens with a place to fulfill their hardware needs. It also sold automobile accessories and other household goods. This building later housed a pizza parlor, a medical-supply store, and several other businesses. On the outside, the structure stills looks much as it does in this picture.

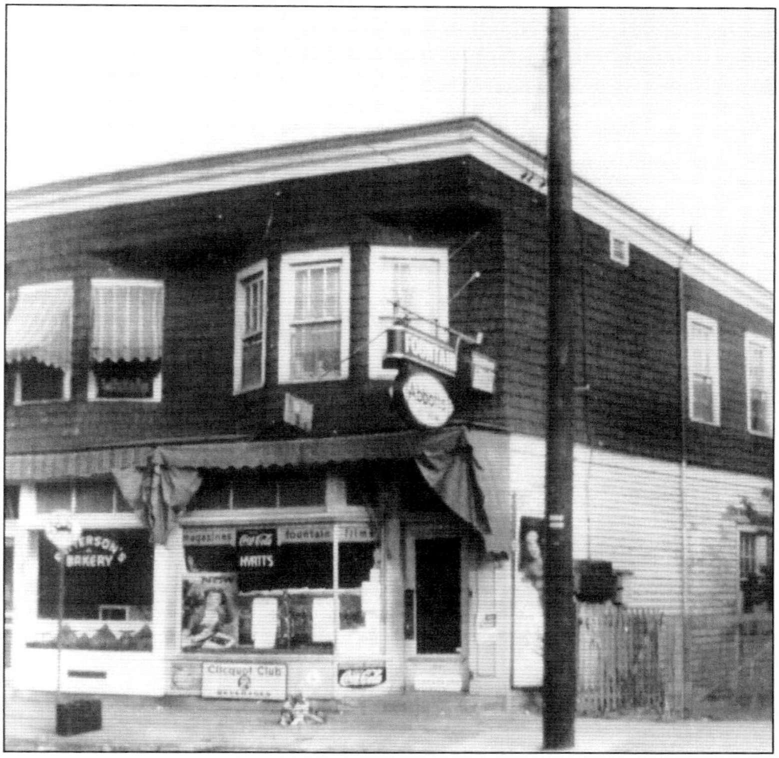

This building, located on Shore Road, served as Patterson's Bakery on one side and Hyatt's on the other side. George and Ellen Hyatt owned Hyatt's and were well-known residents of Somers Point. George became a respected councilman for the city of Somers Point, and Ellen went on to work for the Somers Point Sewerage Authority. (Courtesy Ruth Mulford Newsome.)

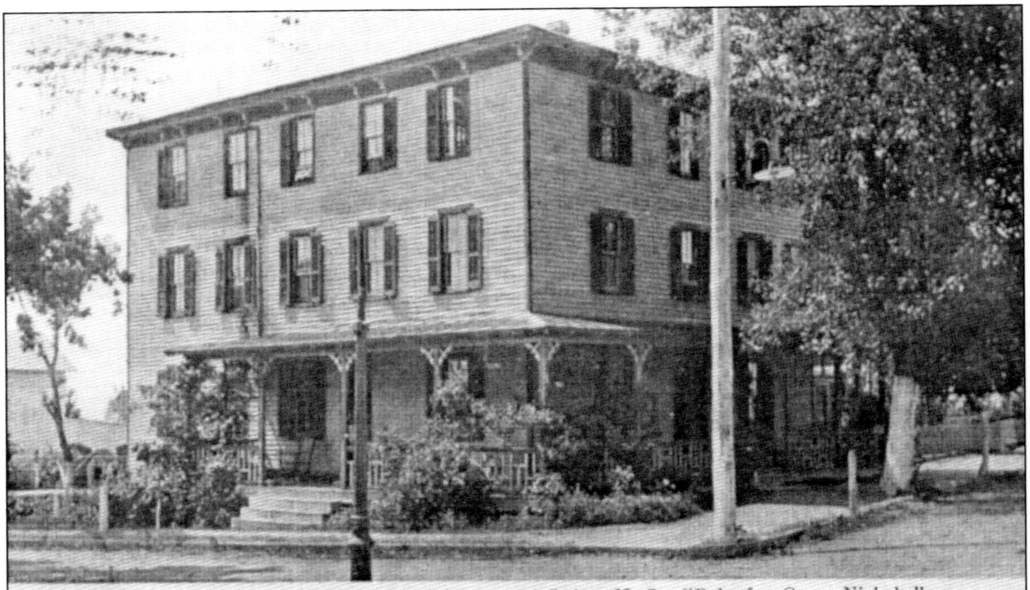

"TREEN VILLA" BOARDING HOUSE, Somers Point, N. J. "Pub. for Oscar Nichols."

Proprietress Deborah A. Treen ran Treen Villa, located on Shore Road at Annie Avenue. Treen Villa offered reasonable boarding rates and also served dinner. A 1911 advertisement shows that one could buy dinner at the villa for 50¢.

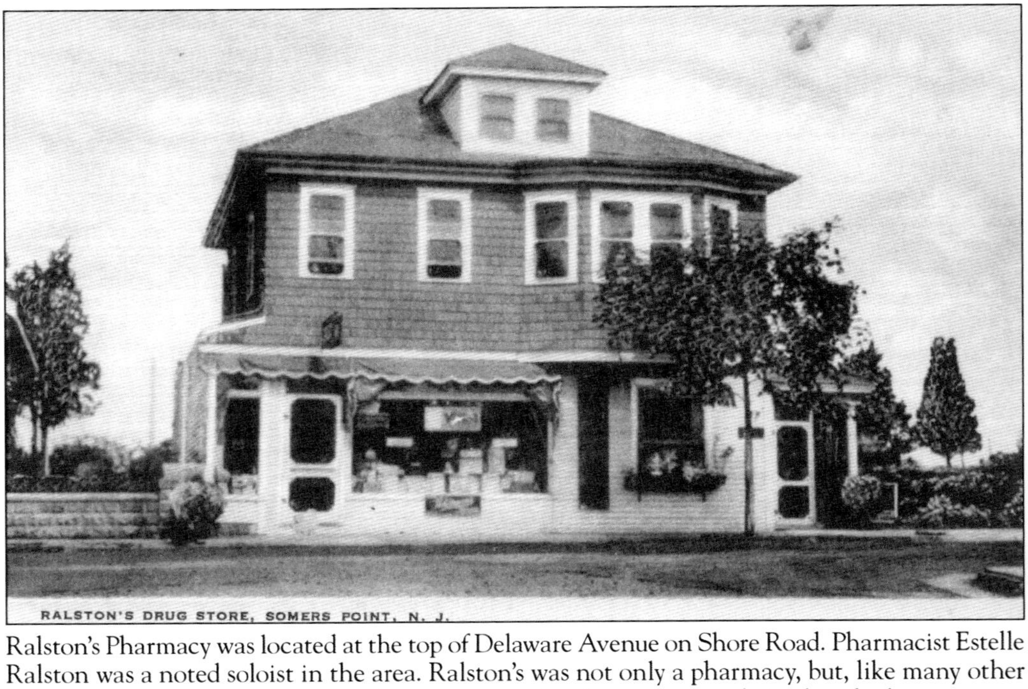

RALSTON'S DRUG STORE, SOMERS POINT, N. J.

Ralston's Pharmacy was located at the top of Delaware Avenue on Shore Road. Pharmacist Estelle Ralston was a noted soloist in the area. Ralston's was not only a pharmacy, but, like many other stores at the time, also had a soda fountain and offered ice cream and simple refreshments.

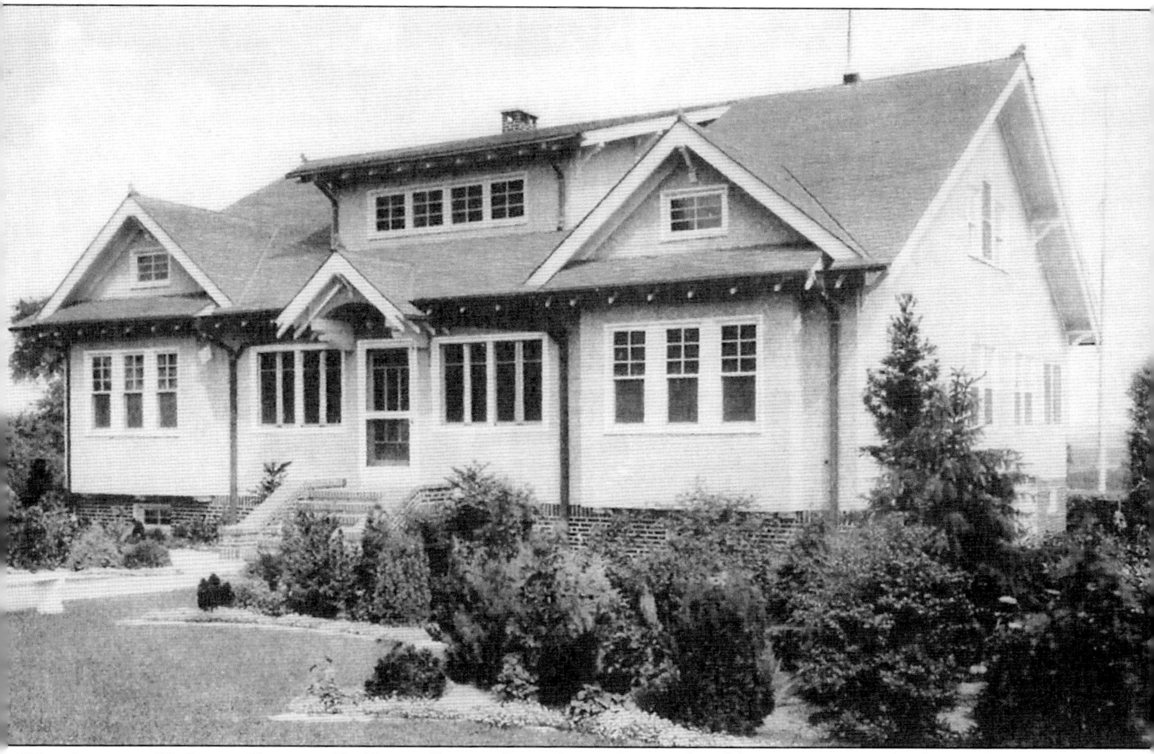

The home of Mayor George Goll was located at the corner of Gibbs Avenue and Shore Road. At the time that Goll lived there, the property took up the whole block between Gibbs Avenue and New York Avenue. Goll was mayor of Somers Point from 1924 to 1928 and also served as the vice president of the First National Bank of Somers Point at the time of its opening in 1924. Some older residents remember him standing at his gate on Halloween and handing out nickels to the trick-or-treaters.

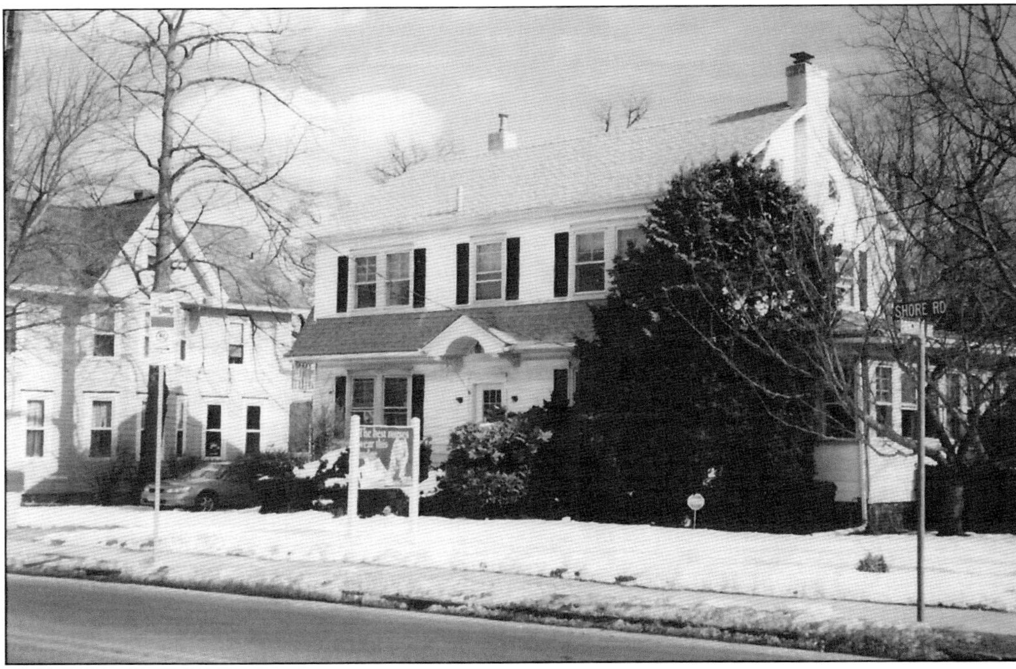

This property, located at the corner of Brighton Avenue and Shore Road, was the home and office of Dr. R. Rostin White. Dr. White was the head surgeon at Atlantic Shores Hospital and Sanatorium (later Shore Memorial Hospital) from 1930 into the 1950s. (Courtesy Joan Bird Wilson.)

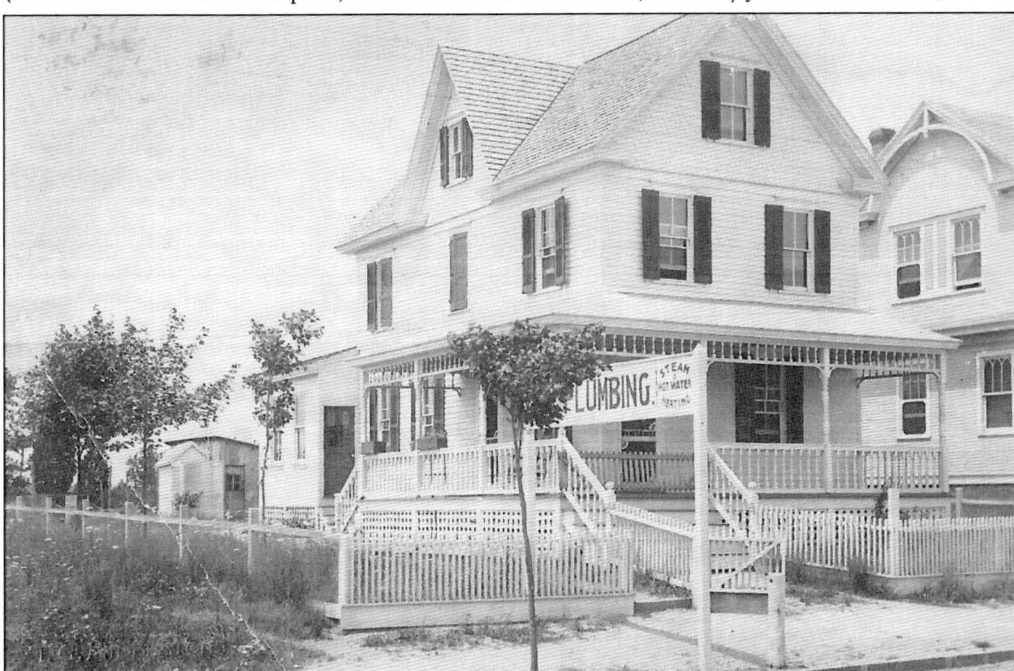

Walter A. Smith Plumbing and Heating was located on Shore Road with the phone number "7."

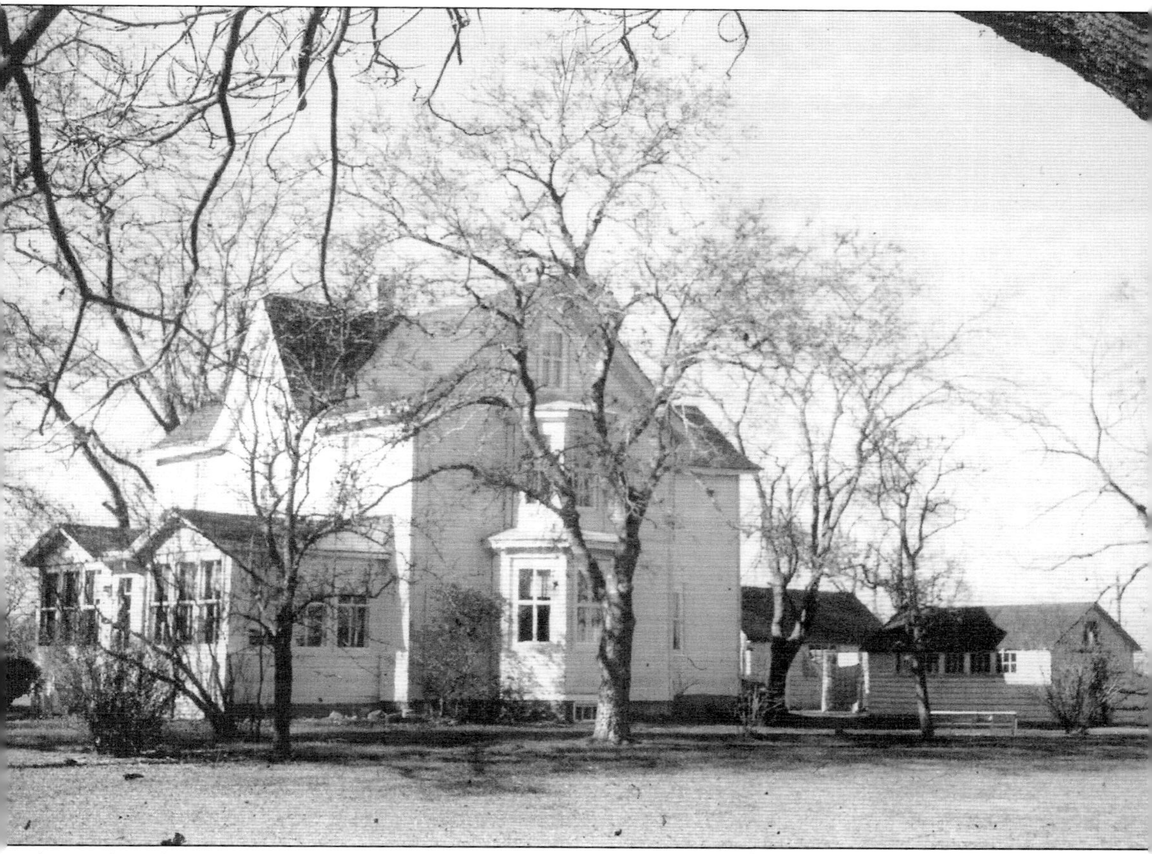

The Deborah Jane Somers Anderson house is located on the site of the birthplace of Master Commandant Richard Somers, who died at Tripoli Harbor during the First Barbary War in 1804.

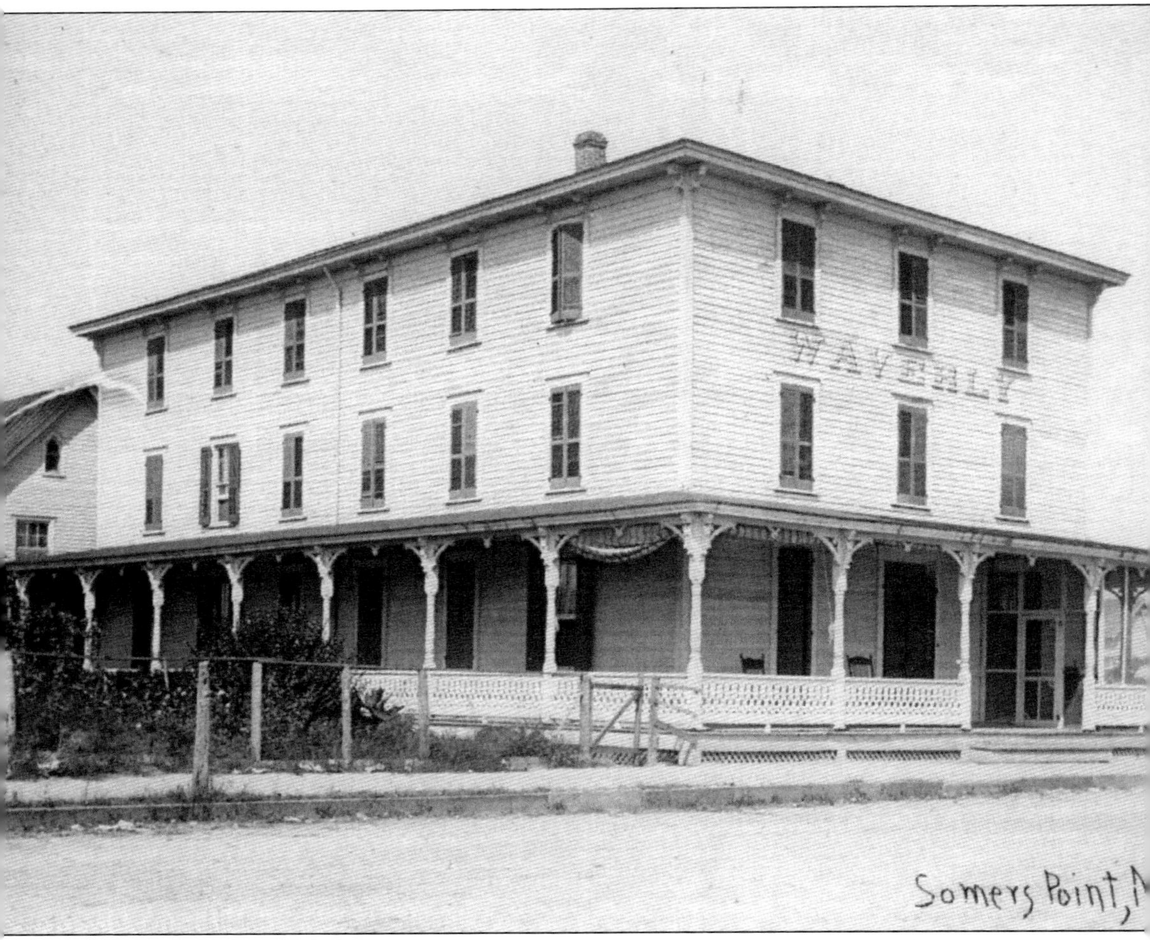

The Waverly Hotel was located at the top of Somers Avenue, across Shore Road. The proprietor was William B. Steelman, who charged $7 or $8 per week to stay there. This hotel was later torn down to make room for a parking lot.

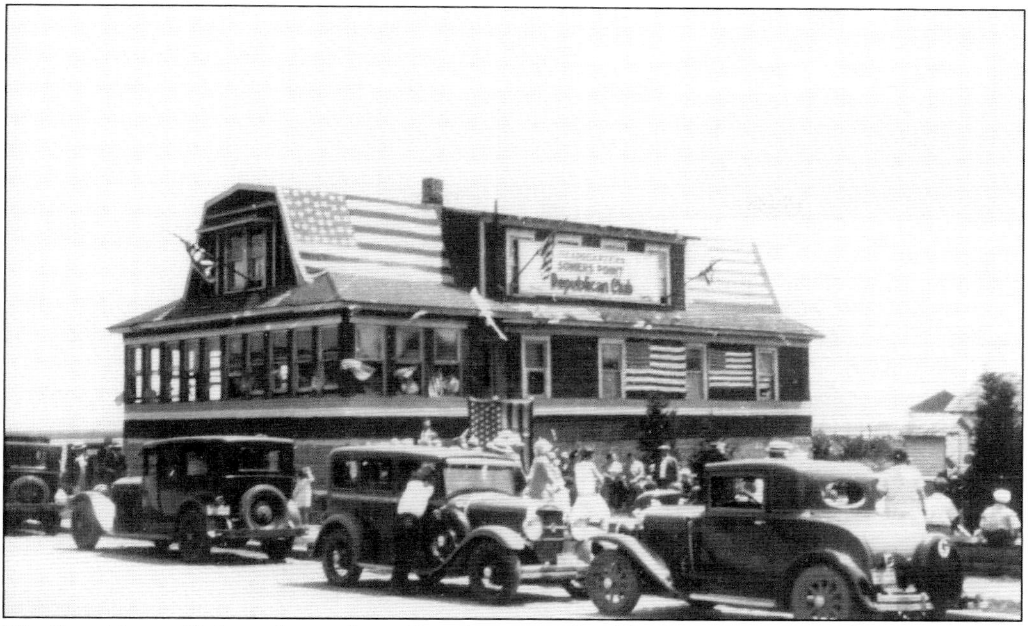

The Republican Club was located near Bay Avenue and Gibbs Avenue. Decorated with American flags and a Somers Point Republican Club sign, this building would have been hard to miss. (Courtesy Ruth Mulford Newsome.)

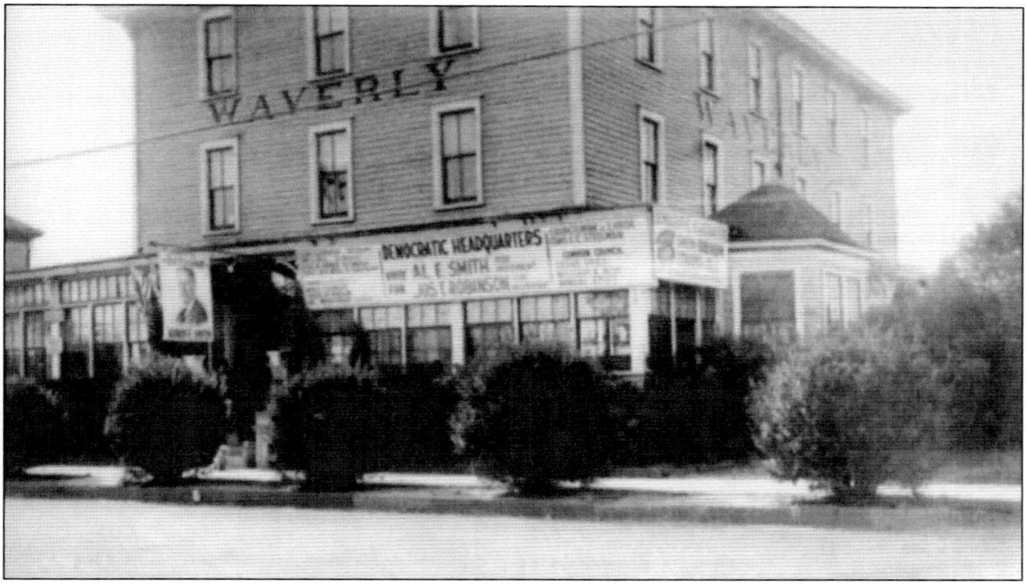

Well-decorated and touting the names of the Democratic candidates, the local Democratic headquarters during the presidential election of 1928 was located at the Waverly Hotel on Shore Road. The results for president did not go in the Democrats' favor (Republican Herbert Hoover won), but it is unclear which party took the win in Somers Point. (Courtesy Ruth Mulford Newsome.)

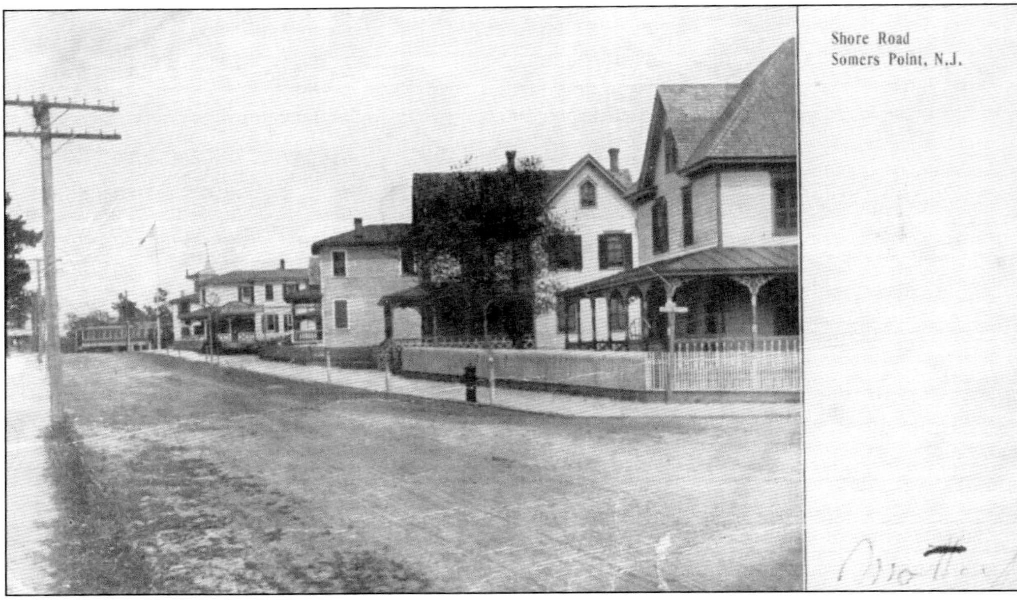

A view of Shore Road looking north from Delaware Avenue shows a trolley turning the corner at New Jersey Avenue and Shore Road. This trolley was part of the Atlantic Suburban Line that ran down Shore Road before turning onto New Jersey Avenue and then continuing on Bay Avenue. The Atlantic Suburban Line ran from October 22, 1903 until March 31, 1929. All of the buildings on the right-hand side still stand today.

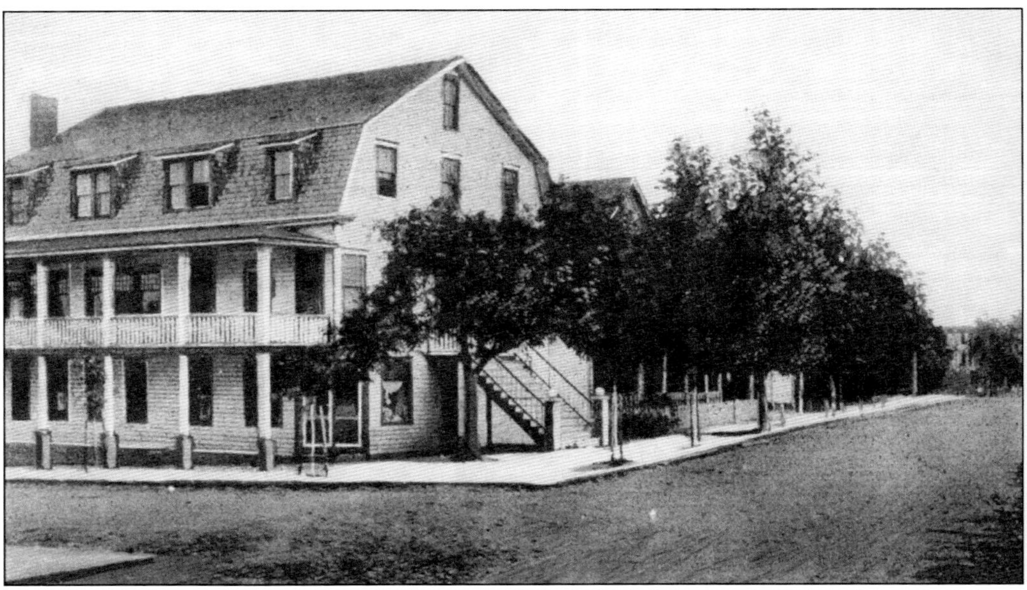

This view of the corner of Delaware Avenue and Shore Road shows a building that is still there today. What started out as a private home and dry goods store is now occupied by Gregory's, a popular restaurant and bar since 1946.

Six

PATRIOTISM

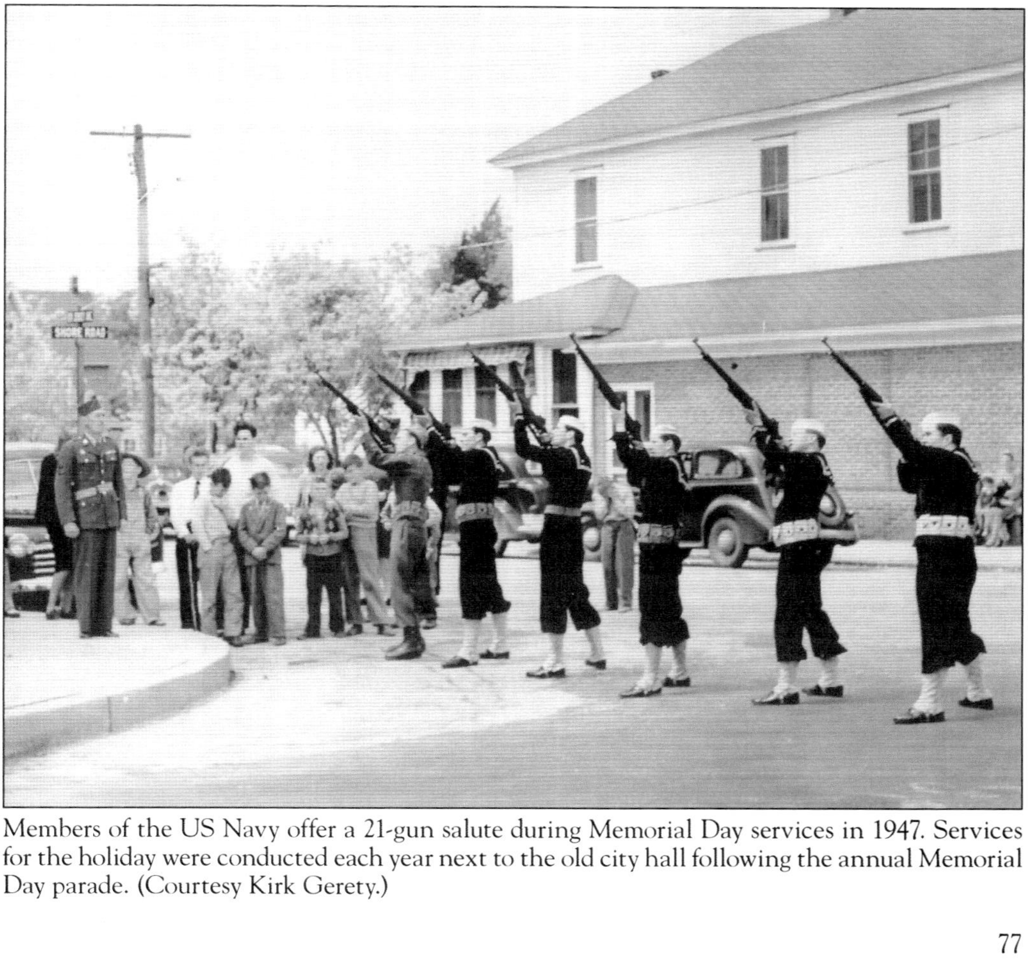

Members of the US Navy offer a 21-gun salute during Memorial Day services in 1947. Services for the holiday were conducted each year next to the old city hall following the annual Memorial Day parade. (Courtesy Kirk Gerety.)

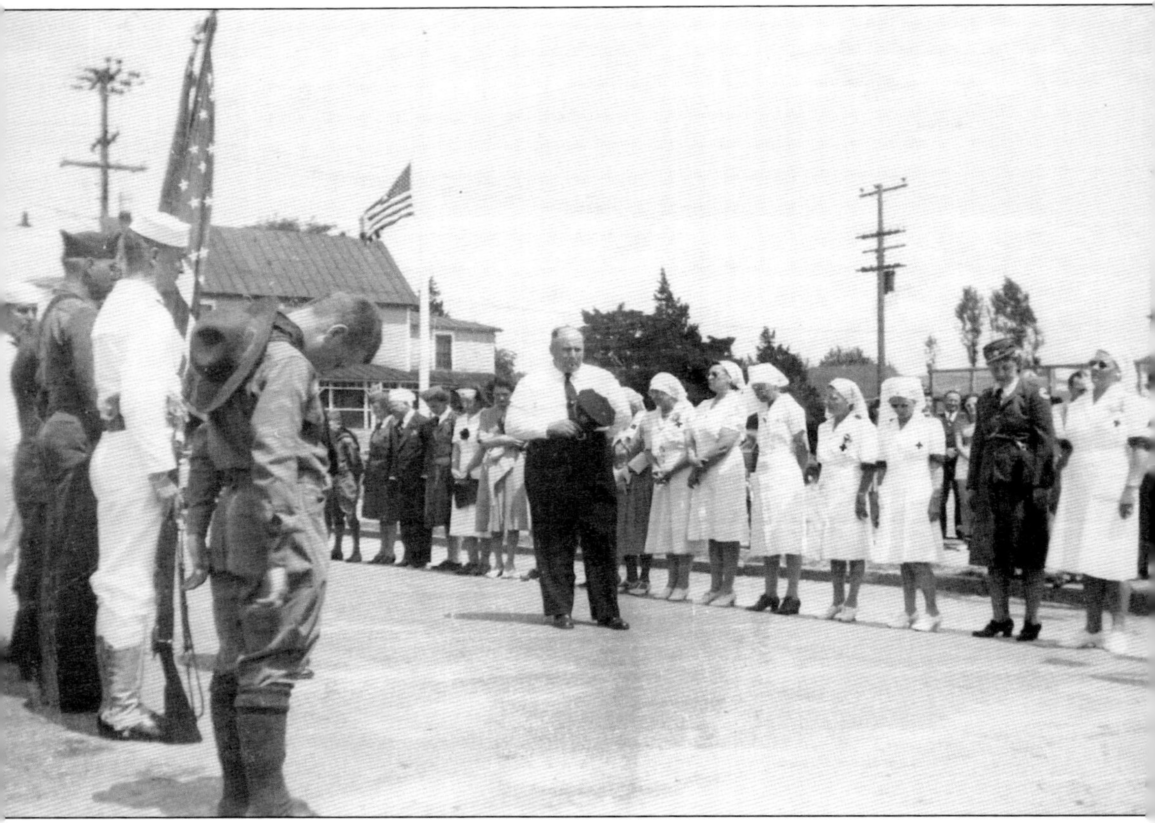

Police chief William Morrow speaks during a Memorial Day service at the beach, near the War of 1812 Monument. The Boy Scouts would traditionally throw a wreath into the bay to commemorate servicemen lost at sea. (Courtesy Kirk Gerety.)

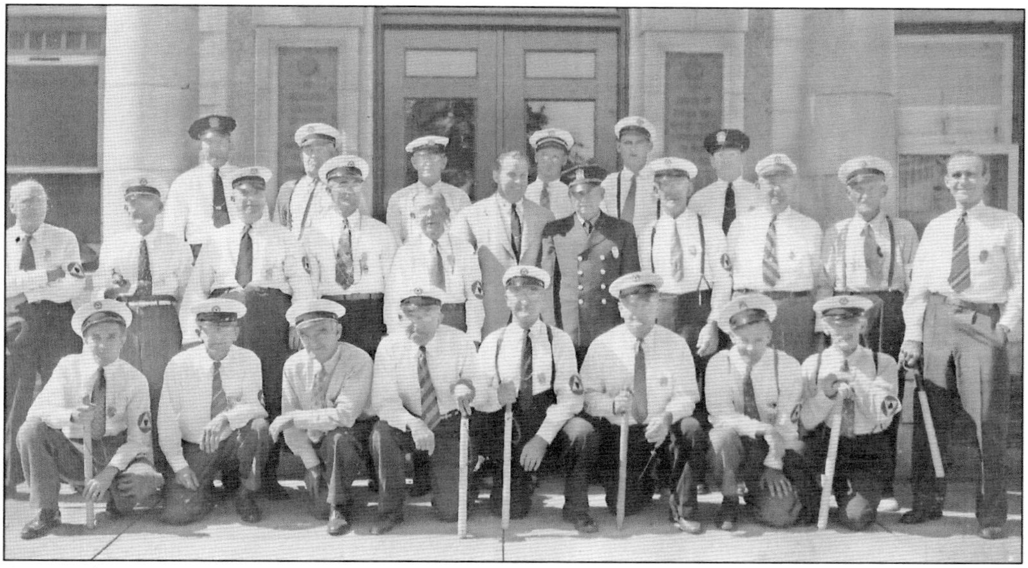

Air Raid Precautions wardens pose in front of the old city hall. Somers Point's air raid wardens were responsible for patrolling the streets during air raid blackouts to make sure that no light was visible from the outside of buildings and that no cars or people were out on the street.

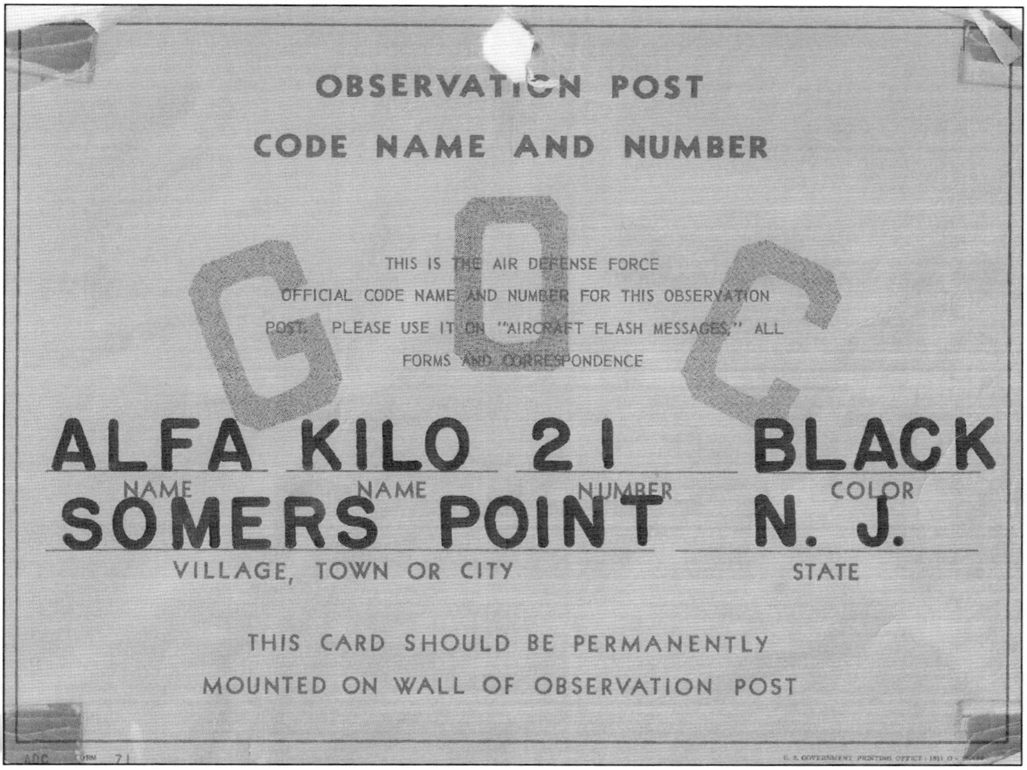

This Observation Post Code Name and Number card was displayed at the observation post in Somers Point during World War II. This shows the code name and number that was to be used on all correspondence that was generated from this post.

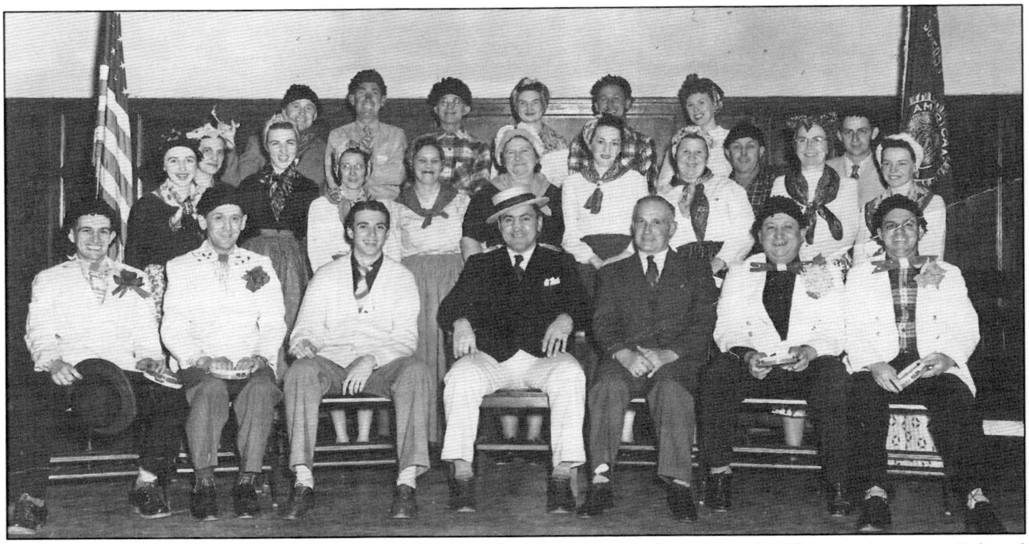

The Clark-Eliason American Legion Post 352 held minstrel shows at the Dawes Avenue School to raise money to build a post home. Pictured here are, from left to right, (first row) Norman Rowland, Sherman Winslow, Ronald Medlock, Clem Stevens, Willard Turner, Parker Mulford, and Bill Vieth; (second row) Ann Rowland, unidentified, Doris Sumner, Edith Moncrief, Ruth Mulford, Helen Summers, Frances Mathis, Lillian Tallman, Bill Moncrief, Margaret Winslow, Herman Meskers, and Ruth Turner; (third row) Ken Turner, Andy Sumner, John Summers, Lucy Chamberlain, Autsie Elwell, and Norma Meskers. (Courtesy Ruth Mulford Newsome.)

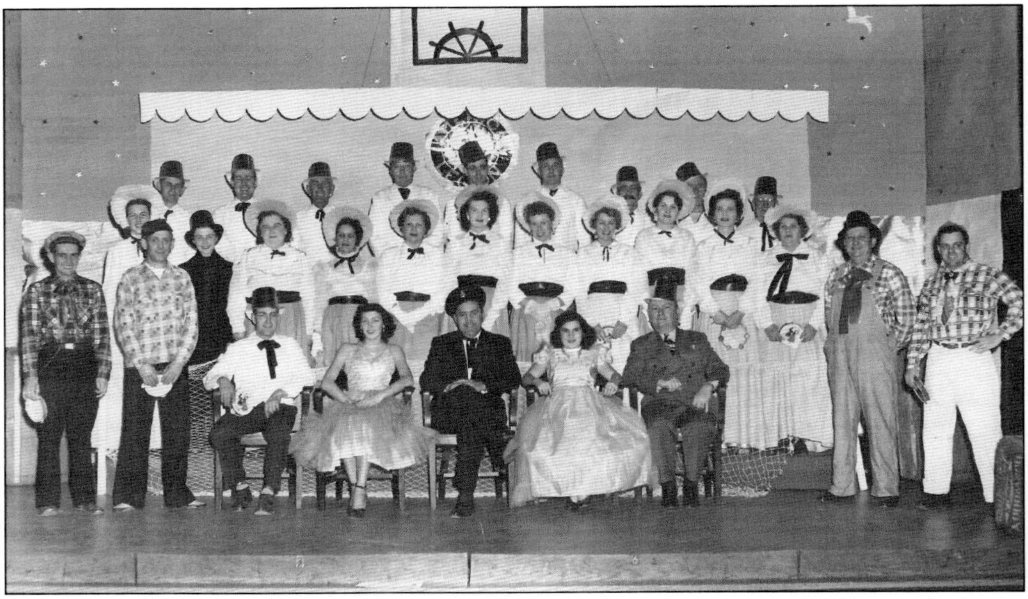

Pictured here in another Showboat minstrel show in 1952 are, from left to right, (first row) Charles Jones, Billy Sue Headley, Clem Stevens, Betty Esposito, and unidentified; (second row) Norman Rowland, Sherman Winslow, Ann Rowland, Helen Summers, Ruth Mulford, unidentified, Lucy Chamberlain, Norma Meskers, unidentified, Geneva Stevens, D. Hoffman, Myrtle Debus, Parker Mulford, and Bill Vieth; (third row) Doris Sumner, Herman Meskers, unidentified, Andy Sumner, three unidentified, John Summers, and two unidentified. (Courtesy Ruth Mulford Newsome.)

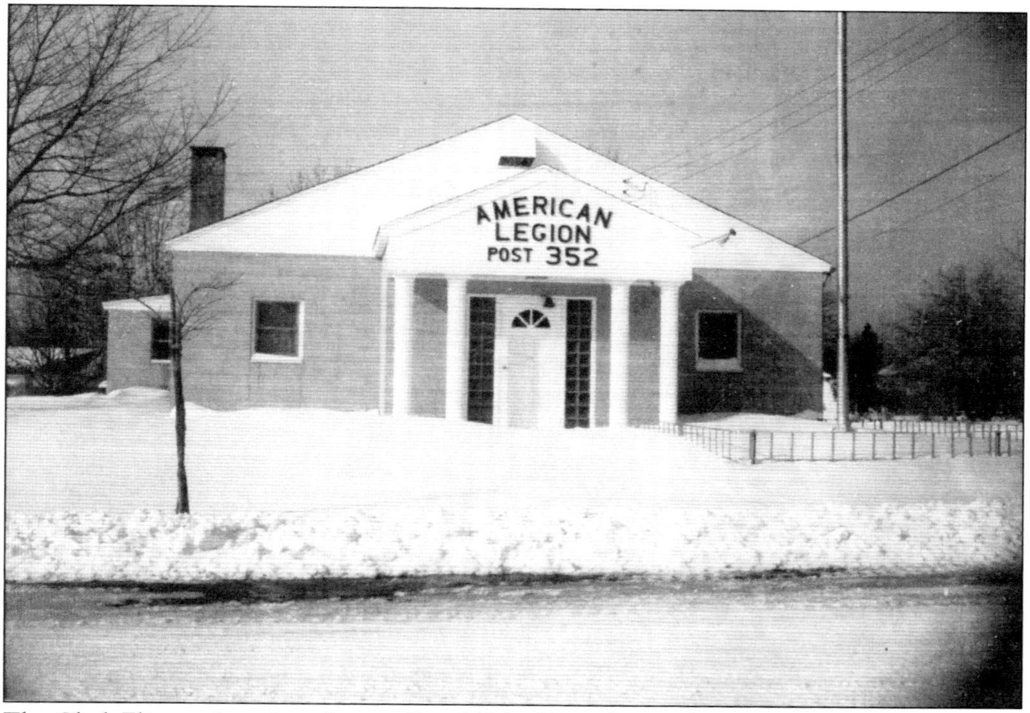

The Clark-Eliason American Legion Post 352 building shown above is located on First Street. Proceeds from fundraising, including the shows pictured on the previous page, enabled American Legion members to construct this building. Below is a picture of the bar in the new building. The post is named for Edmund L. Eliason Jr. and H. Paul Clark, two local servicemen killed during World War II. (Both, courtesy Ruth Mulford Newsome.)

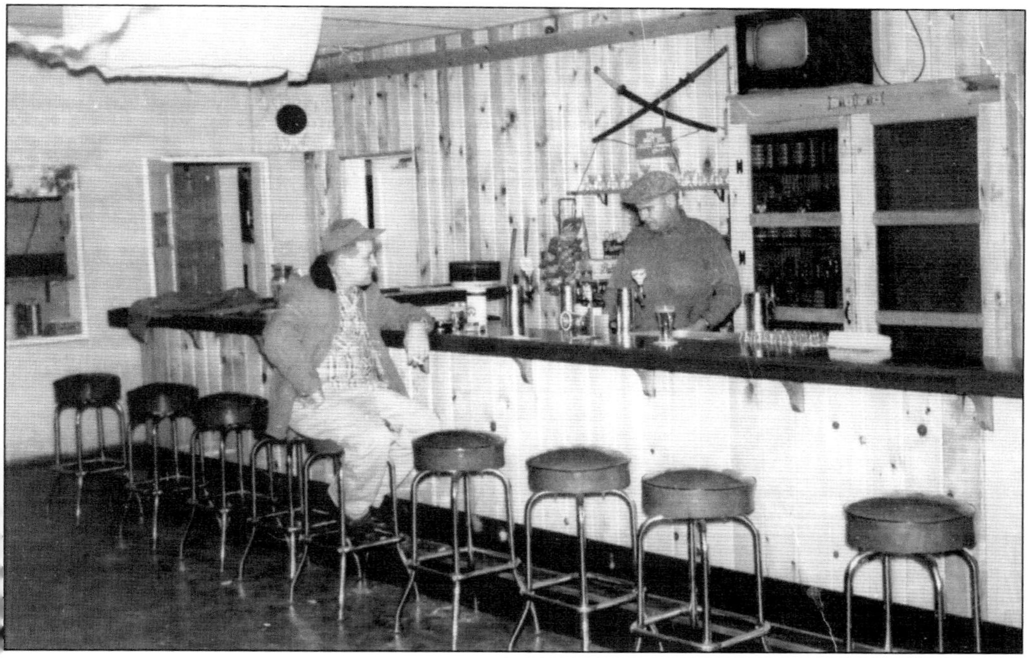

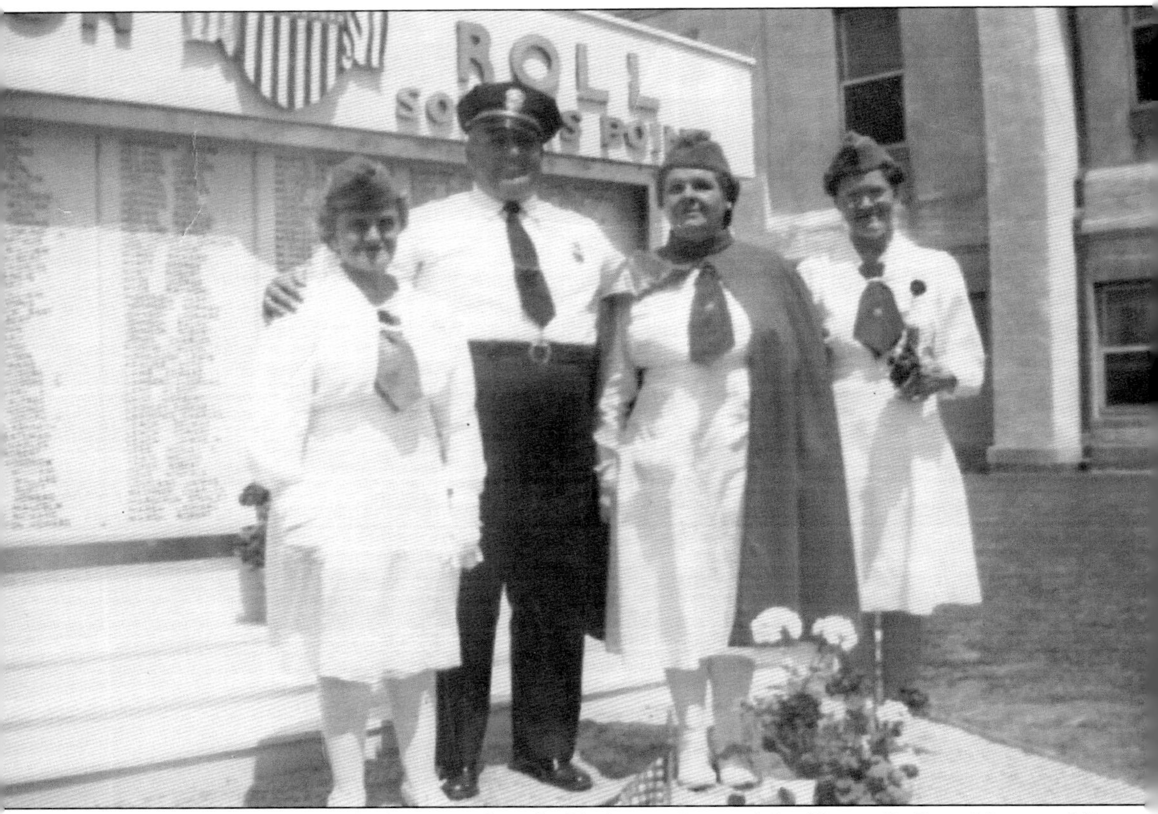

Bill Morrow stands with three unidentified ladies in front of the Honor Roll on Memorial Day. The Honor Roll was located next to the old city hall and listed all of the men from Somers Point who had gone to war during World War II. Although many people remember the Honor Roll being at this location, no one seems to remember it being removed, and what happened to it remains a mystery. (Courtesy Kirk Gerety.)

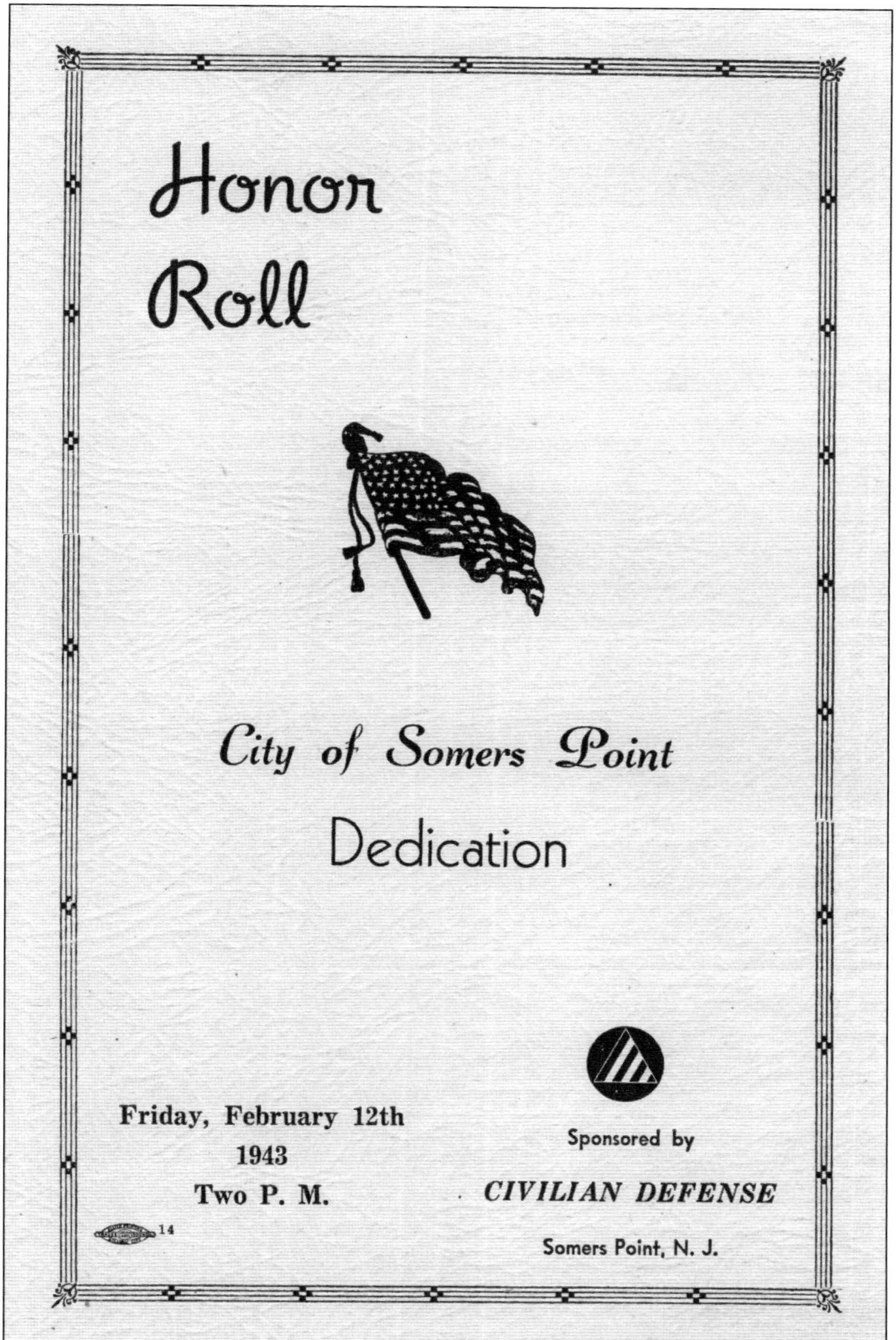

Honor Roll

City of Somers Point

Dedication

Friday, February 12th
1943
Two P. M.

Sponsored by
CIVILIAN DEFENSE
Somers Point, N. J.

This is the front of the program from the dedication of the Somers Point Honor Roll, which was held on February 12, 1943. (Courtesy Kirk Gerety.)

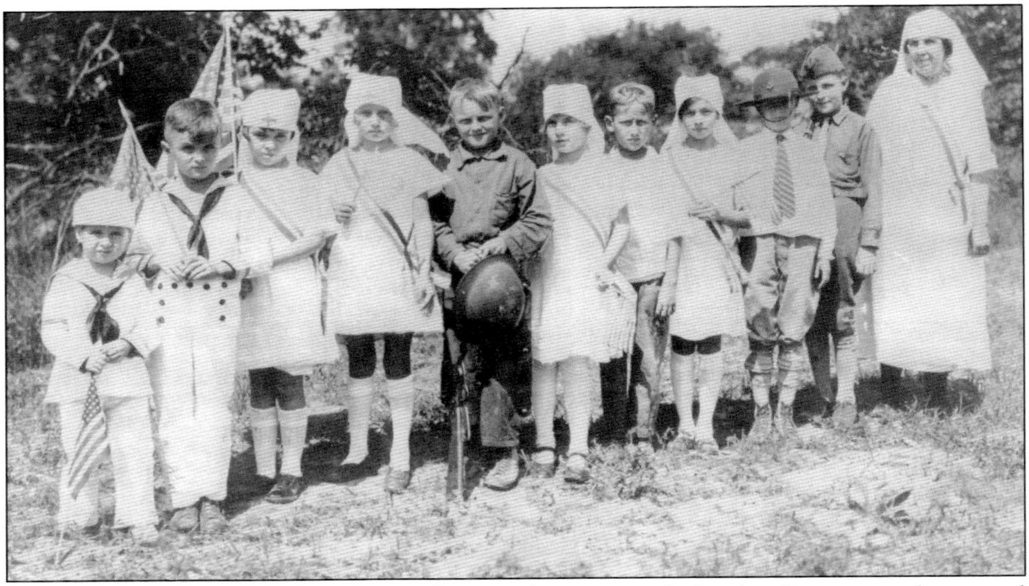

Schoolchildren dressed in patriotic outfits pose for a picture before heading out to the annual Memorial Day parade. (Courtesy Ruth Mulford Newsome.)

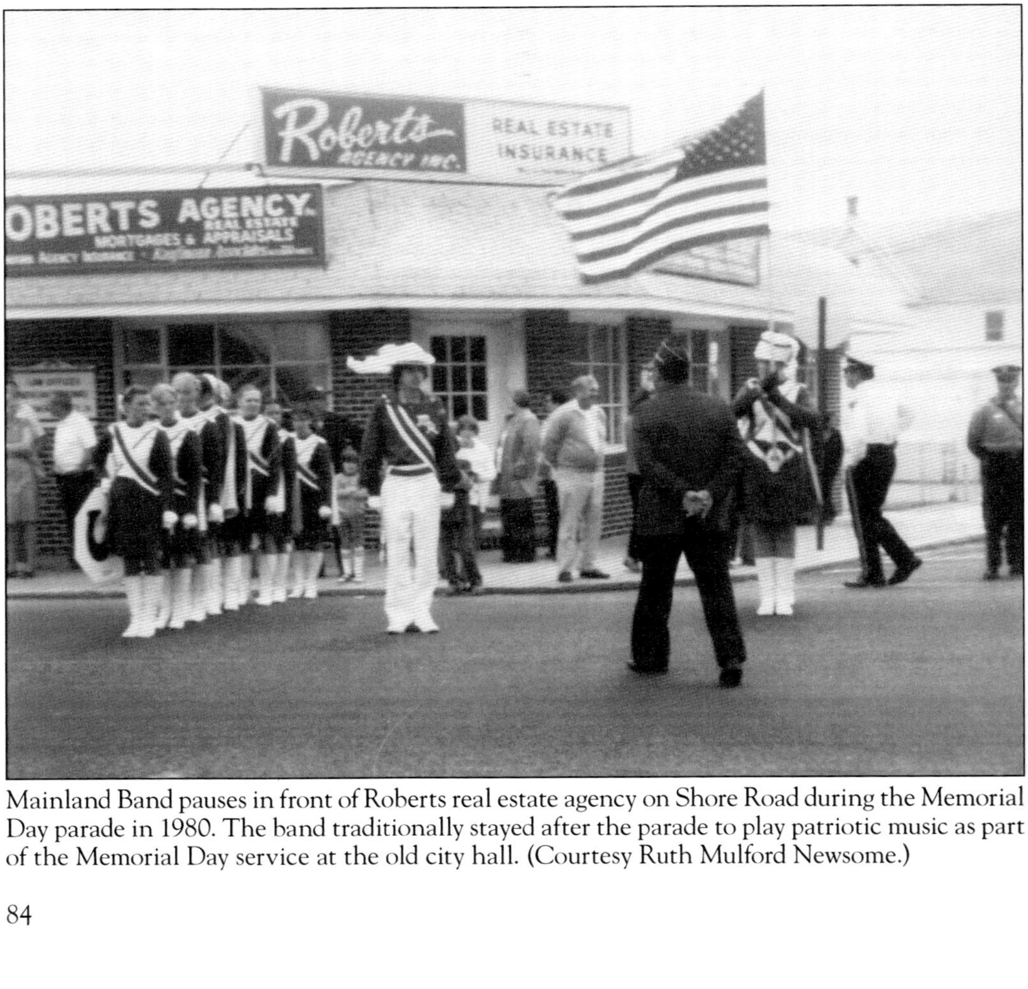

Mainland Band pauses in front of Roberts real estate agency on Shore Road during the Memorial Day parade in 1980. The band traditionally stayed after the parade to play patriotic music as part of the Memorial Day service at the old city hall. (Courtesy Ruth Mulford Newsome.)

Seven

CHURCHES

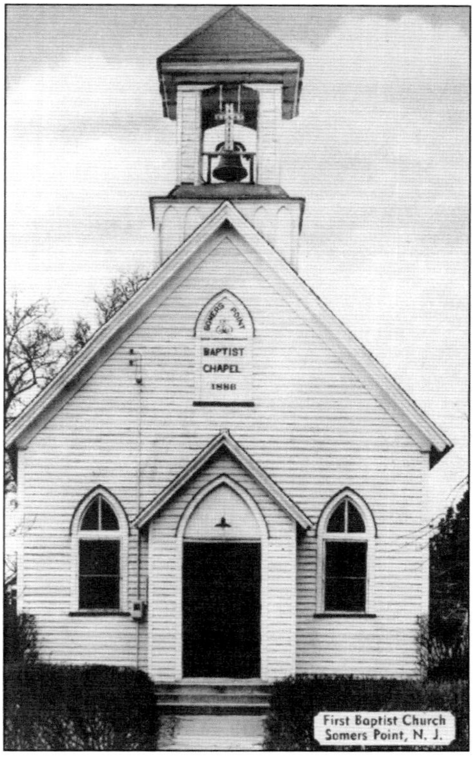

Somers Point Baptist Church on Shore Road was built in 1886. The building served as the church until the early 1960s, when it was sold to the City of Somers Point. The congregation met temporarily at Dawes Avenue School until the new church was built on New York Avenue.

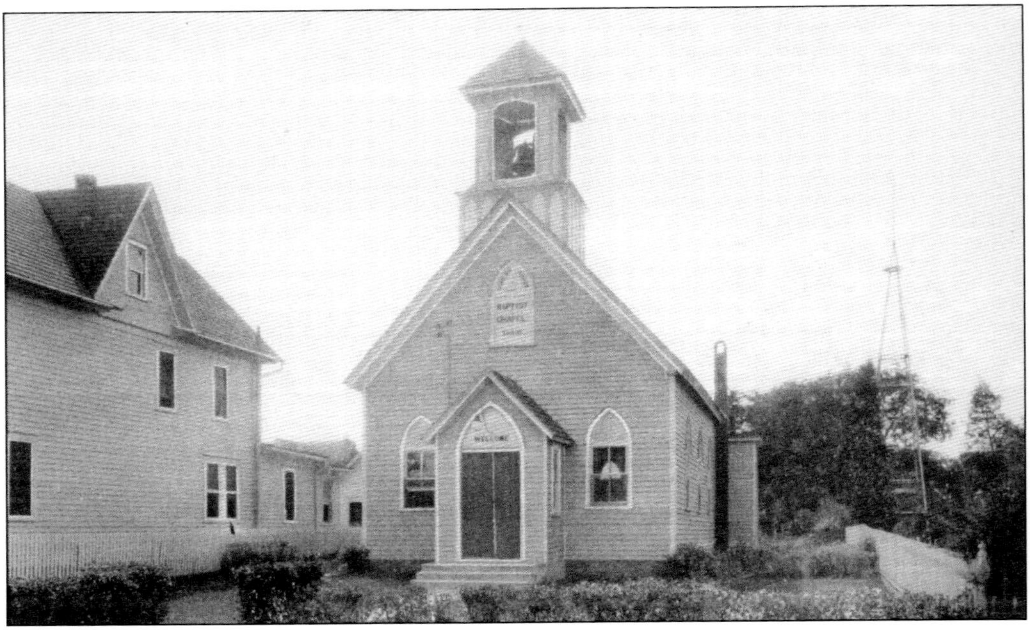

The Somers Point Baptist Church stands on property purchased on April 24, 1886, from Jesse Somers by the West Baptist Association for the price of $250. The church building was erected by free labor, also in 1886. The certificate below shows the information on the bell that is still located at the church building. (Both, courtesy Ruth Mulford Newsome.)

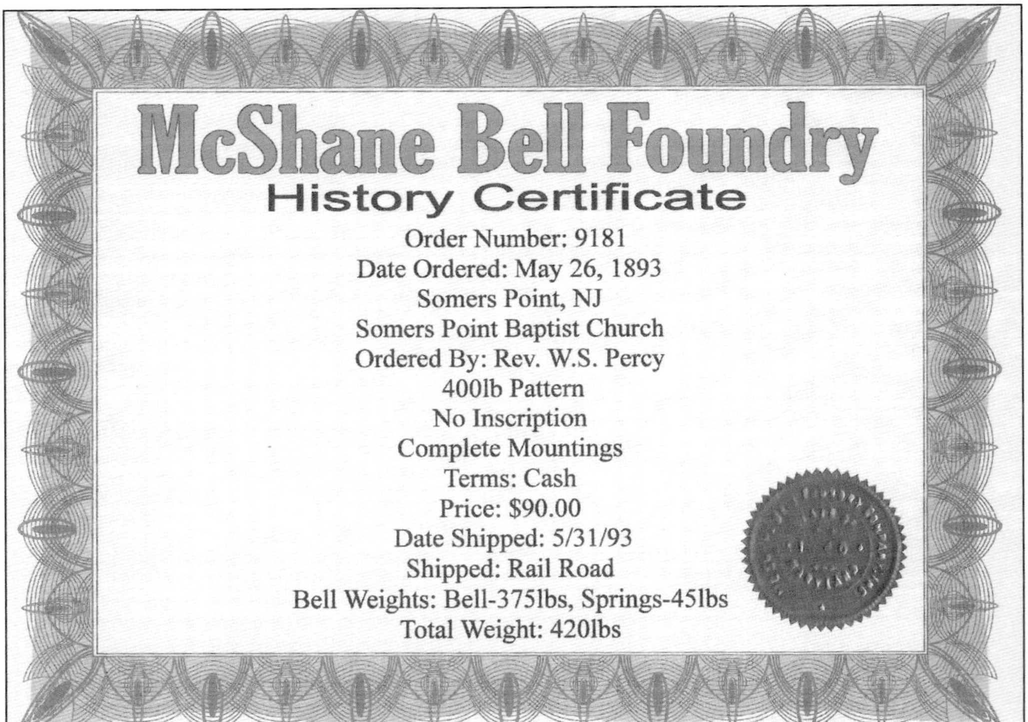

McShane Bell Foundry

History Certificate

Order Number: 9181
Date Ordered: May 26, 1893
Somers Point, NJ
Somers Point Baptist Church
Ordered By: Rev. W.S. Percy
400lb Pattern
No Inscription
Complete Mountings
Terms: Cash
Price: $90.00
Date Shipped: 5/31/93
Shipped: Rail Road
Bell Weights: Bell-375lbs, Springs-45lbs
Total Weight: 420lbs

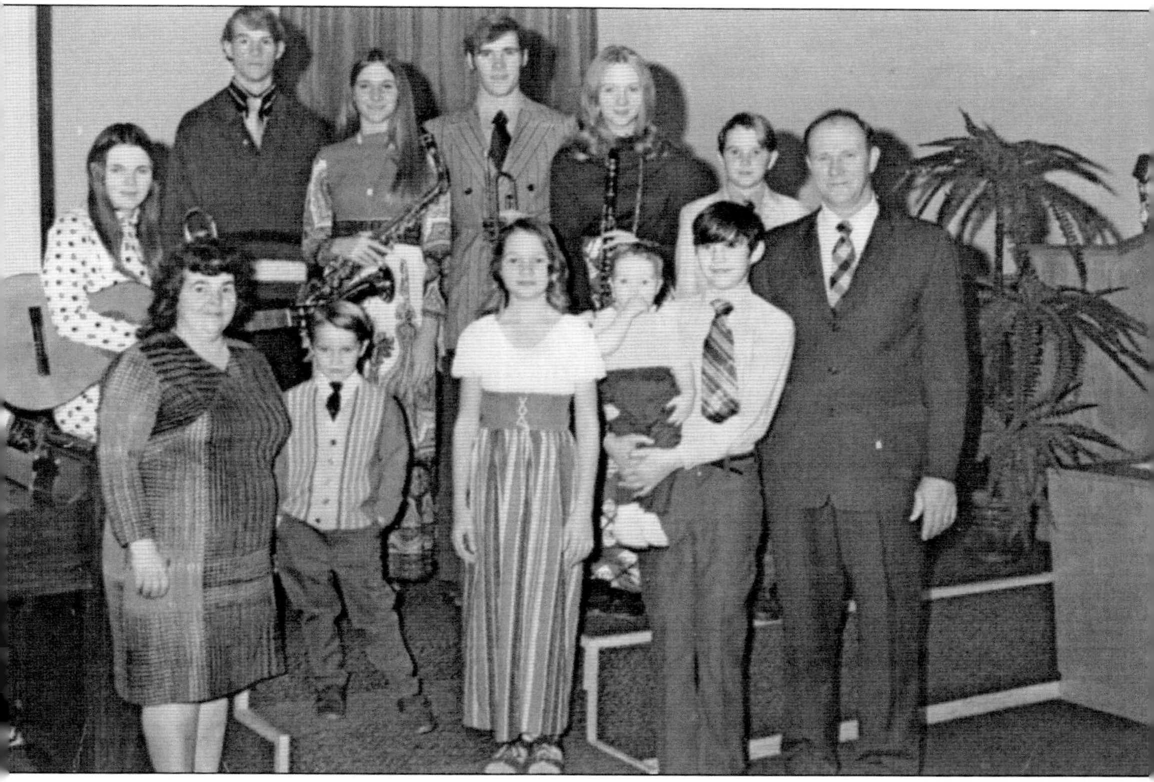

Rev. Gene Corbett and his family are pictured here: from left to right, (first row) Carol, Orin, Sola, Tenny, and Lael; (second row) Melody, Luke, Daurolyn, Drue, Roxy, Dathan, and Pastor Corbett. Reverend Corbett was the last pastor at the Baptist church located on Shore Road. After the building was sold to the city, church services were conducted at Dawes Avenue School while a new church was being built on New York Avenue. (Courtesy Ruth Mulford Newsome.)

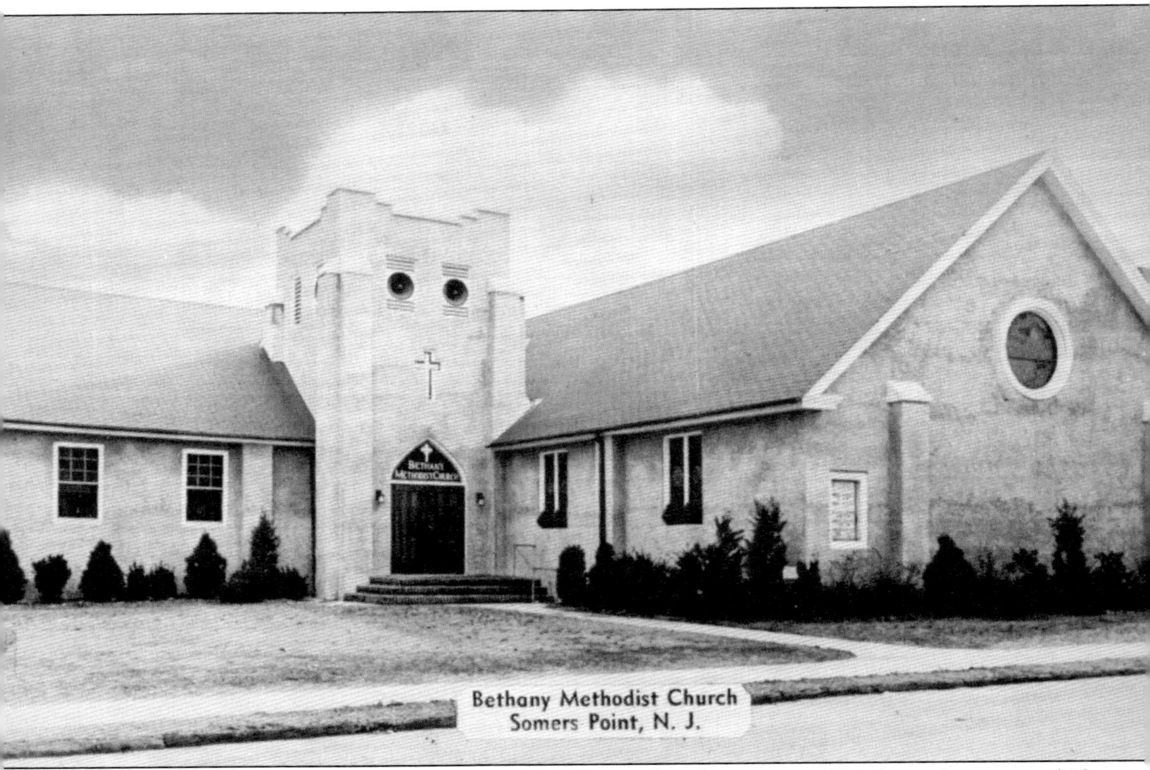

Bethany Methodist Church, built in 1949, is located at the corner of Brighton Avenue and Shore Road. The congregation relocated to a newer building in 1982, and the name has since been changed to United Methodist Church. This building was purchased by Shore Memorial Hospital.

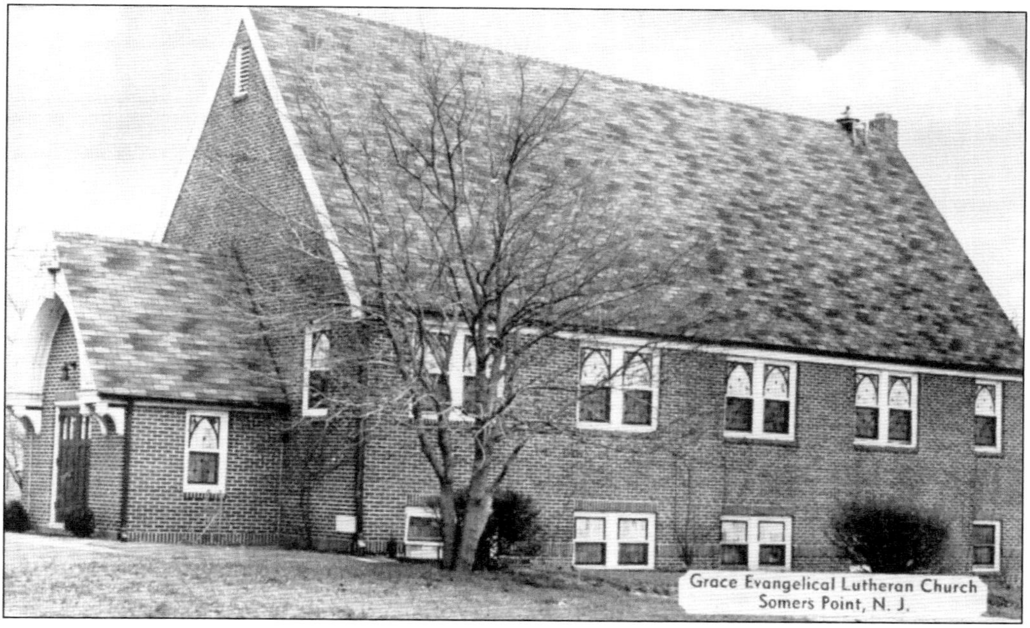

Pictured above, Grace Evangelical Lutheran Church is located at the corner of Meyran Avenue and Shore Road and was originally built in 1927. The picture below shows the interior of the church as it looked when it was decorated for the Christmas season.

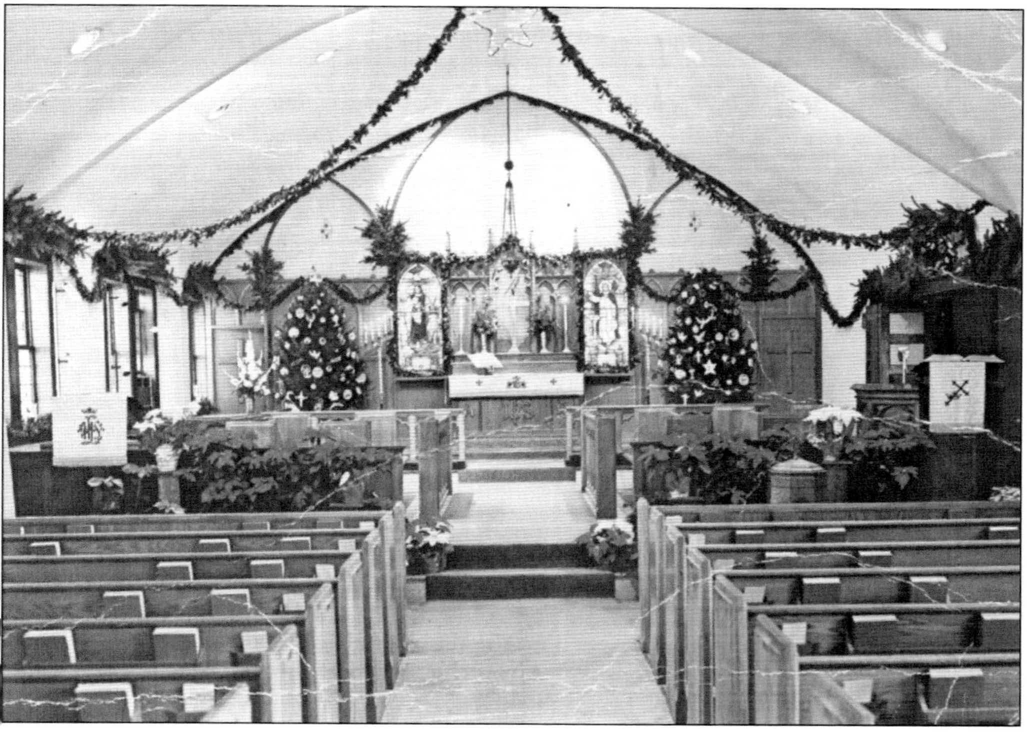

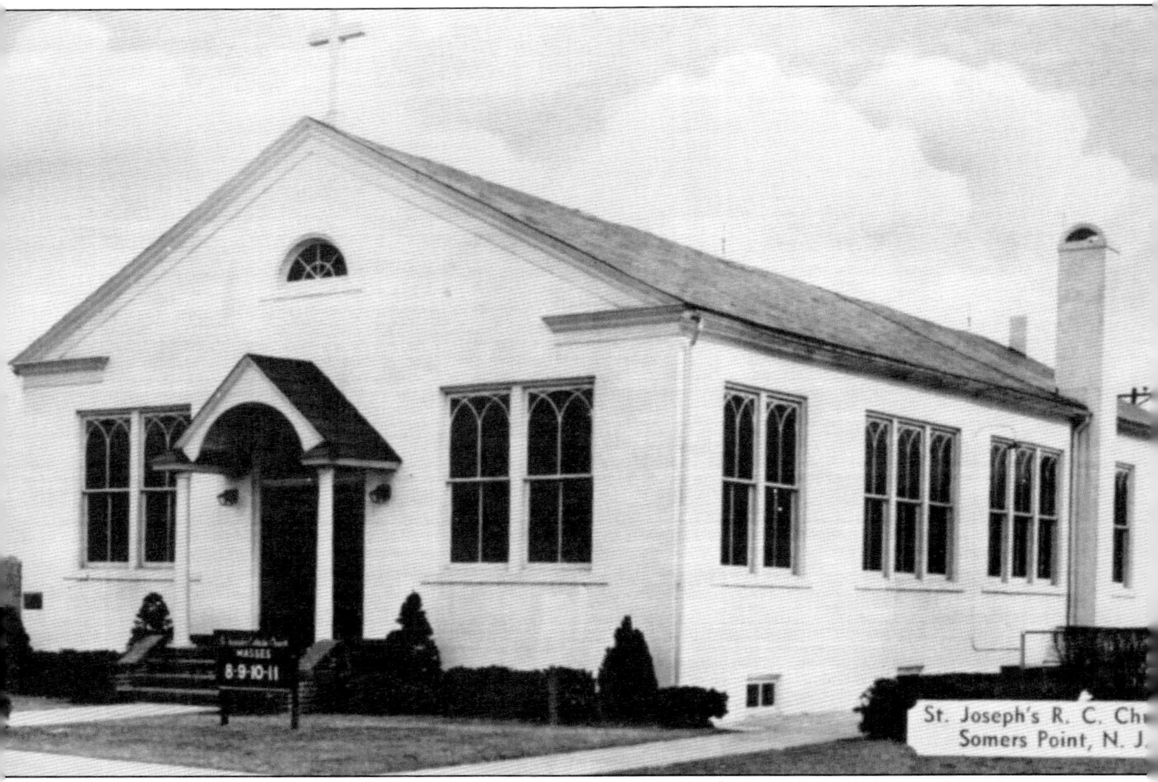

This picture shows the original St. Joseph's Roman Catholic Church located at the corner of Harbor Lane and Shore Road, built in 1922 when the church was still under the care of St. Augustine's in Ocean City. St. Joseph's became its own parish July 13, 1946. Ground-breaking for the new church was held on April 29, 1956. This original building still stands today and is still used by the church.

Eight

SPORTS

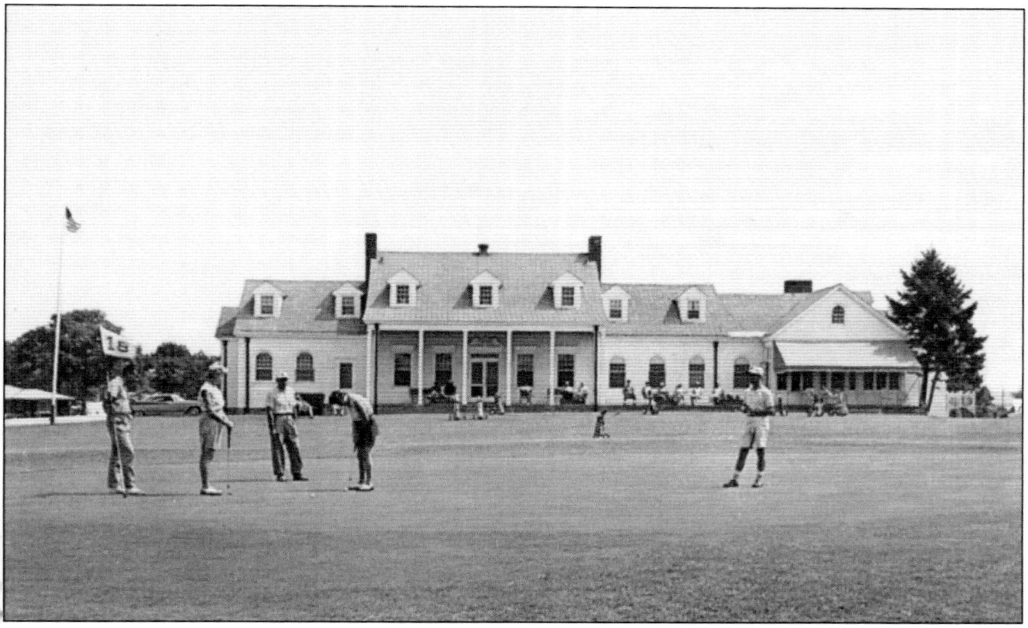

Golfing at the Ocean City–Somers Point Golf Course has long been a popular pastime in Somers Point. In this image that shows the old clubhouse, golfers wait their turns to putt at the 18th hole.

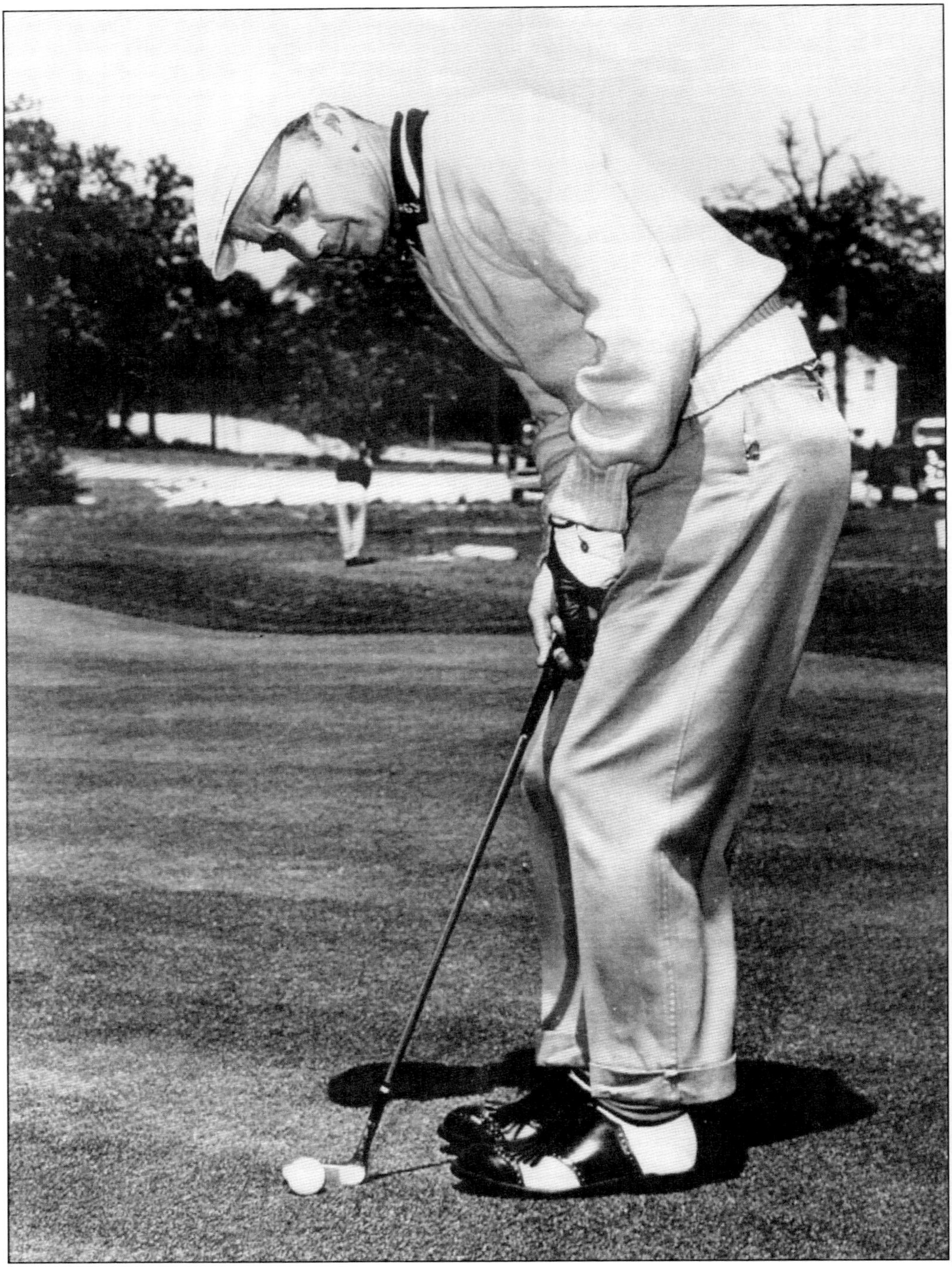

Harry Elwell Jr. moved to Somers Point as a teenager, and his love of golf started when he became a caddie at the Ocean City–Somers Point Golf Course. Through the years, his game progressed and he became one of the most prominent golfers in the area. He competed in many area tournaments and won several, becoming the club champion at the Ocean City–Somers Point Golf Club on several occasions. (Courtesy Ruth Mulford Newsome.)

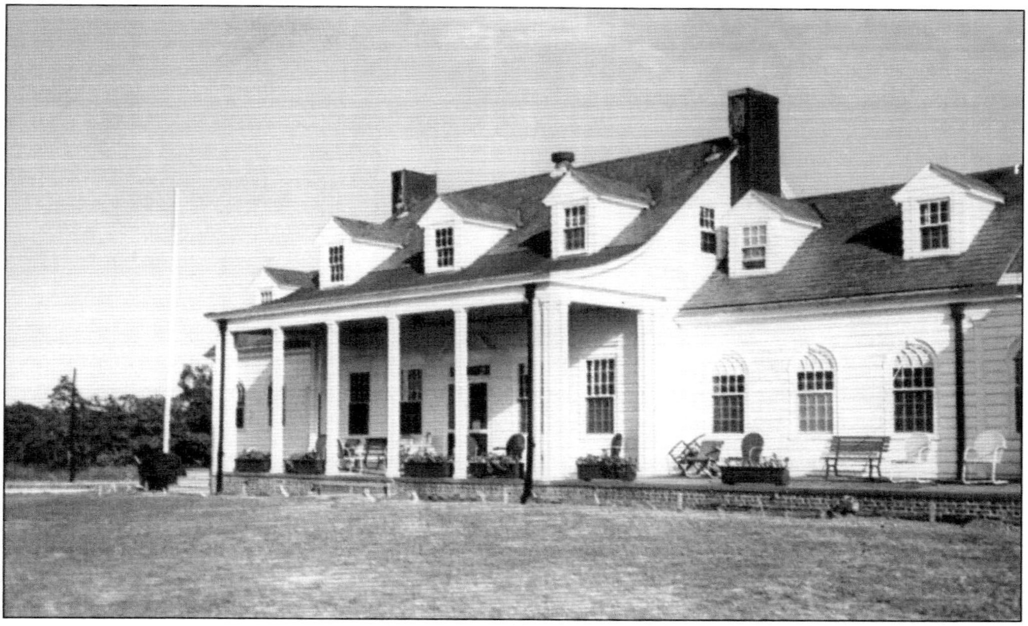

The Ocean City–Somers Point Golf Club was originally built by Harvey Young Lake, an Ocean City resident, as a nine-hole course to be used by his family and friends. When the course became too expensive to keep private, he decided to take on partners and make it a public course, expanding it to an 18-hole course. Above is a picture of the clubhouse as it looked in later years. The picture below shows the clubhouse being built.

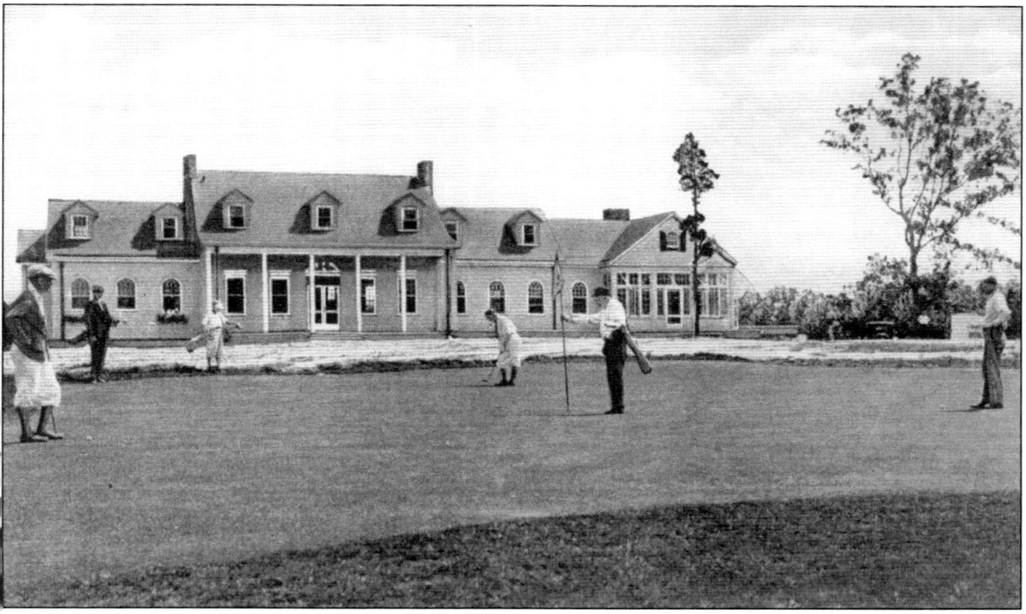

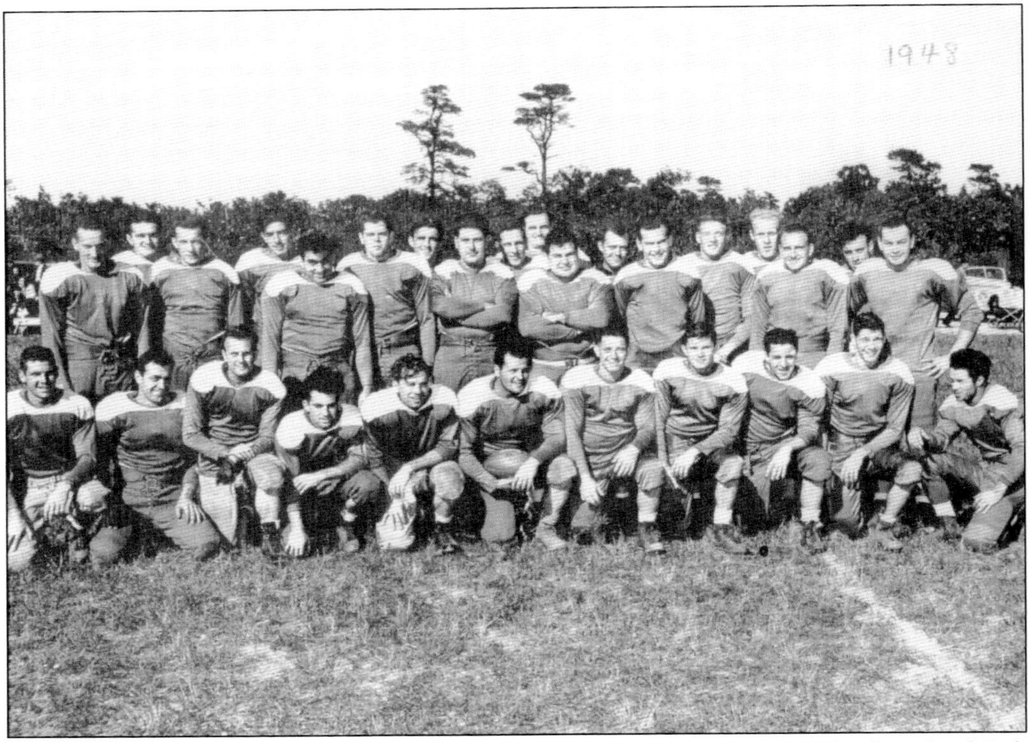

This is the Somers Point football team from 1948. Pictured are, from left to right, (kneeling) Bob Gifford, Charles Jones, ? Sheppard, Joseph Veit, Harry Ford, Jim Marshall, Frank Galente, Bill Coffey, Frank Sannino, Gus Balleit, and Bill Schafe; (standing) Jim Mahoney, Walter Corwell, Leonard Marsh, Tom Neill, Mike Allegretto, Colin McGinnis, Paul Becotte, Alfred Wood, Chuck ?, Charles Gray, Andrew Scola, Edward Corman, Mort Thompson, Sam McDowell, Fred Chapman, Robert Fugee, unidentified, and Jake Schuff. (Courtesy Joan Bird Wilson.)

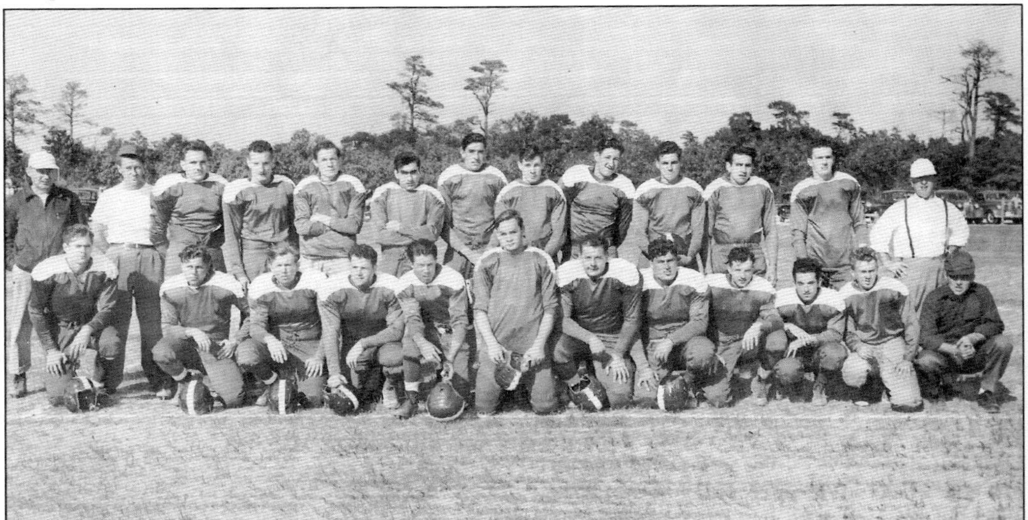

The year that this photograph was taken of this Somers Point football team is unknown. (Courtesy Kirk Gerety.)

Somers Point boys get ready to start the game with a jump shot. Richard Gray (left) and Wade Moncrief (right) are centers for their respective teams. Charlie McClure holds the ball. (Courtesy Kirk Gerety.)

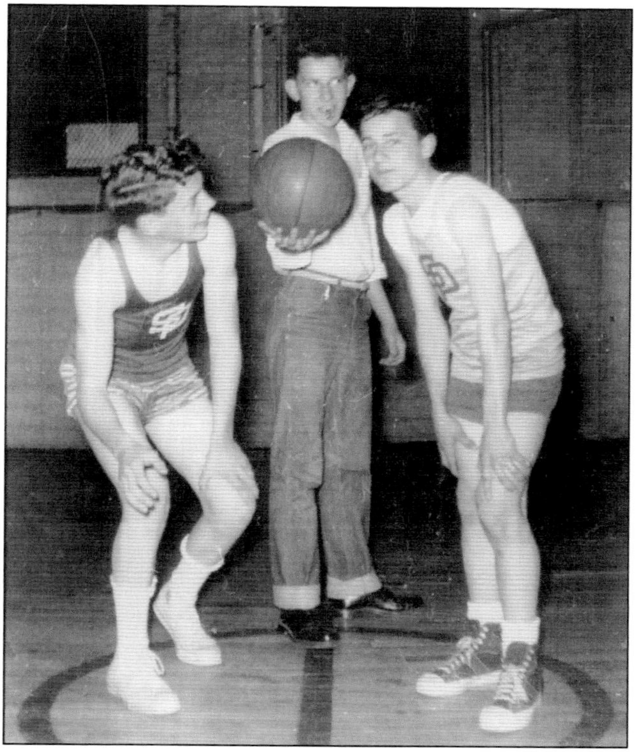

The Somers Point basketball team holds trophies after a championship. Identified are George Gerety (second row, second from left), Bill Morrow (second row, fifth from left), and Joseph DiOrio (on the far right). (Courtesy Kirk Gerety.)

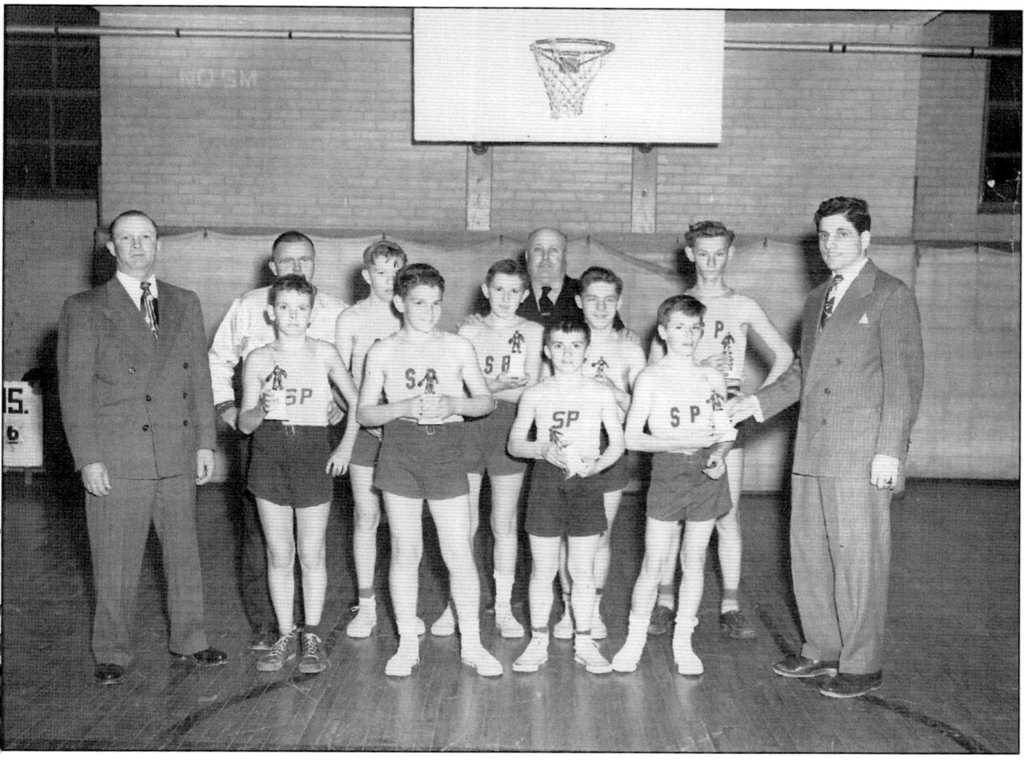

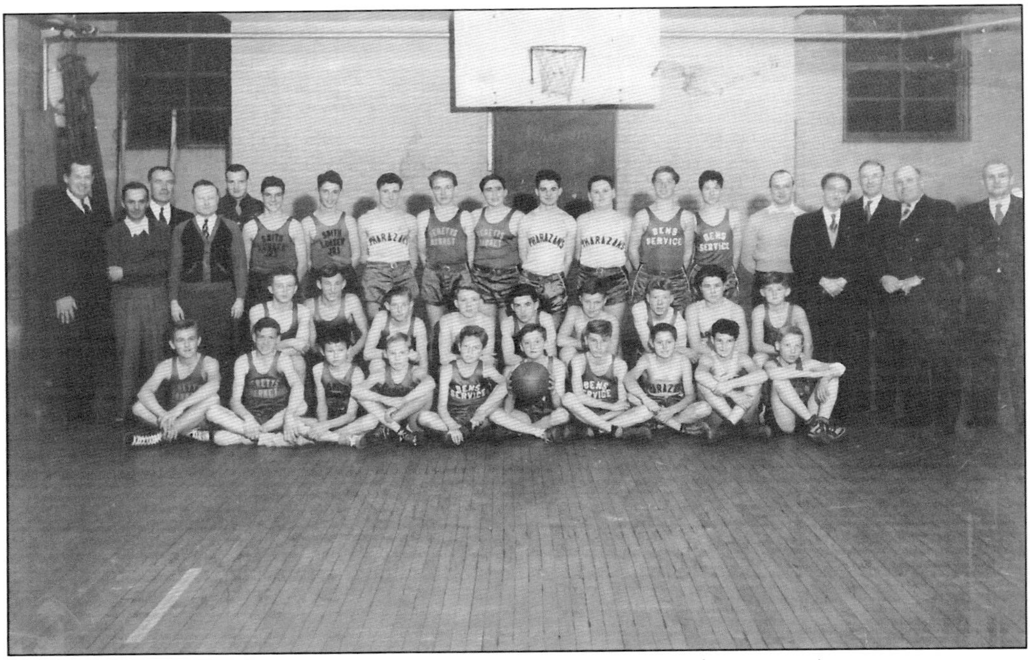

The Somers Point Boys Club basketball league is shown here at the Dawes Avenue gymnasium. The Somers Point Boys Club was run by Somers Point police chief William Morrow and was popular with the local boys. (Courtesy Kirk Gerety.)

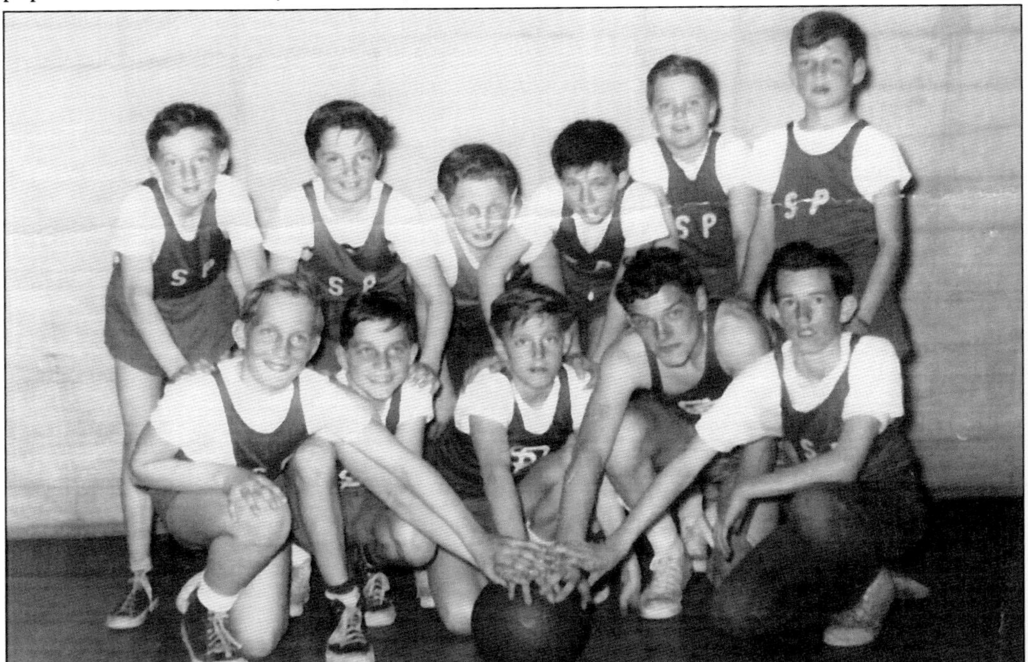

Boys basketball team the Blues poses during the 1954–1955 season. Identified are (front row) Joseph Huber (second from left), Richard Gray (second from right), and Robert Lukasiewicz (far right); (back row) Butch Ellis (second from left). (Courtesy Kirk Gerety.)

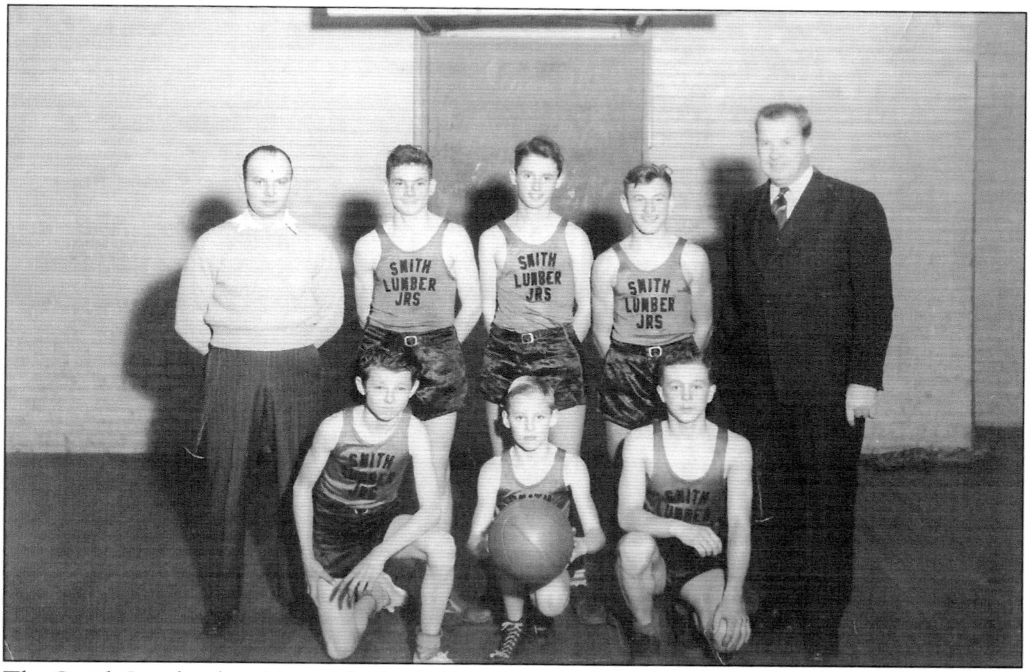

The Smith Lumber boys' junior basketball team poses for a team picture. Coach Charles Smith stands at left and mayor Fred Chapman stands at right. (Courtesy Kirk Gerety.)

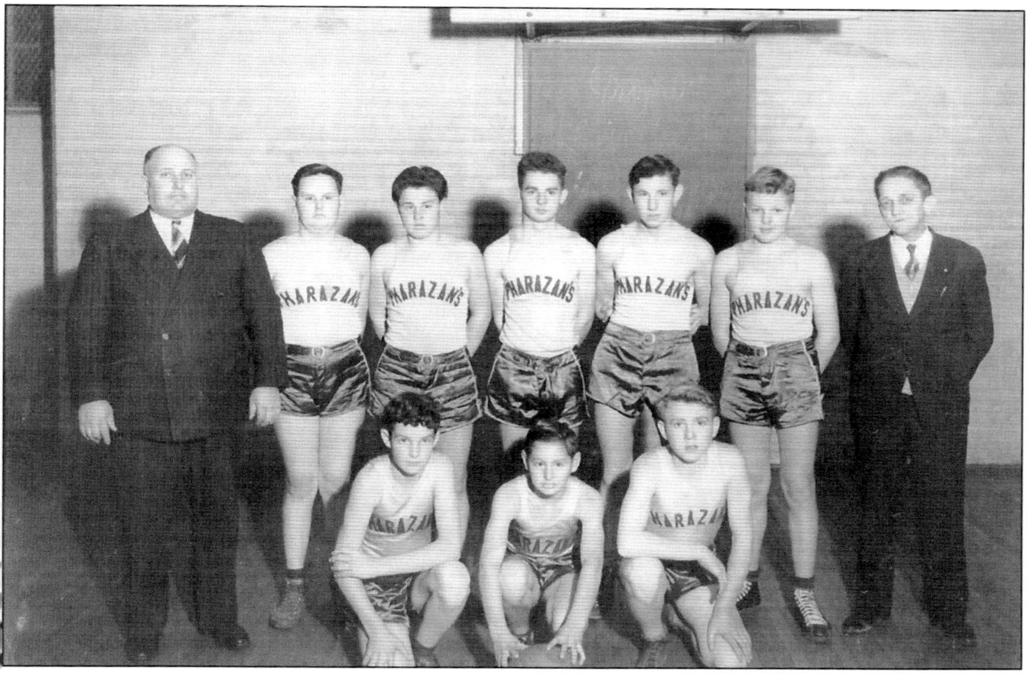

Here, the boys' basketball team sponsored by Pharazan's poses for its team picture. Bill Morrow is at left. (Courtesy Kirk Gerety.)

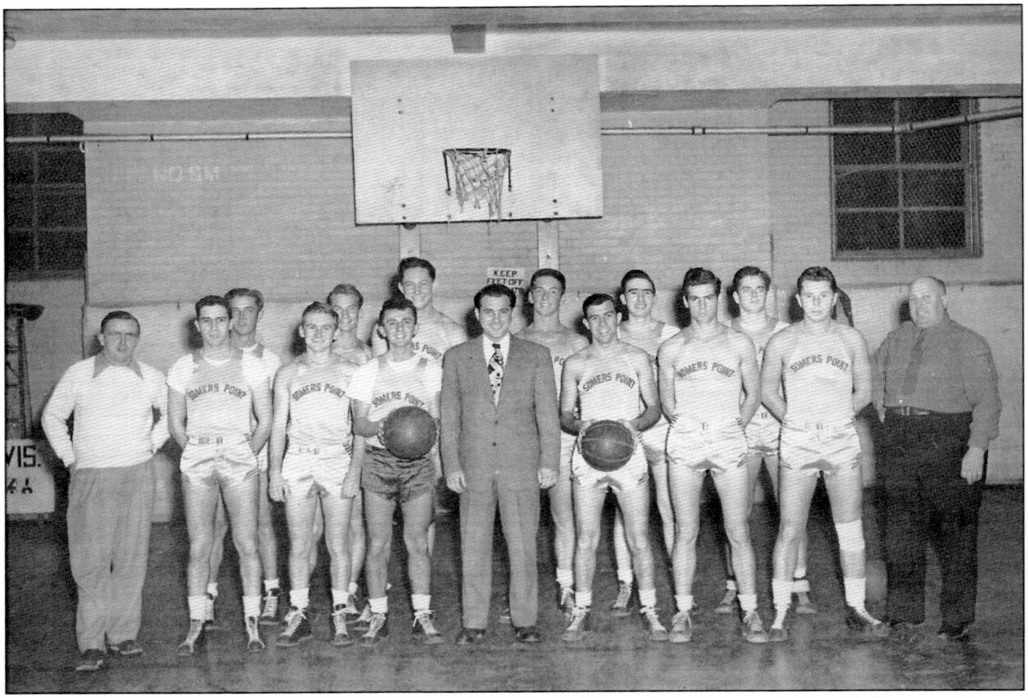

This Somers Point basketball team poses in the Dawes Avenue gymnasium. Coach George Gerety is at left, and Bill Morrow is at right. (Courtesy Kirk Gerety.)

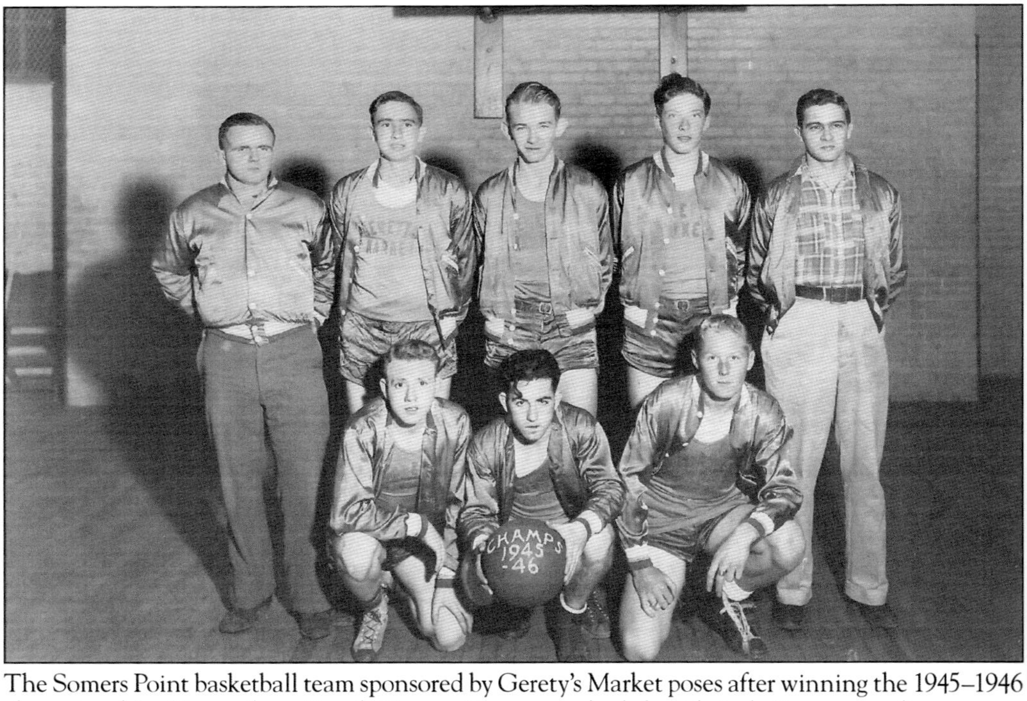

The Somers Point basketball team sponsored by Gerety's Market poses after winning the 1945–1946 championship. Pictured are Coach George Gerety on the left with Jack Gerety standing next to him. Joseph Gerety is standing on the far right. (Courtesy Kirk Gerety.)

Somers Point baseball player Robert Gifford (left) shakes hands with the opponent of the day, a true sign of good sportsmanship. It is unknown who won the game. (Courtesy Kirk Gerety.)

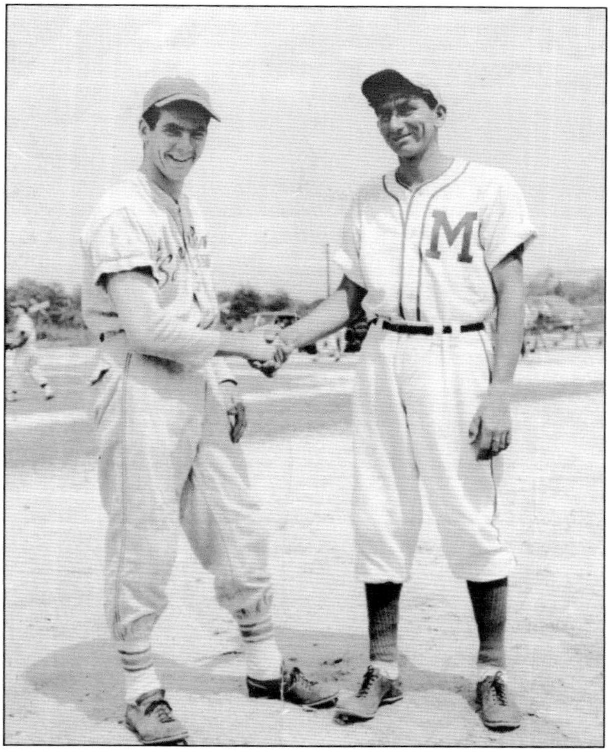

The Somers Point Chiefs pose as they prepare to take the field. (Courtesy Kirk Gerety.)

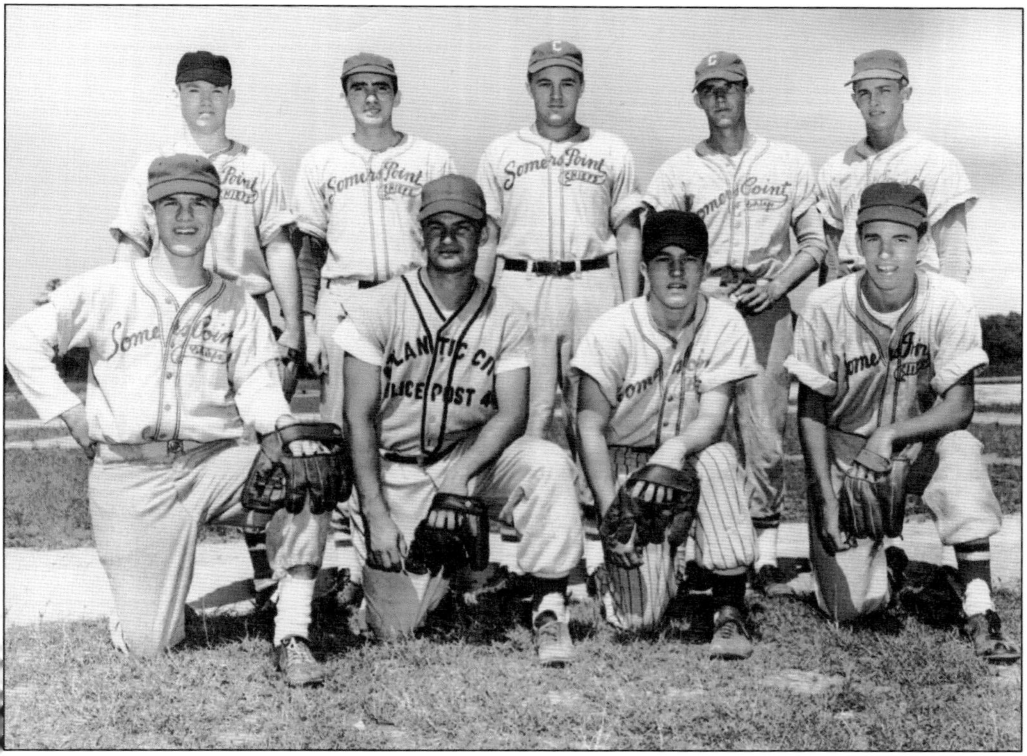

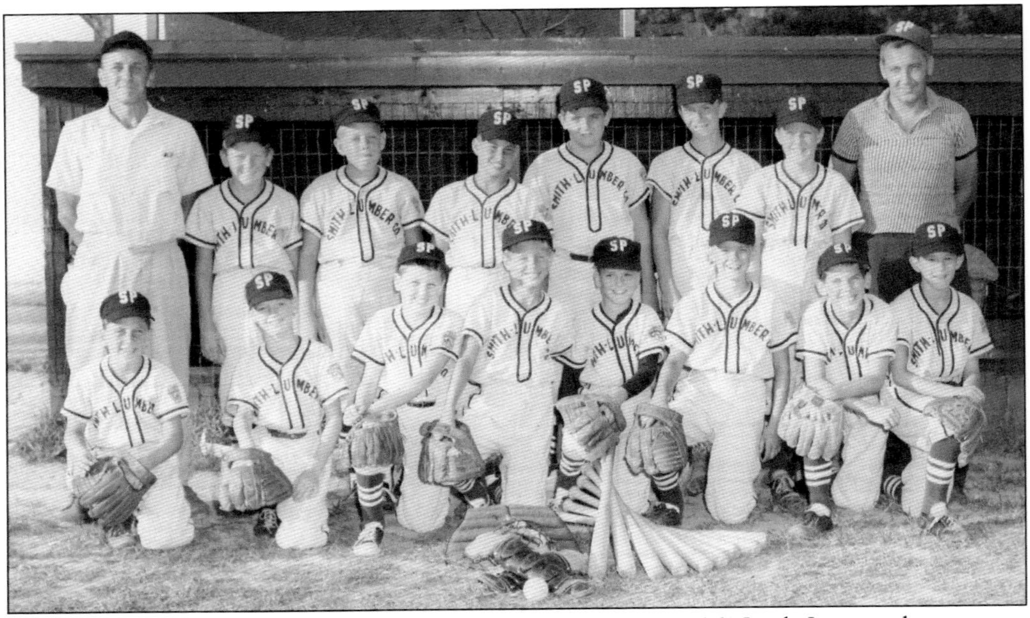

1961 Little League champs Smith Lumber pose next to the dugout. Pictured are, from left to right, (kneeling) Dennis DiOrio, Billy McCrossan, John Miller, Pat Crawford, Jeff Miller, John Spurlock, Joe DiOrio, and Phillip DuMars; (standing) Dean Werb, Jerry Smart, Gary Werb, Guy Brown, Marshall Schaffer, Bob Dougherty, Jim McCue, and Vic Crawford. (Courtesy Jeffrey Miller.)

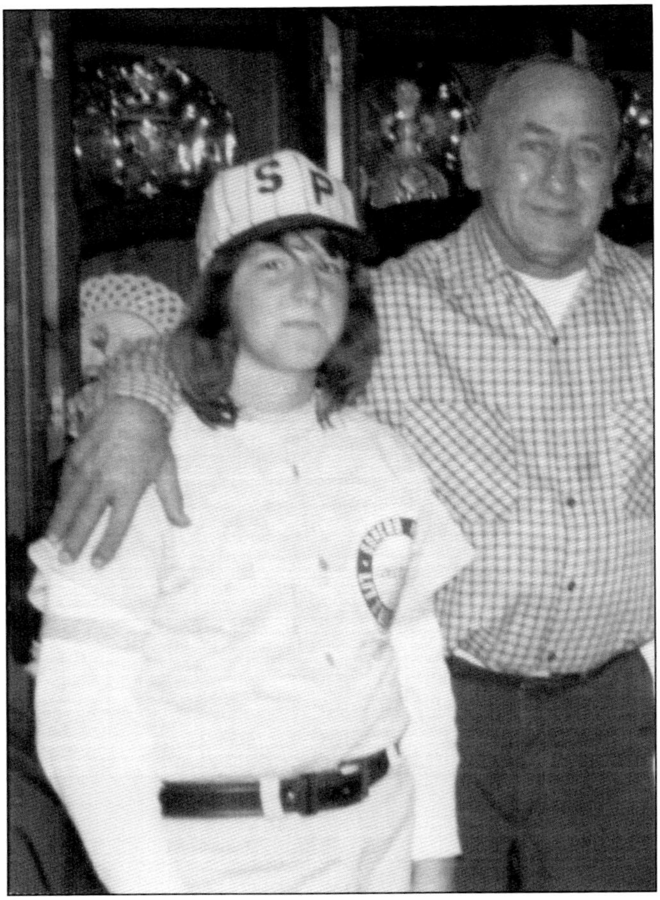

Elizabeth "Beth" Shuman stands with Autsie Elwell. The first girl to play Little League in Somers Point, Shuman played for Coach Fowler on the Lovett Pumps team. She excelled at the game, playing not only first base but also serving as pitcher and going on to play on the all-star team. (Courtesy Ruth Mulford Newsome.)

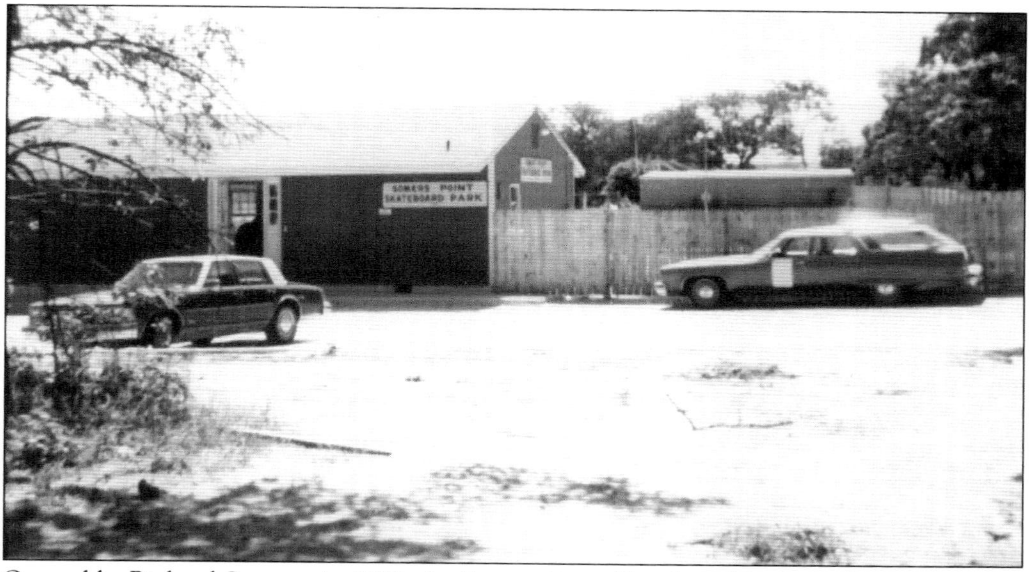

Opened by Richard Stretton in 1978, the Somers Point Skateboard Park was located adjacent to the pit at what is now Ramona Court off of Fifth Street. It took nearly 40,000 square feet of concrete to compete the park, which consisted of multiple moguls, hills, curves, and slalom runs. The park also had a 52-foot bowl that stood 12 feet high in the middle of the park. The park only lasted a few years and eventually gave way to residential development. (Both, courtesy Ruth Mulford Newsome.)

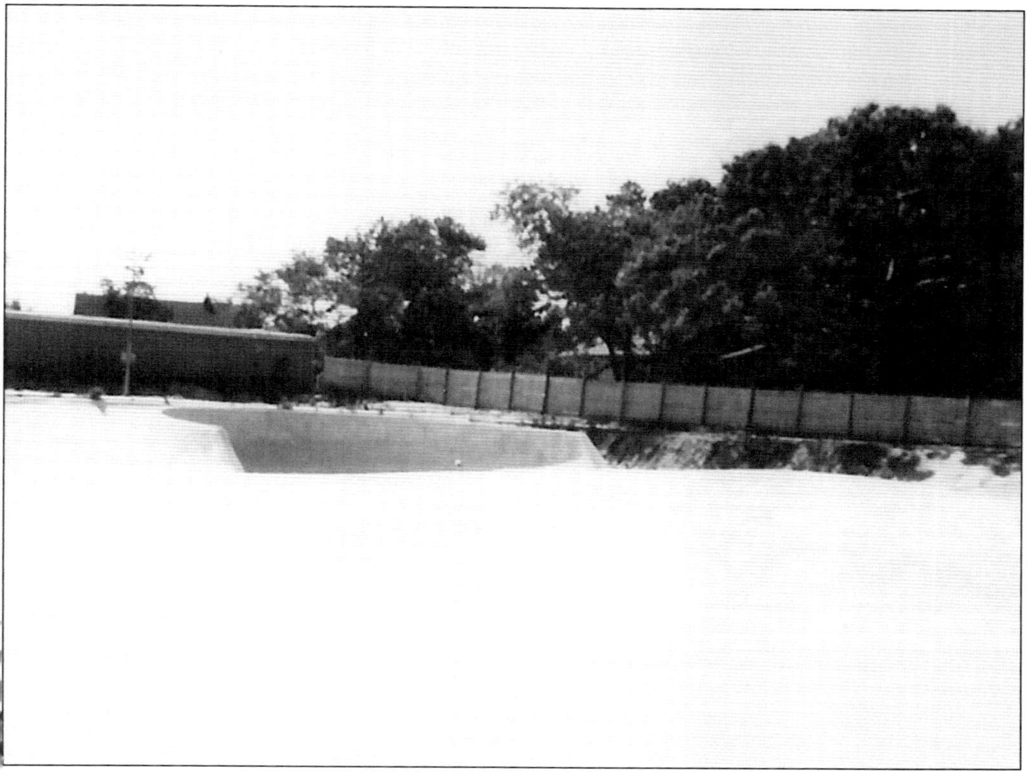

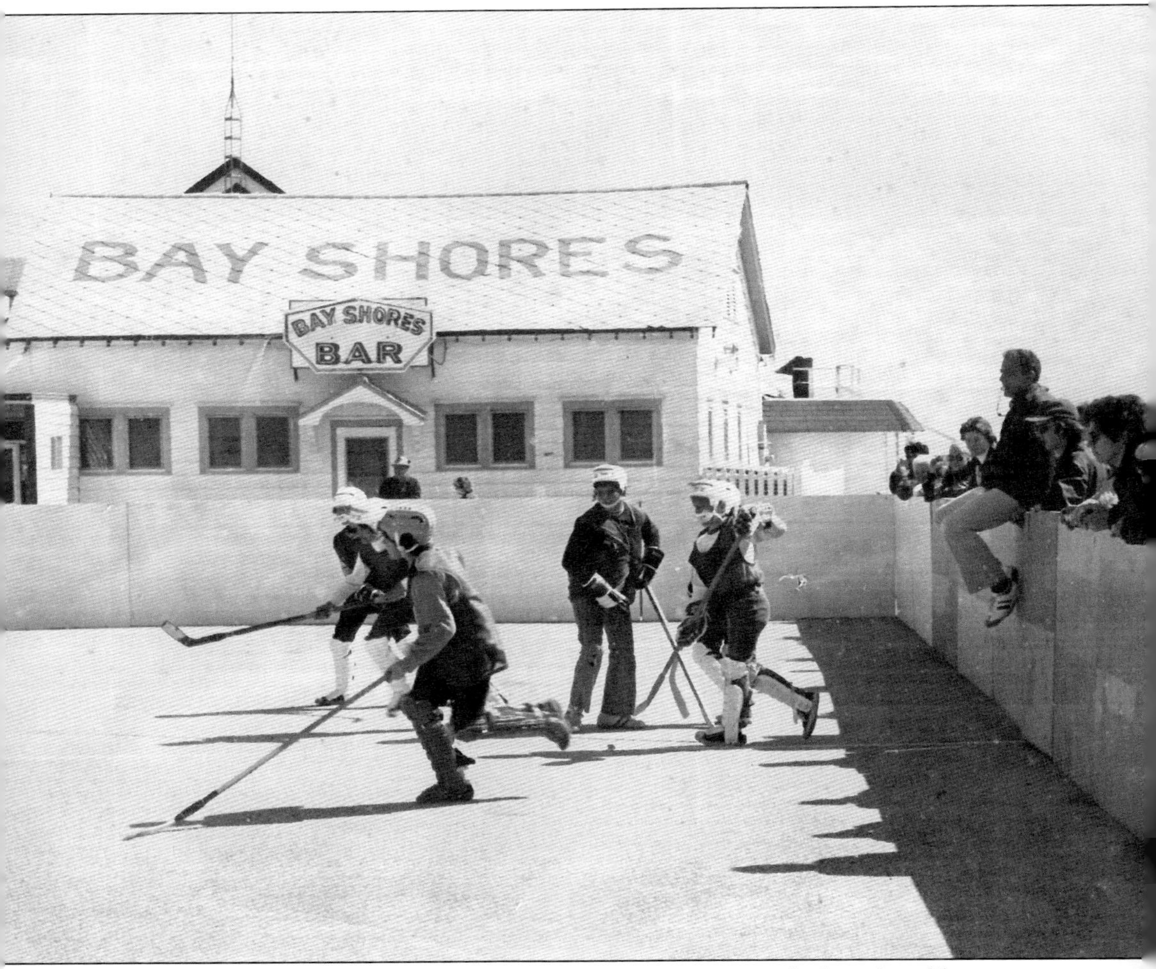

Although street hockey is currently a big sport in Somers Point, finding this old picture was quite a surprise. No one seems to remember this, but evidently street hockey was organized earlier than local residents recall. An organized league may have run this street hockey court located in the parking lot of Bay Shores. (Courtesy Ruth Mulford Newsome.)

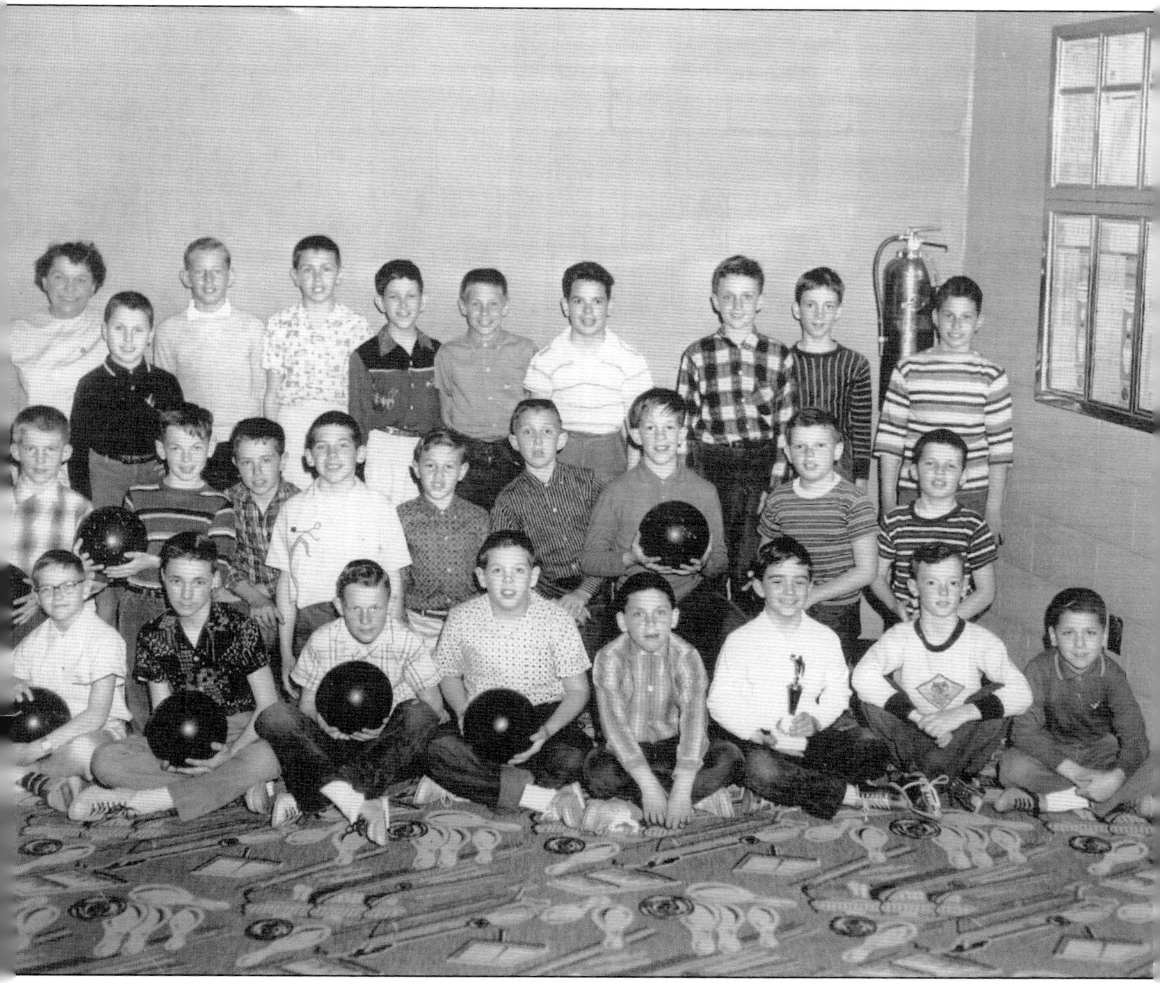

Bowlers in the boys' league at the Somers Point Bowling Alley pose for a picture. Shown are, from left to right, (first row) George Gumann, two unidentified, Gary Werb, Dennis DiOrio, unidentified, Bill McCrossan, and Jeff Miller; (second row) two unidentified, Mike Keller, Joe DiOrio, three unidentified, Joe Maenner, and Chris Maenner; (third row) Anne Werb, John Miller, seven unidentified, and Guy Brown. (Courtesy Jeffrey Miller.)

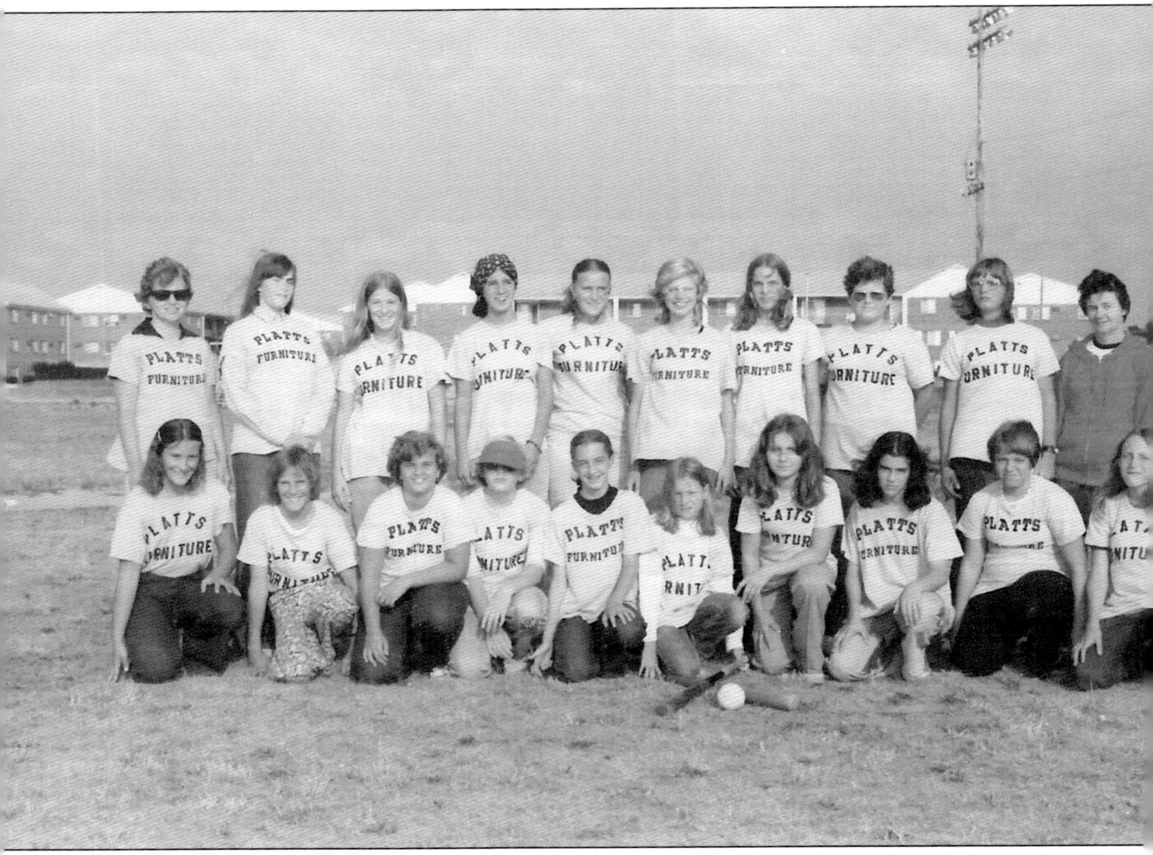

This Somers Point Platt's Furniture senior league softball team includes, from left to right, (first row) Carol Snow, Linda Snow, Denise Costanza, Patty Jacobs, Lynn Newsome, Shelly Jacobs, Tracey Rossi, Terry Gravina, Patty Martin, and Nancy Gallagher; (second row) coach Carol Jacobs, Laura Weir, Elizabeth Adams, Diane Morshead, Donna Snow, Kathy Dembroski, Sally Dickens, Rosalie Rogers, Kathy Murphy, and scorekeeper Ruth Newsome. This team won the senior league softball championship in 1976. (Courtesy Ruth Mulford Newsome.)

Nine

Memories of School Years

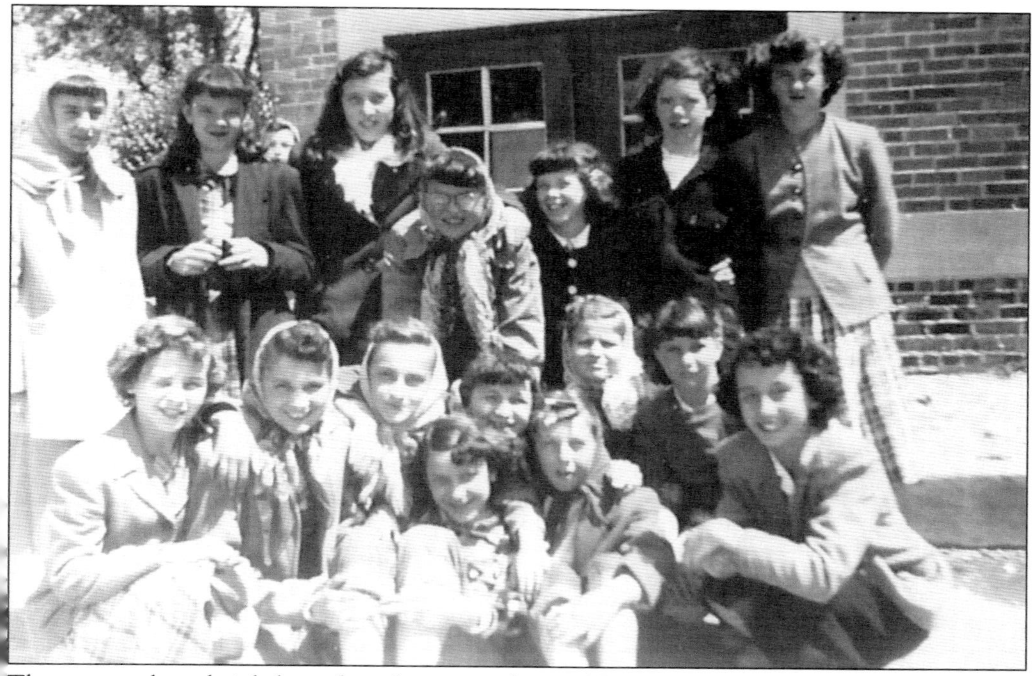

These seventh-and-eighth-grade girls pose in front of Dawes Avenue School in 1948 or 1949. They are, from left to right, (first row) Miriam Eckhart, Pat Ellis, Pauline Landry, Betty Meyers, Anna May Harrington, Joan Bird, Barbara Ludwig, Lucy Sullivan, and Judy Balsley; (second row) Ruth Mulford, Jean Force, Betty Pidcock, Nancy Sullivan, Lillian Bazard, Barbara Merrill, and June Searfoss. (Courtesy Ruth Mulford Newsome.)

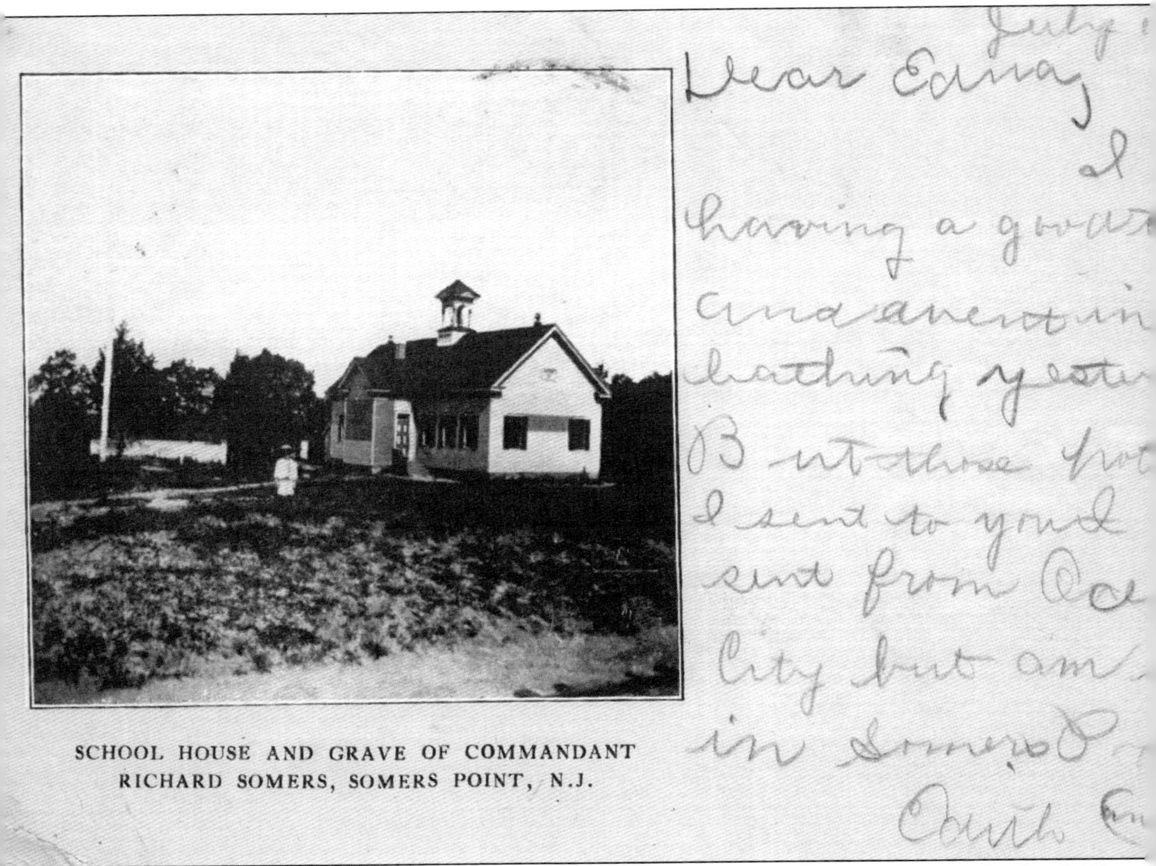

The old schoolhouse pictured was located on New York Avenue prior to the current school. This building was moved to make room for the current New York Avenue school. In the distance on the left is the wall around the graveyard located on the school grounds. This postcard indicates that this is the grave of Commandant Richard Somers, when in fact, Richard Somers, who died fighting the Barbary pirates on September 4, 1804, is buried in Tripoli, Libya.

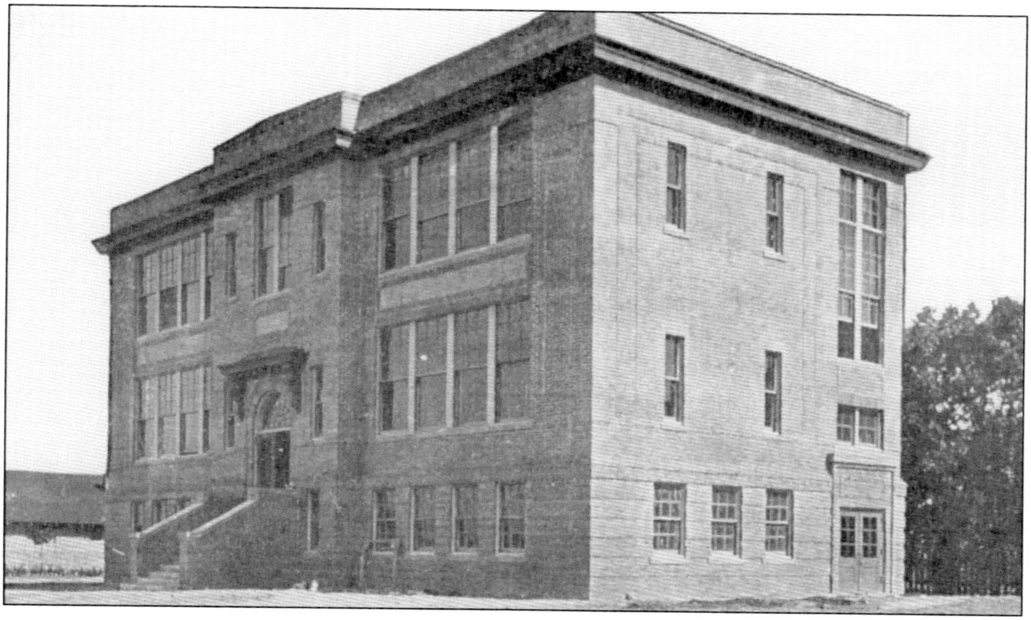

The New York Avenue School was constructed with bricks in 1914. Pictured above, it was built to enable all area students to attend school at the same location. This school also housed the city's first public library. The picture below shows the New York Avenue School after an addition in 1924. The coping still surrounds the property today.

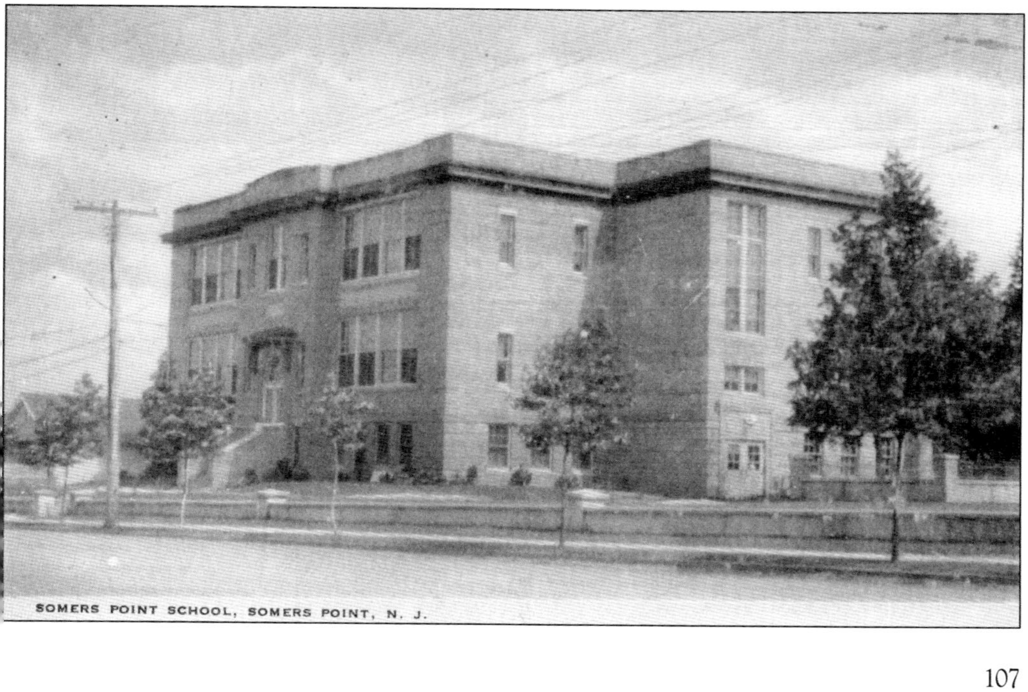

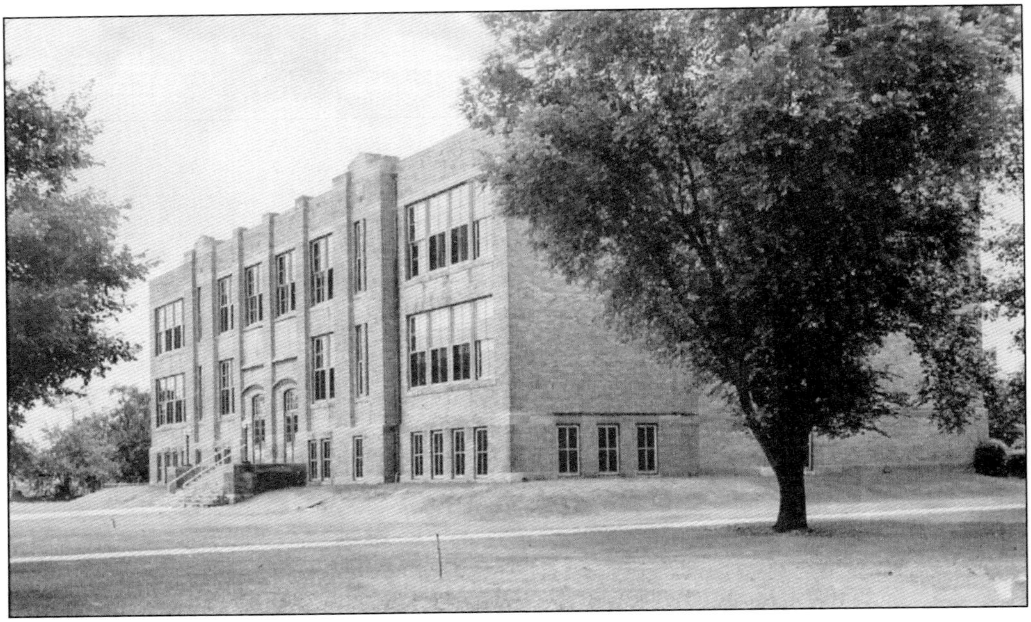

These photographs show the Dawes Avenue School looking much the same just prior to demolition (below) as it did in its earlier years (above). The school was built of brick in 1929. Unlike the New York Avenue School, Dawes Avenue School boasted an auditorium that was not only used by the school district but by other community organizations as well. (Below, courtesy Joan Bird Wilson.)

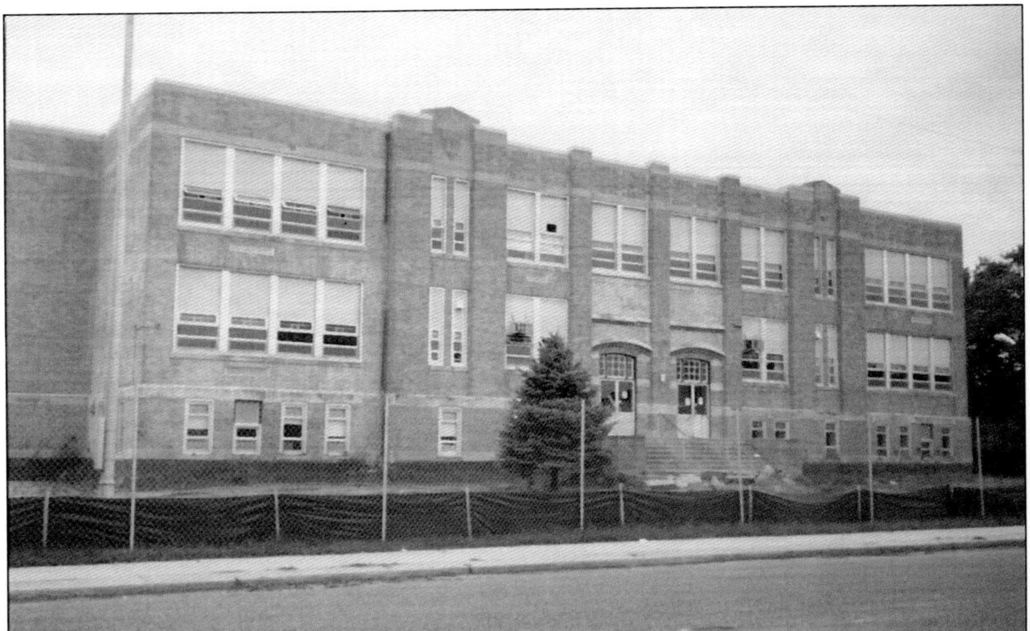

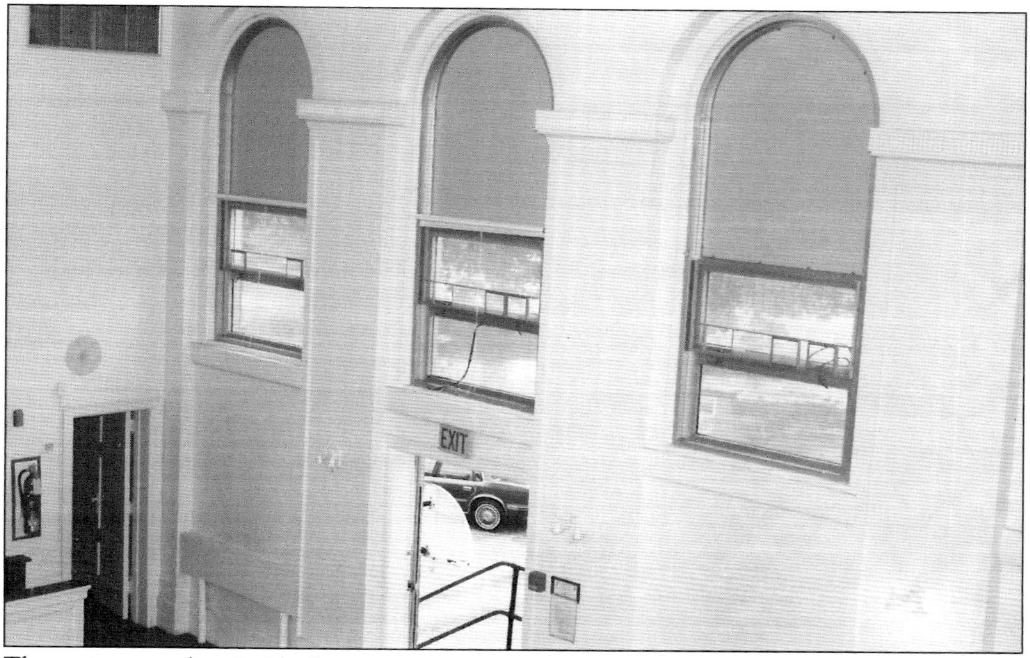

These pictures taken inside the Dawes Avenue School prior to its demolition show the windows at the balcony level, close to the front of the auditorium, and the balcony seating in the auditorium. (Both, courtesy Joan Bird Wilson.)

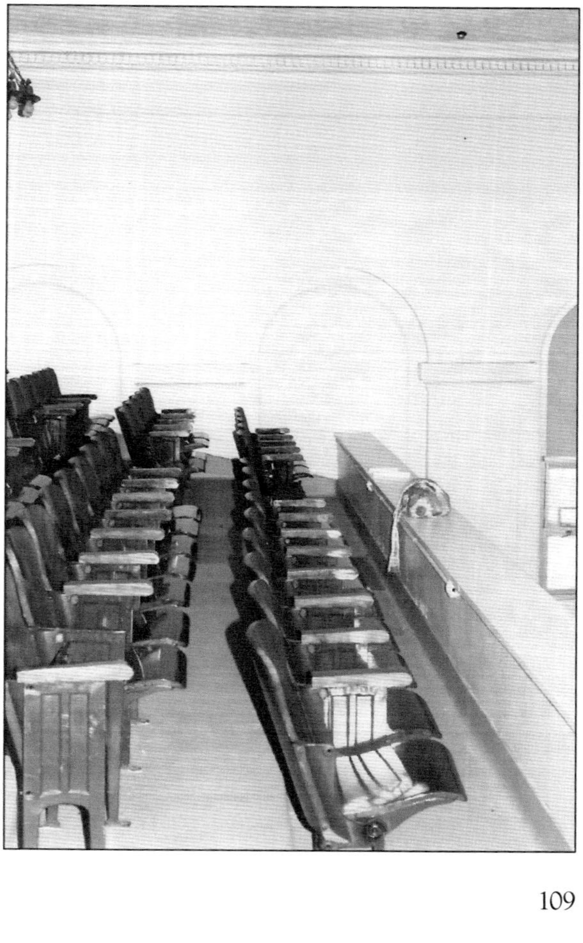

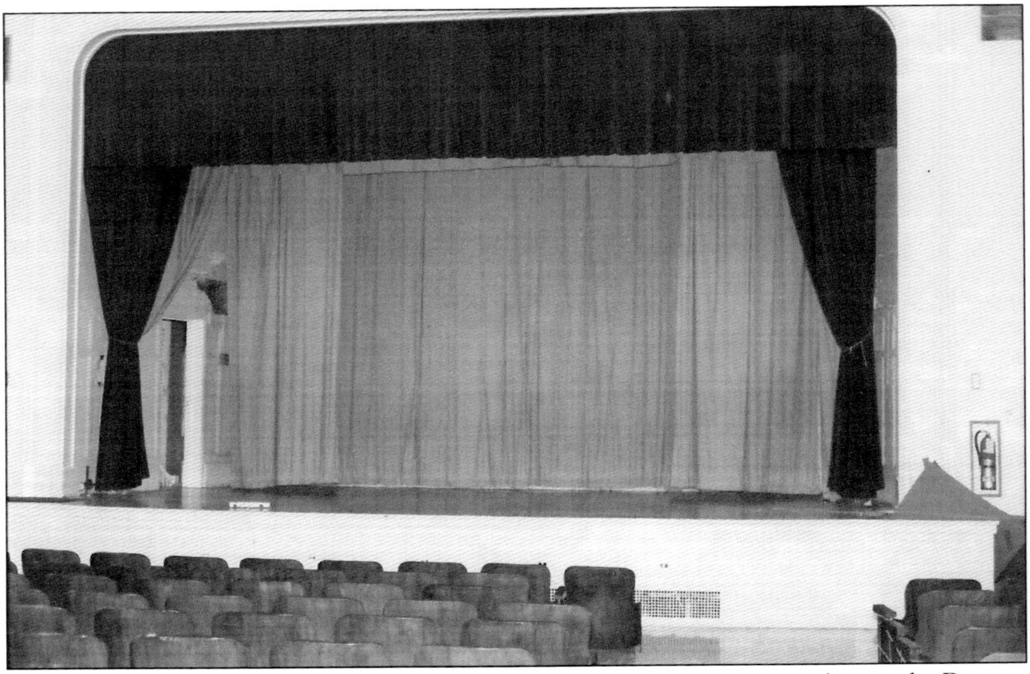

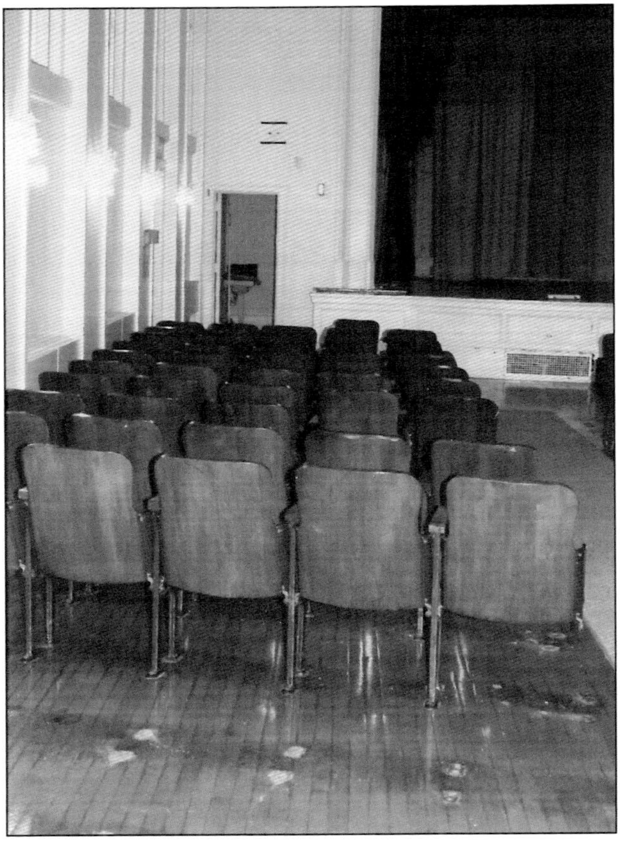

More pictures taken in the Dawes Avenue School Auditorium show the stage and some of the seating on the lower level. Members of the community enjoyed many performances in this auditorium. After the demolition of this school, the city now lacks a real auditorium but instead uses an all-purpose room with a stage at the Jordan Road School. (Both, courtesy Joan Bird Wilson.)

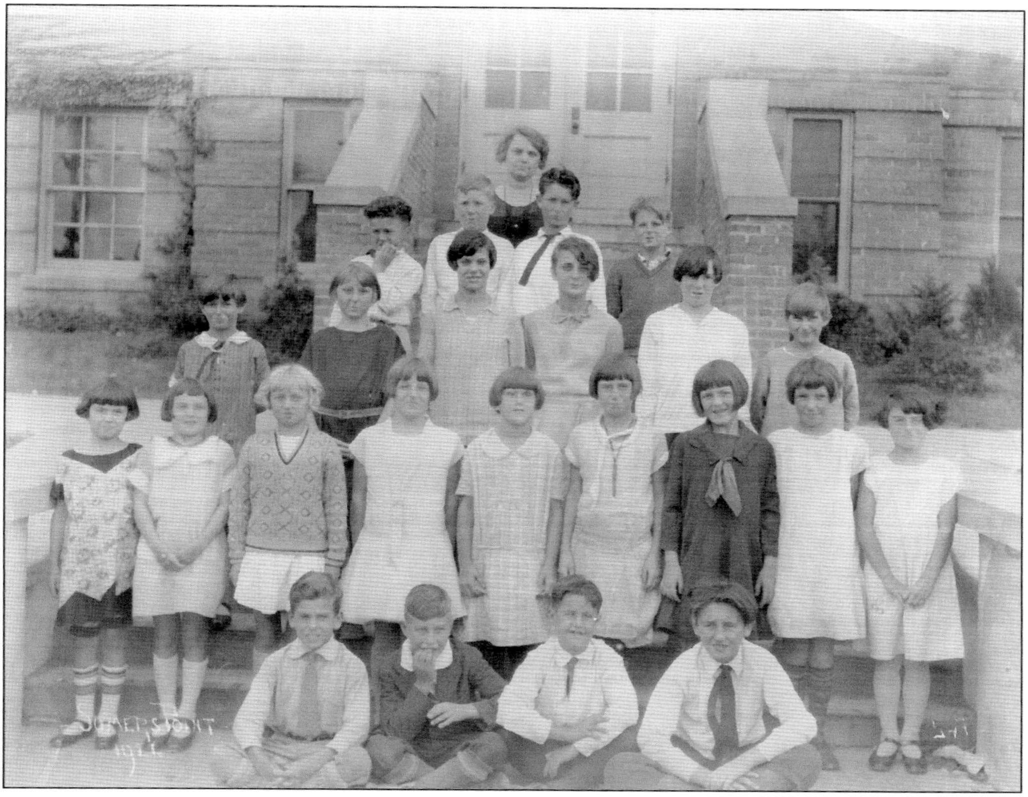

The fifth-grade class at New York Avenue School poses for its picture on the front steps in the 1920s. The front of New York Avenue School has not changed since this picture was taken, and use of the front doors resumed just recently.

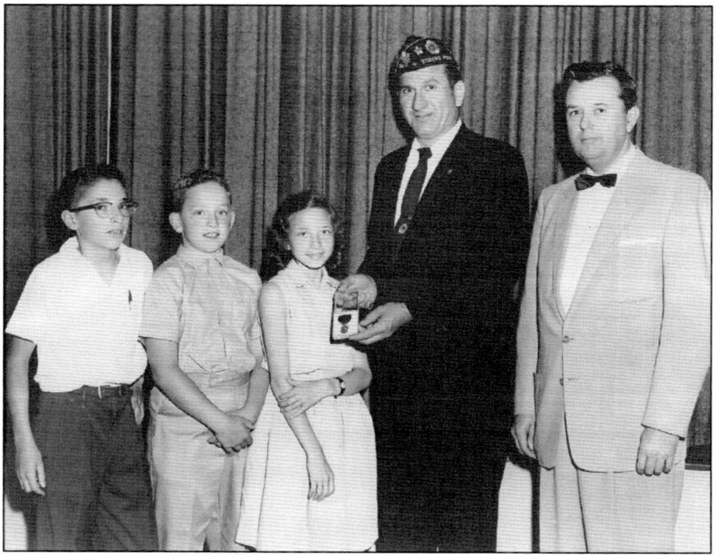

In the spring of 1959, the American Legion held an essay contest for the sixth, seventh and eighth grades, entitled "Why We Should Display Our Flag on Holidays." Shown here are, from left to right, eighth-grade winner George King, seventh-grade winner Bob Loper, sixth-grade winner Elaine Rohland, Legionnaire Marinko "Mike" Mrvica, and school superintendent Herbert Searle. (Courtesy Bob Loper.)

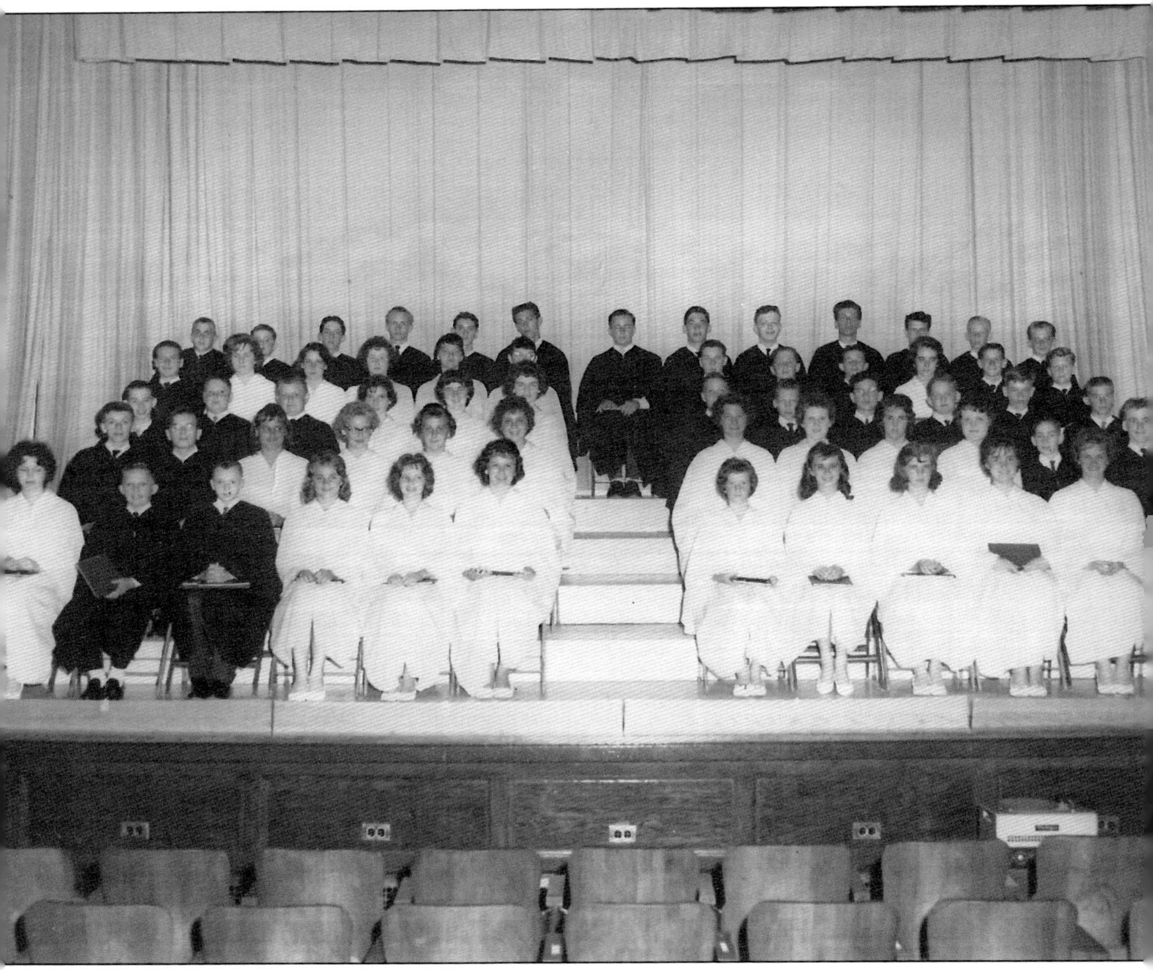

The eighth-grade graduating class of 1961 poses for a class photograph at the Dawes Avenue School. Pictured are, from left to right, (first row) Mary Balachowsik, Jim Day, Jim Photis, Dottie Scherfel, three unidentified, Janis Potter, two unidentified, Barbara Goetsch, and unidentified; (second row) three unidentified, Pam Ratzlaff, Linda Back, two unidentified, Phyllis Grubb, two unidentified, Jim Bates, and Steve Colao; (third row) Joe Wittenweiler, five unidentified, Ken Litwak, Rick Miller, Cliff Bailey, Bob Loper, Roger Broschard, and unidentified; (fourth row) Walter Cottrell, Marsha Oberle, Nancy Sadowl, two unidentified, Peggy Broadwater, Tom Star, and five unidentified; (fifth row) Bill Phillips, Howard Barrett, David Banholzer, unidentified, Jerry Regina, Skip Castaldi, four unidentified, Ed Berge, Tom Fisher, and Rick Brewster. The unidentified class members pictured include Bob Berger, Joe Brennan, Helen Burke, Bobbie Burleson, Mary Carmona, Bill Cawley, Luanne Clunn, Wayne Cox, Curtis Dull, Carol Faisst, Carolyn Fields, Terry Frits, Carolyn Headley, Diane Headley, David Henry, Carol Hone, Joe Horwath, Bonnie Juliano, Kathy McBride, Patty McMahon, Alvin McNeill, Judy Montgomery, Jim Moore, Richard Newsome, Susan Orchard, Ed Pritchard, Christine Ricketts, George Roff, Mitch Somers, Cathy Vieth, Lance Weight, Valerie Wojciechowski. In charge of the graduation was teacher Bessie Gath. Today, with the absence of an auditorium, classes graduate at the Jordan Road School. (Courtesy Bob Loper.)

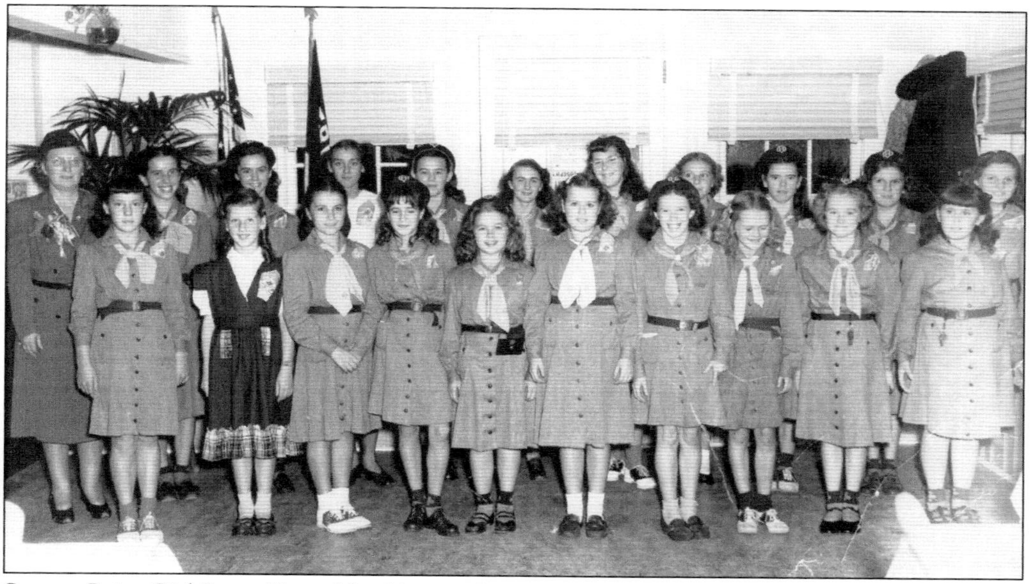

Somers Point Girl Scout Troop No. 16 poses for a group picture at Art's Restaurant after a dinner presented by the Sinawik Club. Shown are, from left to right, (first row) Barbara Hand, Mary Lou Farrell, Pat Ellis, Kathleen Keyes, Alice Koch, Barbara Gaskill, Lillian Bazard, Wilberta Hyatt, Barbara Scull, and Jean McCausland; (second row) leader Florence Herbert, Frances Meskers, Eleanor Mapes, Billy Sue Headley, Barbara Ford, Ruth Mulford, Ruth Ayers, Betsy Martin, Barbara Merrill, Dorothy Herbert, and Barbara Farrell. (Courtesy Ruth Mulford Newsome.)

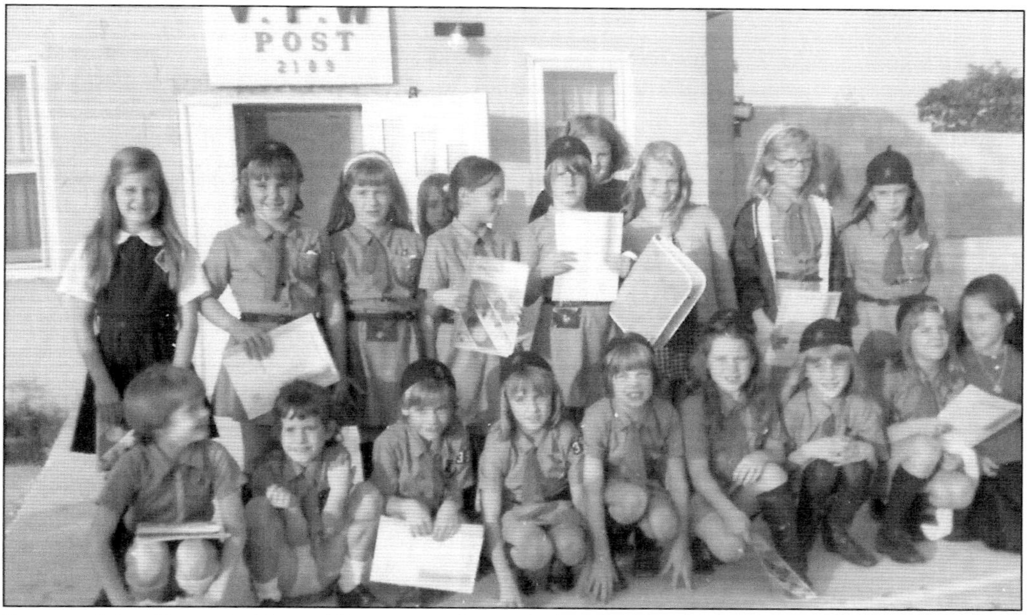

Somers Point Brownie Troop 75 poses in front of the VFW in 1971. Pictured are, from left to right, (first row) unidentified, Anne-Marie Scholler, Patty Steele, Lynn Newsome, Debbie Branin, Janice McHale, Tammy Capps, Mary Beth Dwyer, and unidentified; (second row) unidentified, Gina McBride, Elizabeth Adams, unidentified, Carmen Sanchez, Elizabeth Shuman, unidentified, Joann Starr, Lynne Ireland, and Wendy Michelette. (Courtesy Ruth Mulford Newsome.)

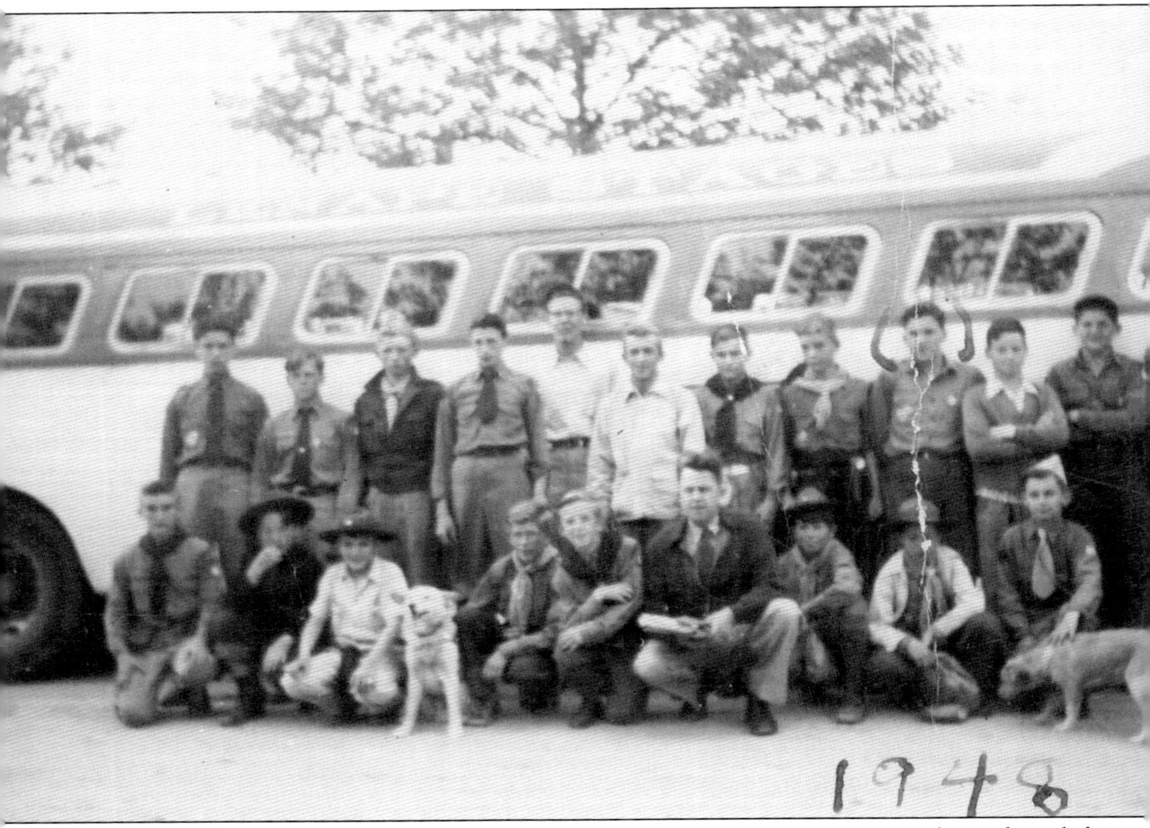

Somers Point Boy Scouts board a bus on their way to a field trip. Pictured are, from left to right, (kneeling) Jack Hickman, Bill Winslow, Buddy Sauers, Howard Broschard, Clyde Fenske, Scoutmaster Bill Moncrief Sr., Joe Gaskill, Ronnie Bird, and Albert Wright; (standing) Jim Newcomb, Bob Johns, Albert Thurlow, Bill Moncrief Jr., unidentified, Bob Fenske, Ray Wagner, Bill Woolbert, Bill Carr, Jerry Wilson, Tom Eliason, and Ted Evering.

Ten

Advertisements and Entertainment

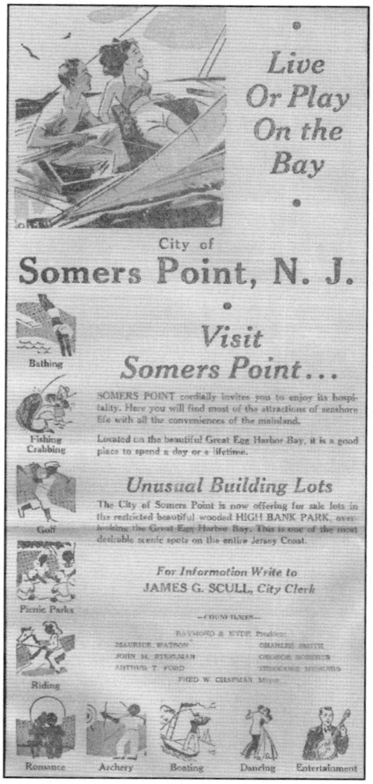

An ad trying to attract visitors and new residents outlines many of the assets Somers Point has to offer. Somers Point still features many of these activities today. Bathing, fishing, crabbing, and boating are all popular pastimes in the surrounding water. Entertainment is available at many restaurants and bars in addition to the very popular free summer beach concerts. Buildable lots are now hard to find in Somers Point, and gone are the stables and horseback riding; but with everything Somers Point has to offer, it is still a great place to "live or play on the bay." (Courtesy Kirk Gerety.)

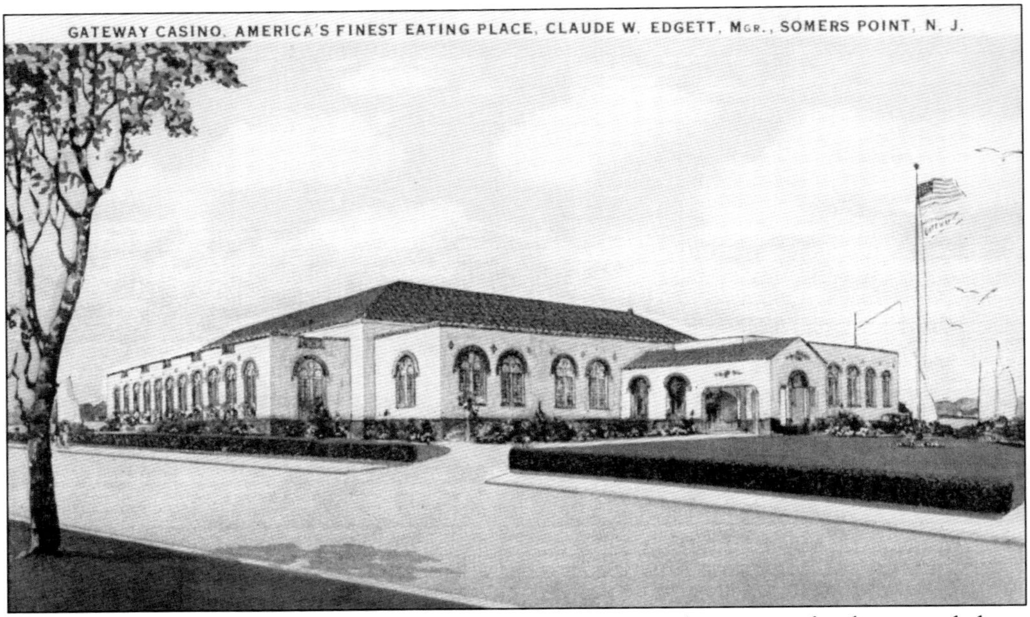

The Gateway Casino opened in 1926 and became a premier destination for diners and those looking for top-rate entertainment, including many of the big bands of the era. The property later became Orsatti's and hosted musical acts such as Frankie Laine and the Ink Spots. After Orsatti's, the property became the Gateway Playhouse, bringing such stars as John Barrymore, Joyce Randolph, and Veronica Lake to its stage. The Under 21 Club also occupied the building, bringing such performers as Chubby Checker, who recorded a live album there. Nonentertainment businesses also occupied the building over time, with the Prudential Insurance Company having offices there prior to moving to Linwood. Wayside Furniture was the last business to occupy the building in March 1968, when the structure burned down due to a gasoline tanker overturning at the traffic circle and catching fire. Gasoline from the tanker poured into the street's drains and carried the fire across the road, catching the former casino building on fire.

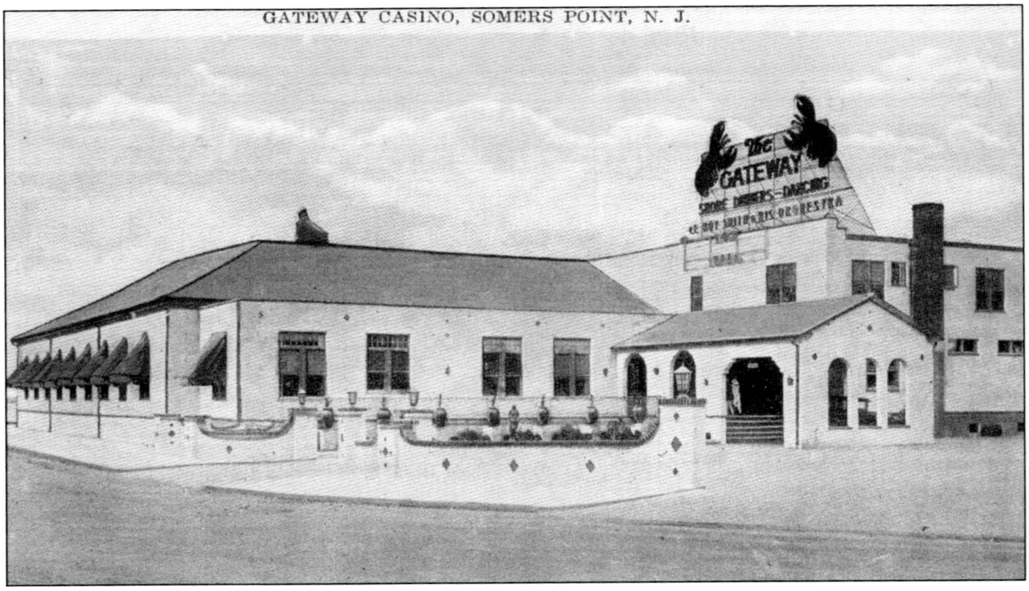

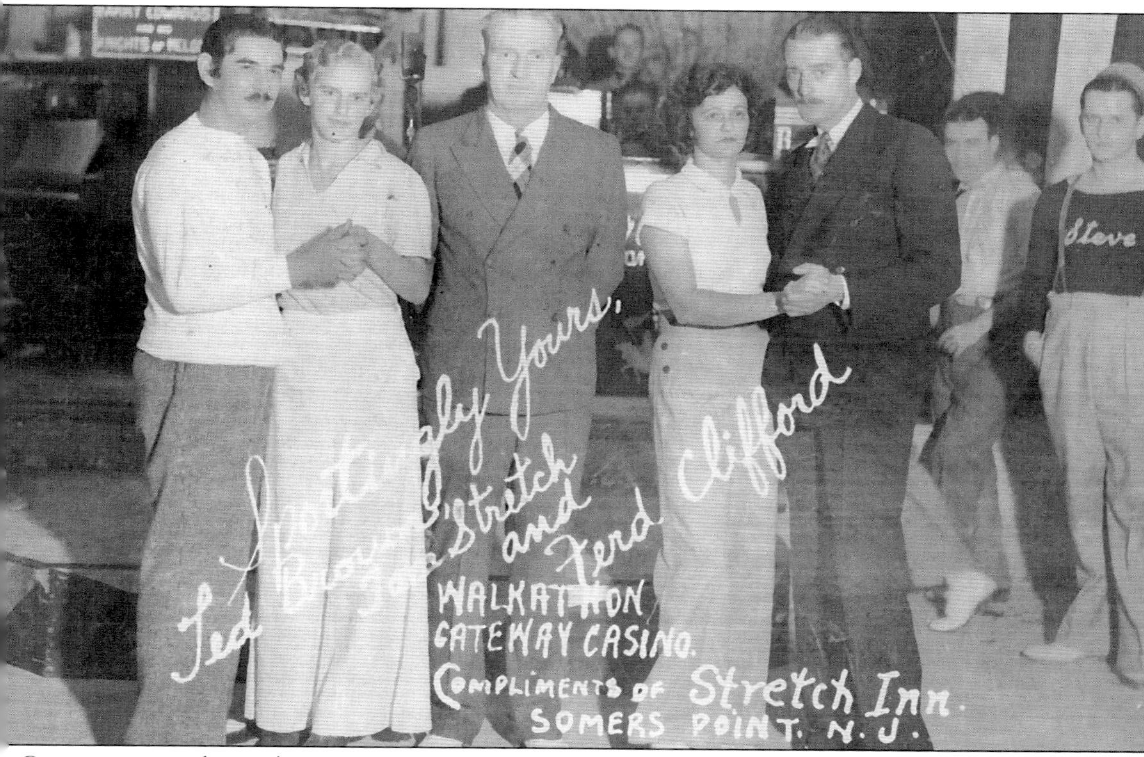

Contestants are shown during one of the many walkathons held at the Gateway Casino. Though this was called a walkathon, it actually involved not walking but dancing. This postcard was put out by Stretch Inn, another business on Bay Avenue.

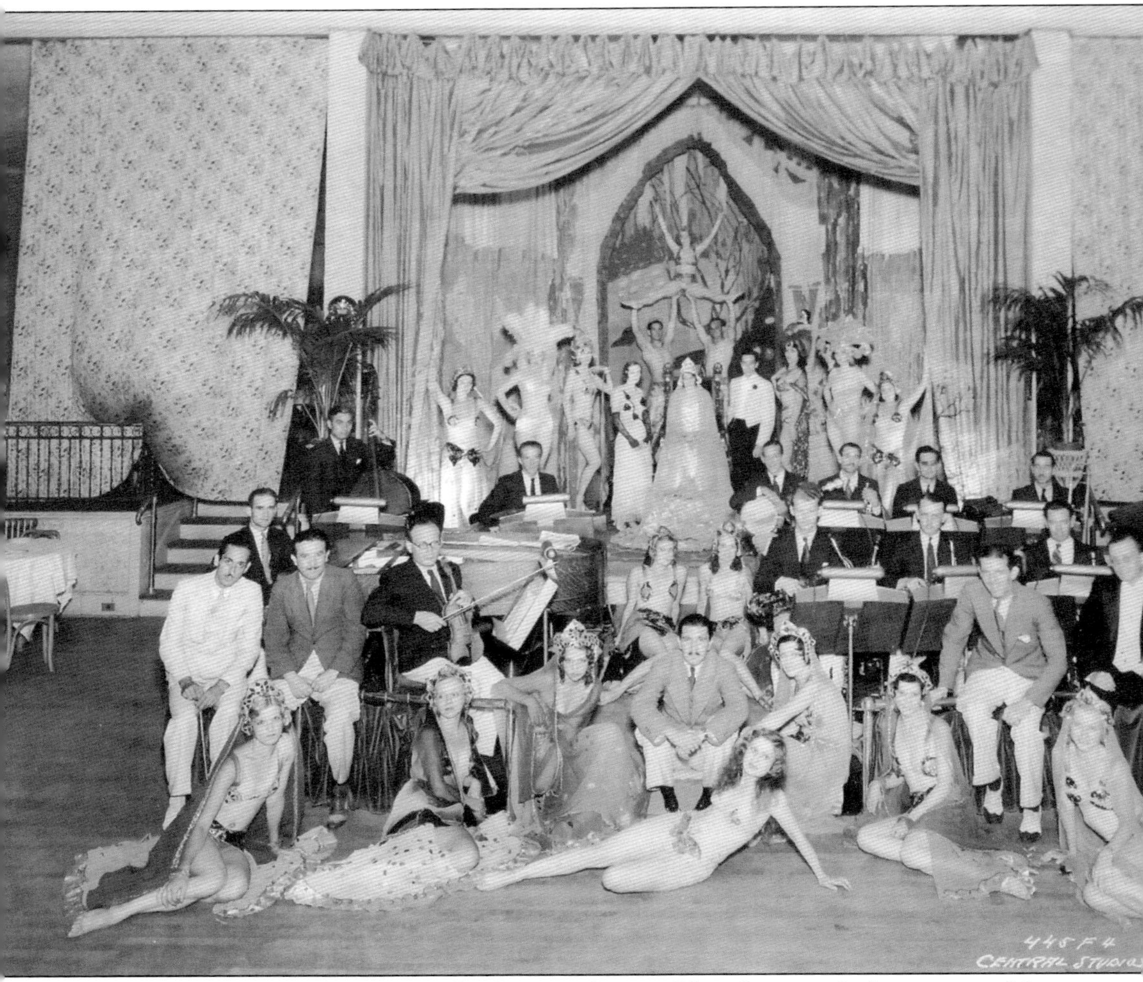

Performers pose on the stage at the Gateway Casino. This photograph shows some of the ornate costumes used in these performances, as well as the number of people needed to put on some of the shows at the Gateway Casino. (Courtesy Ruth Mulford Newsome.)

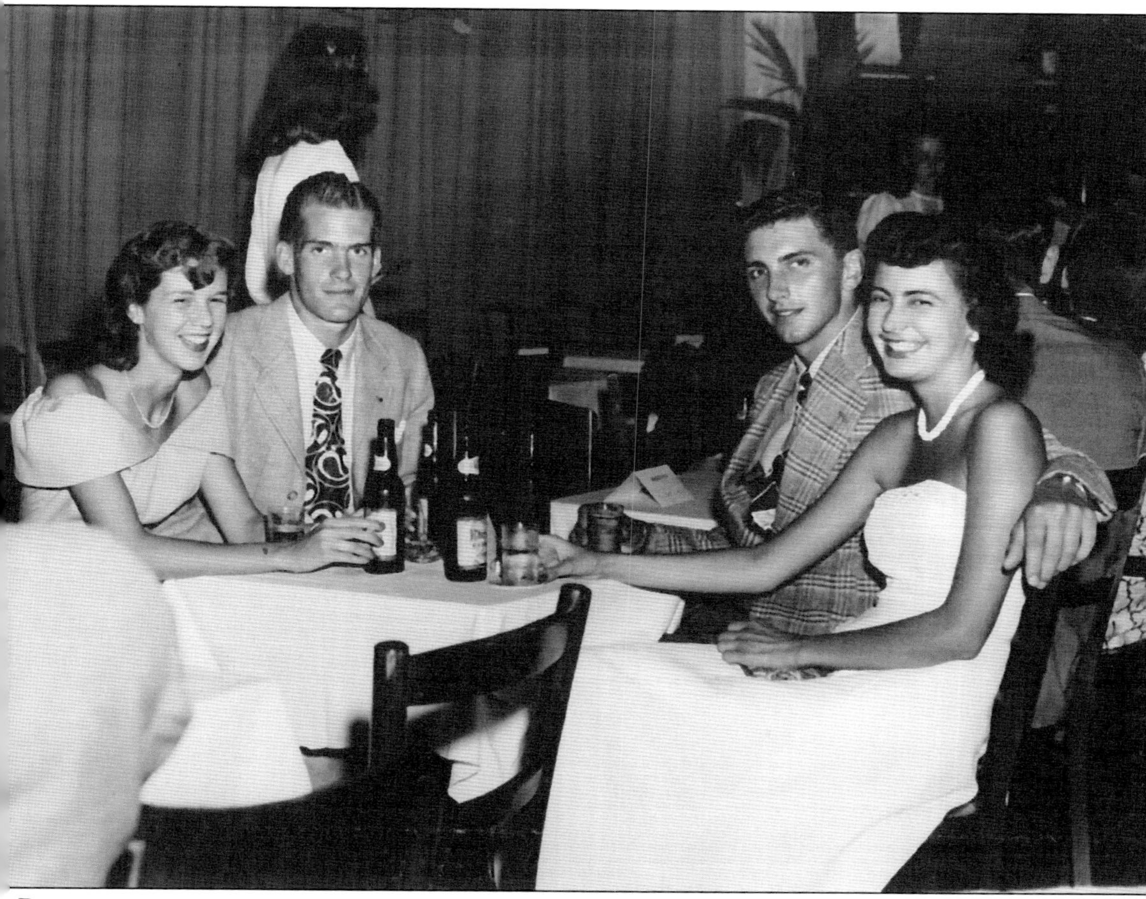

Diners enjoy an evening out at the Gateway Casino. This photograph was taken when the Gateway was owned by Orsatti's. It appears, by the bottles on the table, the drink of choice for the evening is beer.

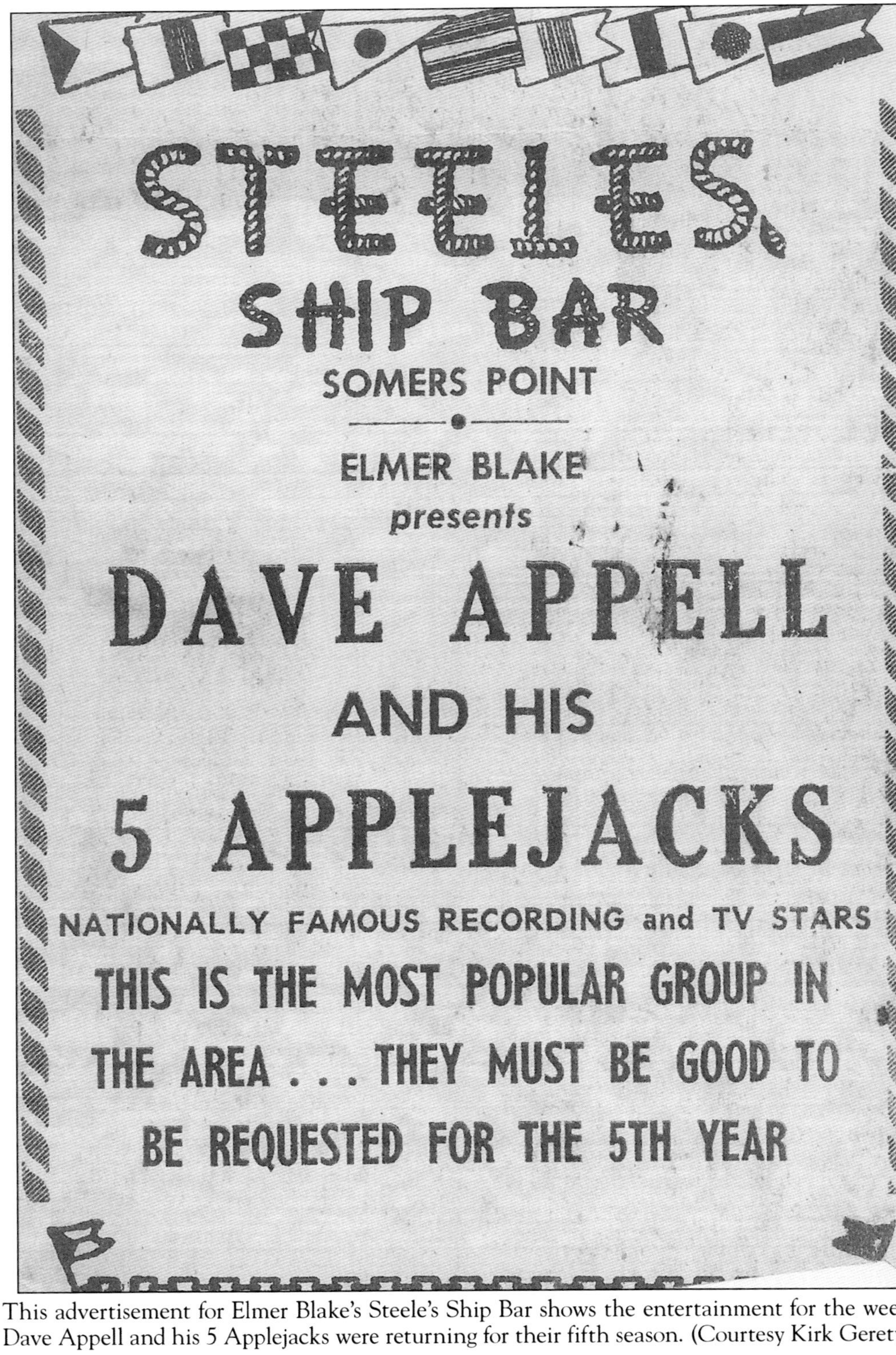

This advertisement for Elmer Blake's Steele's Ship Bar shows the entertainment for the week. Dave Appell and his 5 Applejacks were returning for their fifth season. (Courtesy Kirk Gerety.)

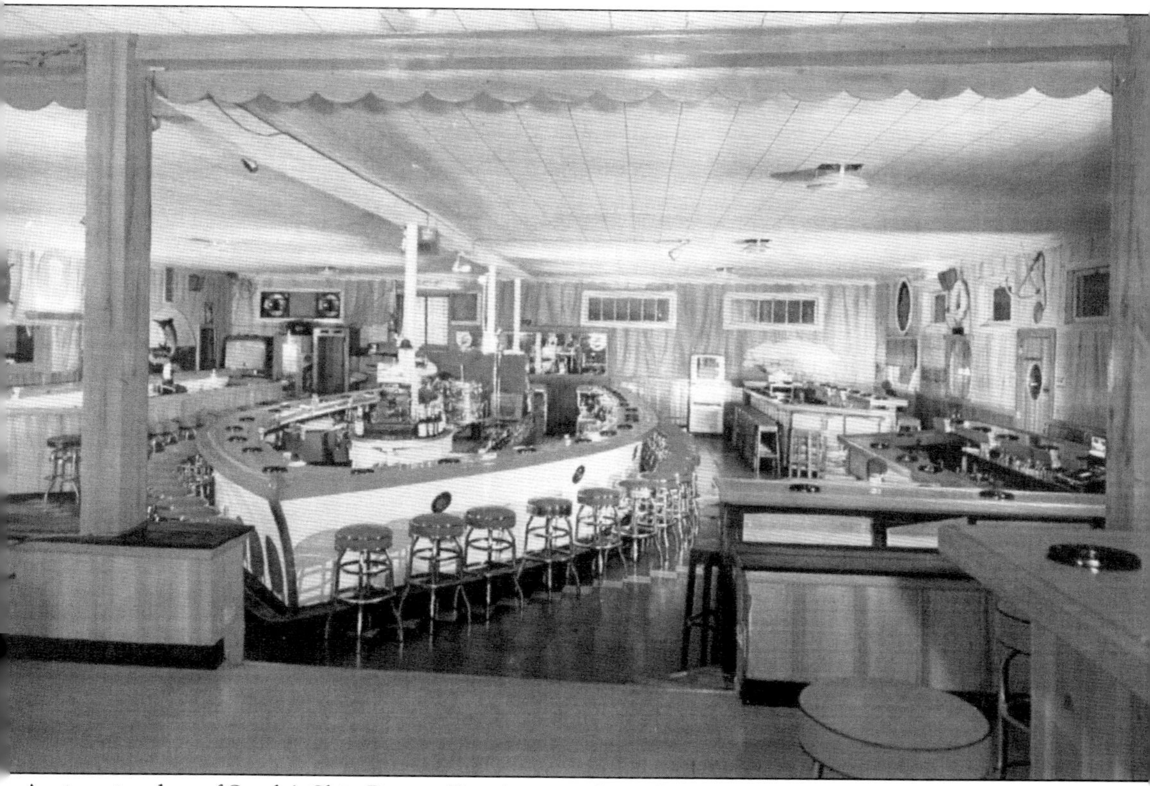

An interior shot of Steele's Ship Bar, on Bay Avenue, shows how it got its name—the large ship-shaped bar in the center of the room.

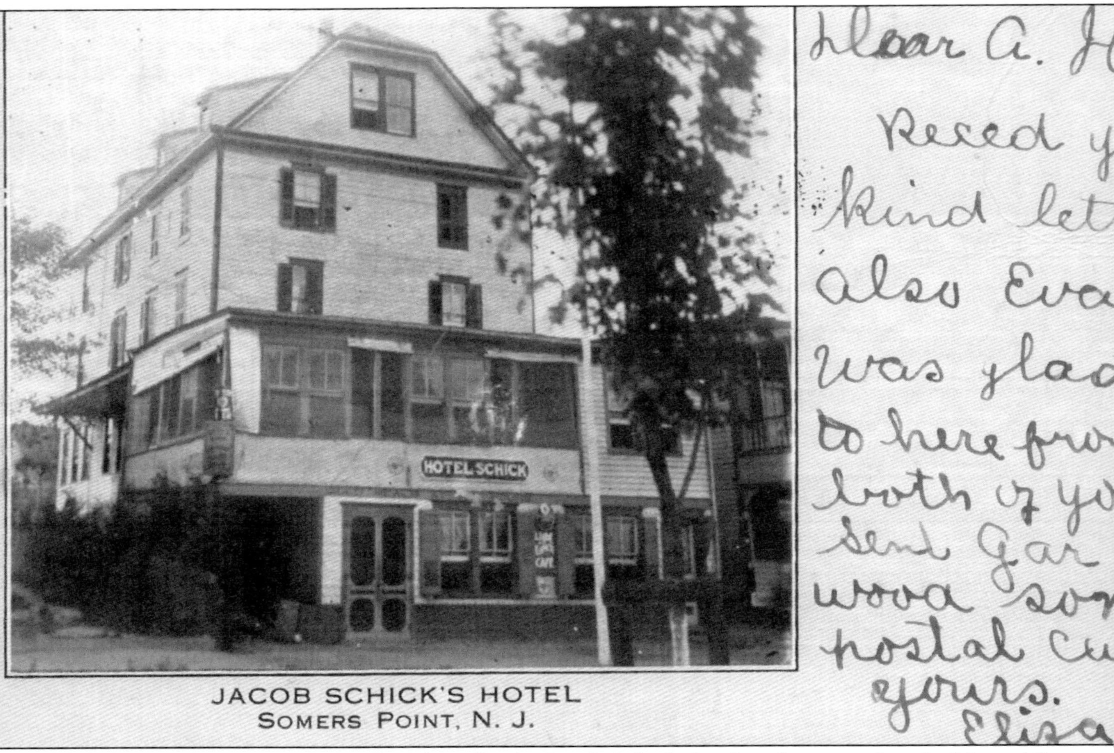

The Hotel Schick was owned and run by the Jacob Schick family, who moved to the United States from Germany. Boasting a rathskeller on the bottom floor and rooms for rent in the back portion of the building, the hotel was a longtime business at the south end of Bay Avenue.

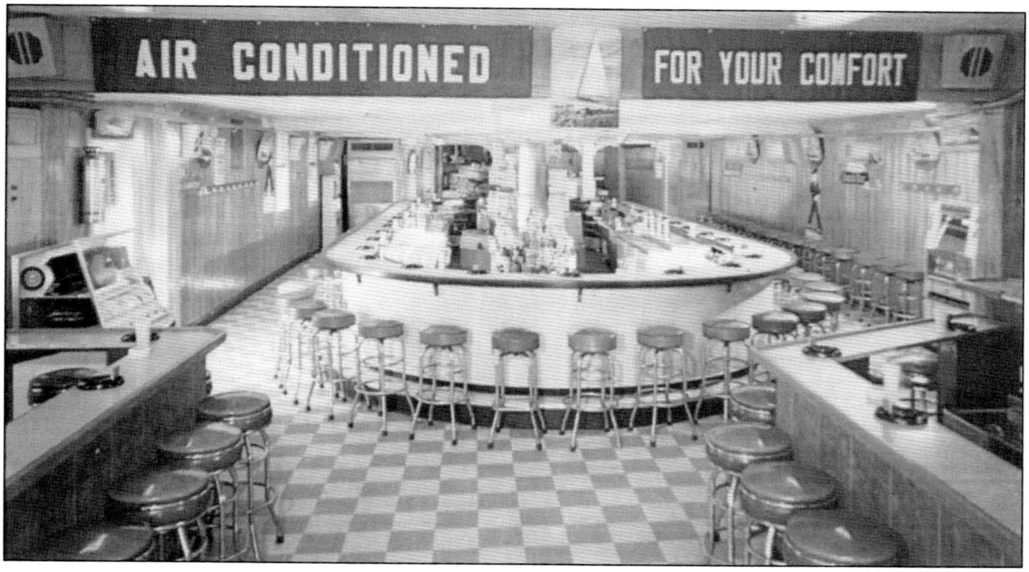

These photographs showing both the interior and exterior of Tony Mart's will bring back a lot of memories for visitors and locals alike. Occupying the former Hotel Schick, Tony Mart's became a centerpiece of Bay Avenue, hosting acts such as Duane Eddy and Levon Helm and the Hawks (the group that later became The Band). The movie *Eddie and the Cruisers* was filmed at this location in the early 1980s, forever immortalizing the memories of those who partied summers away at Tony Mart's. The building was demolished in the early 1980s. (Above, courtesy Tony Mart Collection.)

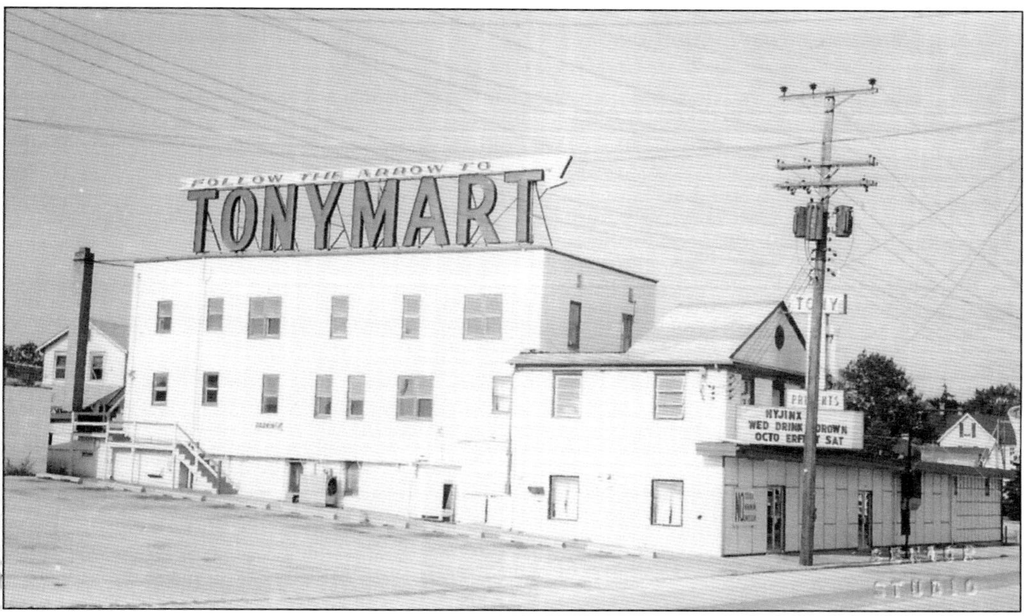

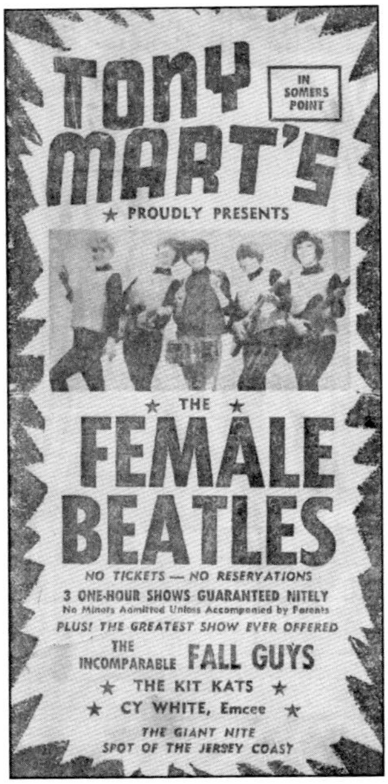

These advertisements for Tony Mart's feature some of the acts that graced the stage and entertained those who made the hot spot their regular hangout. (Both, courtesy Kirk Gerety.)

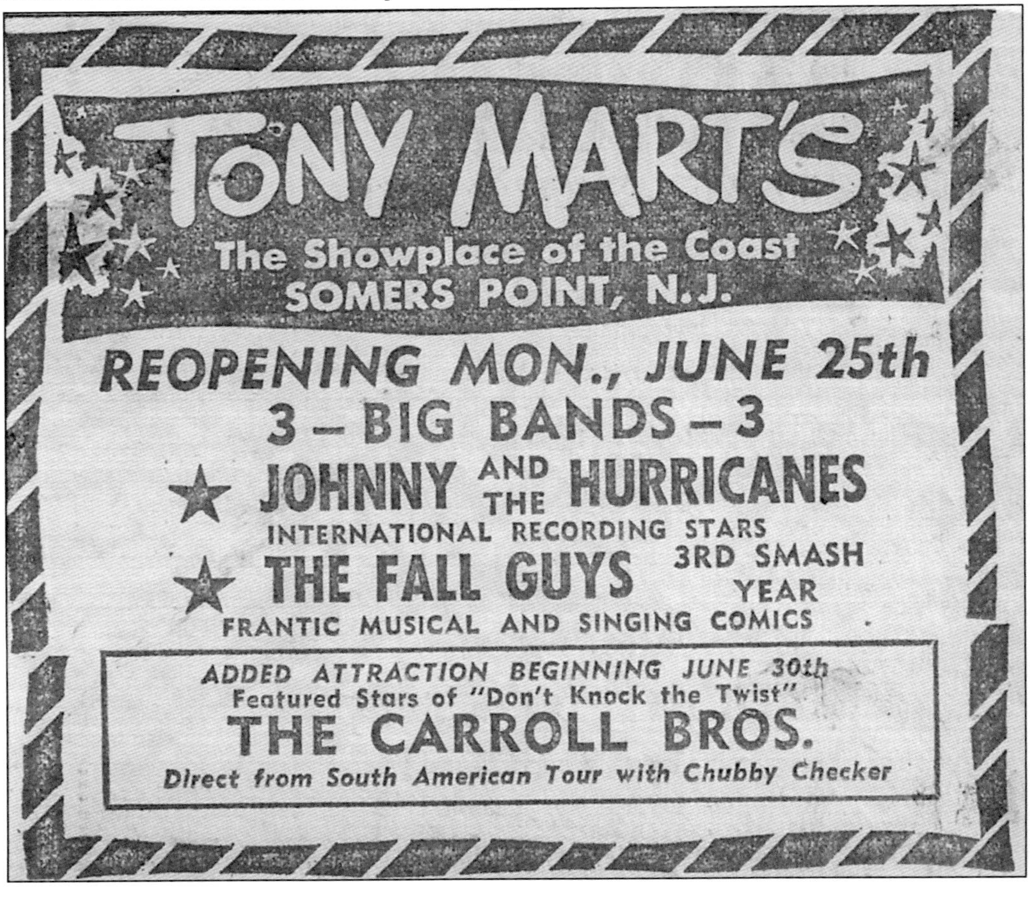

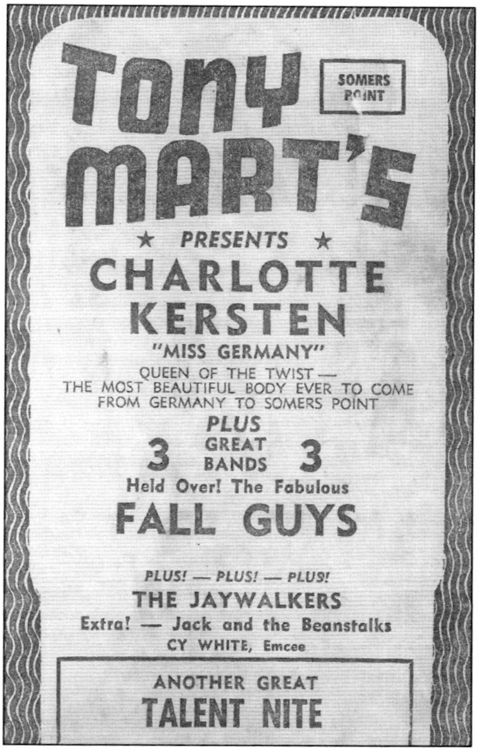

More advertisements for Tony Mart's offer a clear picture of the types of entertainment that could be enjoyed there on a regular basis. (Both, courtesy Kirk Gerety.)

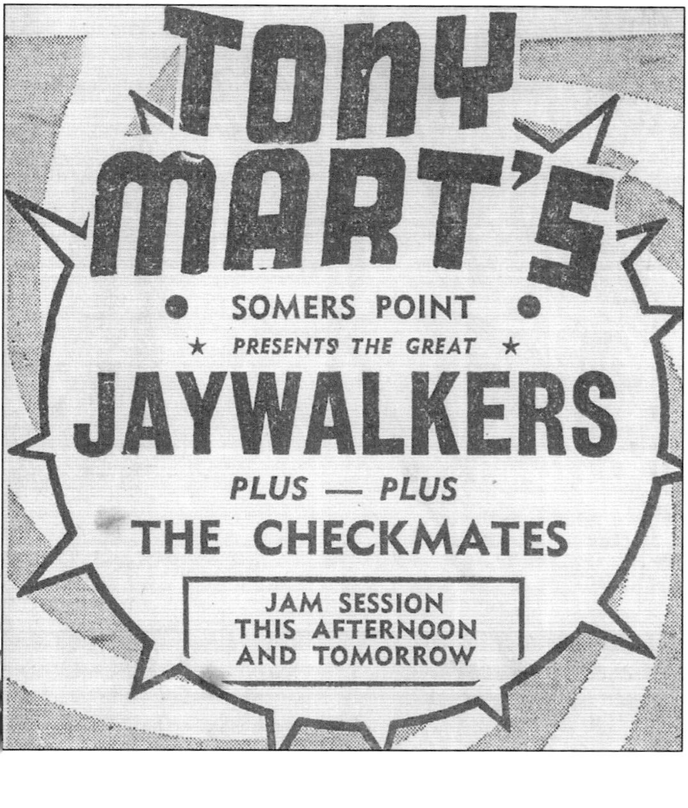

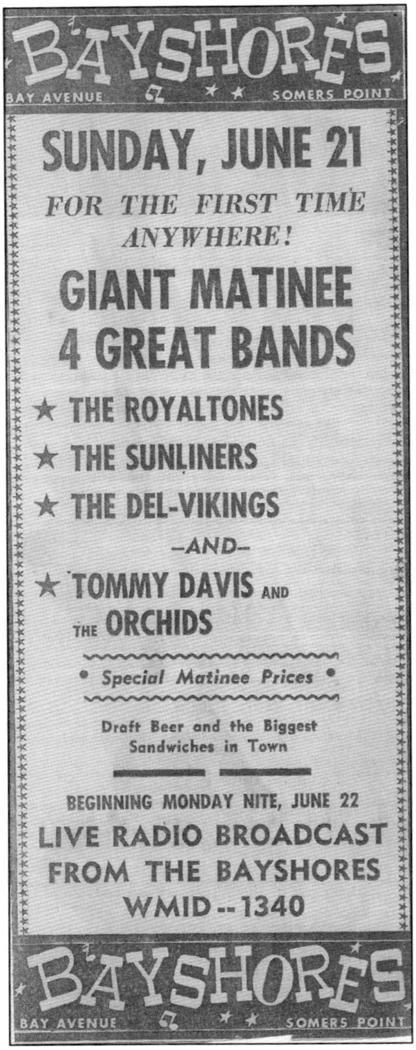

Advertisements for Bay Shores show what was happening on the other side of Bay Avenue. Boasting "draft beer and the biggest sandwiches in town," Bay Shores was a popular area hot spot. In the summer, if a person was not old enough to get in, he or she could sit on the docks and listen to the bands as they played. With Bay Shores and Tony Mart's both gone, the south end of Bay Avenue will never be the same.

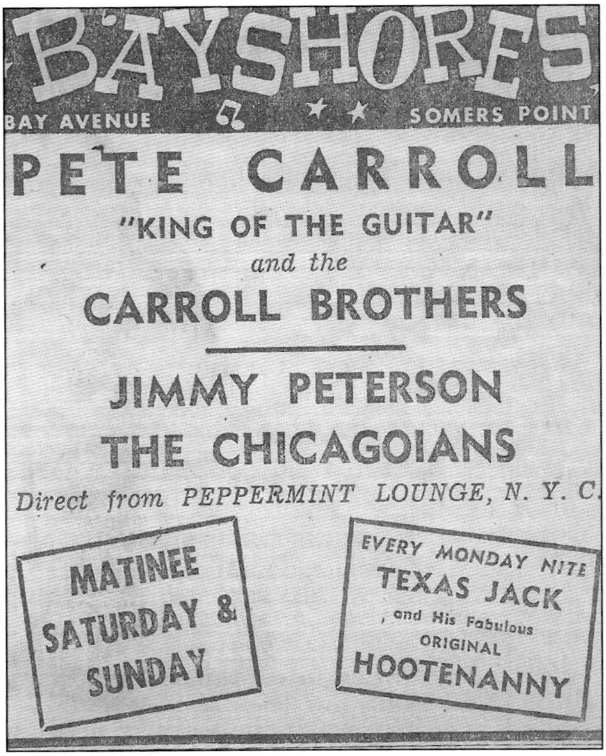

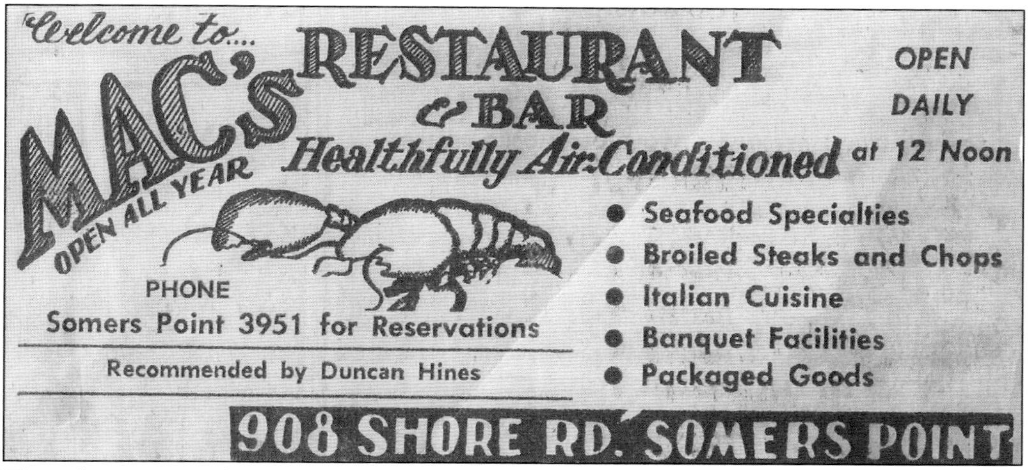

This advertisement for Mac's Restaurant & Bar, located on Shore Road, highlights the type of foods it specialized in, as well as its banquet facilities and a recommendation by Duncan Hines. (Courtesy Kirk Gerety.)

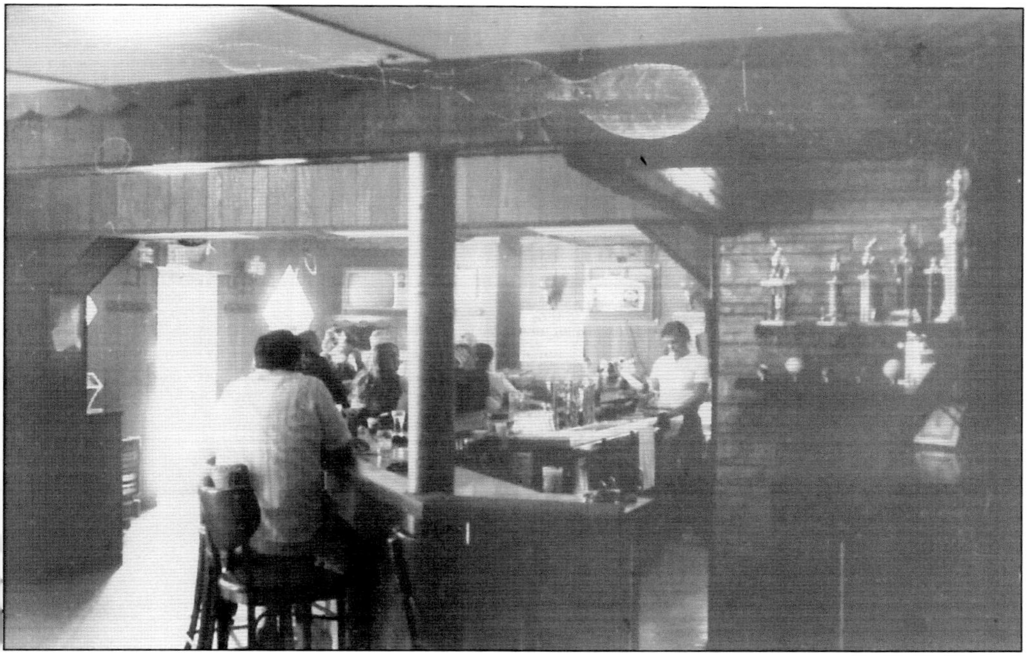
The interior of the Launch Haven Bar, a longtime local neighborhood bar that was beside the railroad tracks at Groveland Avenue. Located in a residential neighborhood, this bar was a popular hangout for the locals, located far away from the entertainment district on Bay Avenue. This building was later demolished to make way for residential units. (Courtesy Kirk Gerety.)

Consistent with our mission to preserve history on a local level, this book was printed in South Carolina on American-made paper and manufactured entirely in the United States. Products carrying the accredited Forest Stewardship Council (FSC) label are printed on 100 percent FSC-certified paper.

MADE IN THE USA